A Doctor's War

A Doctor's War

Letters and Reflections from the Frontlines of World War II

Arthur L. Ludwick, Jr., M.D.,
and Peggy Ludwick

McFarland & Company, Inc., Publishers
Jefferson, North Carolina

Unless otherwise noted, all photographs are from the authors' collection.

For an expanded photo gallery and 90-second book trailer,
visit the book's website: https://adoctorswar.com/

ISBN (print) 978-1-4766-8909-8
ISBN (ebook) 978-1-4766-4729-6

LIBRARY OF CONGRESS AND BRITISH LIBRARY
CATALOGUING DATA ARE AVAILABLE

Library of Congress Control Number 2022034608

© 2025 Margaret J. Ludwick. All rights reserved

*No part of this book may be reproduced or transmitted in any form
or by any means, electronic or mechanical, including photocopying
or recording, or by any information storage and retrieval system,
without permission in writing from the publisher.*

On the cover: Lt. Arthur Ludwick, Jr., U.S. Army War Department
ID card; surgical tools and assorted medals and badges including
the 34th Infantry Division "Red Bull" insignia.

Printed in the United States of America

*McFarland & Company, Inc., Publishers
Box 611, Jefferson, North Carolina 28640
www.mcfarlandpub.com*

To all the men and women who served
so valiantly during World War II,
repeatedly putting their lives at risk in combat;
and to their families back home
who bravely carried on as best they could—

and

To my parents, Jean Hoyer Ludwick and Arthur L. Ludwick, Jr., M.D.,
for their courage through difficult times and resolute commitment
to one another.

Table of Contents

Acknowledgments — ix
Preface — 1
Introduction — 5
Prologue — 19

1. Camp Claiborne, Louisiana: 34th Infantry Division Training, February 1941–December 31, 1941 — 23
2. Northern Ireland: First U.S. Troops to Europe, January 26–December 20, 1942 — 40
3. North Africa: Operation TORCH and Meeting the Desert Fox, January 3–September 22, 1943 — 66
4. Italy: Battle Hardened, September 21, 1943–May 5, 1944 — 127
5. Winding Down: Anzio and Headed Home, March–April 1944 — 189
6. Chronology of Military Service and Major 34th Infantry Division Events: December 2, 1940–November 12, 1951 — 196
7. Walking Wounded — 204
8. Epilogue: Return and Readjustment — 214
9. Behind the Lines: A Daughter's Reflections — 226

Appendices
  A: Silver Star Commendation — 231
  B: German Treatment of American POWs — 233
  C: Capt./Baron Rudolph Charles von Ripper and His "San Pietro, Italy, 1943" Etching — 235
  D: John "Jack" Vail Hoyer — 237
  E: 34th Infantry Division Buddies — 240

Bibliography — 245
Index — 249

Acknowledgments

Much gratitude to all who helped make this book possible:

- Marvin E. Williams, Jr., whose father served with mine during World War II and whose friendship, interest, expert sleuthing, and unwavering support have been invaluable contributions to this project. Our serendipitous meeting on a 34th Infantry Division Facebook page in 2016 has been a gift.
- Jim Bodeen, who on many long, cold ski lift rides up the mountain, talked about the importance of story and writing it down.
- Pat Turner and Jaana Hatton, fellow writers and friends, for reading early drafts and encouraging my slow, steady progress.
- Dennis Held, poet, writer, editor, who taught me some basics, believed in this book, and convinced me that my father's war letters needed to be shared with the world.
- Max G. Geier, Ph.D., professor of history, emeritus, Western Oregon University, for his professional expertise, editing, mentoring, and generous gift of his time.
- Ed Stover, retired journalist, editor, poet—whose keen eye, efficiency with words, and "on call" status were instrumental in moving this project forward.
- Chris Rader, Ed Stover, and Bob White, beta readers, whose constructive input was gratefully received.
- Jeff Ostenson, of North Forty Productions, Wenatchee, Washington, for use of their film production studio and Charles Atkinson, for his time and technical expertise.
- Chris Duren, of Invisible Ink Corporation (invisibleink.com), Yakima, Washington, for his custom maps and graphic design skills.
- Steve Firman, photographer extraordinaire and fellow Wenatchee High School classmate (1966), for his loyalty and help in producing quality prints from old World War II photo negatives.
- Carlos Alvarado, Archivist, @armymedicinehistory, U.S. Army Medical Department Museum and Center of History and Heritage, San Antonio, Texas, for his help in providing information about World War II photos and artifacts.
- Col. (Ret.) Russell Bierl, of the 34th Infantry Division Association and the Iowa Gold Star Military Museum at Camp Dodge Joint Maneuver Training Center, Johnston, Iowa, for access to their archives and answering my many questions.

Acknowledgments

- Write on the River (WOTR), Wenatchee, Washington, for their many excellent writing workshops and dedication to nurturing local writers.
- Kathleen A. Hill, M.A., LMFT, for her insight and encouragement.
- My children: Joshua Henretig, Heather Henretig O'Day, and Benjamin Henretig, for their abiding love for their grandparents, BahBop and MorMor, and their patience with me—always.
- To my guides in Tunisia: Monaam Triki and Abdelmajid Werteni; and my Italian guides and WWII historians: Silvano Casaldi, Luigi Nobile, Luciano Bucci, and Pino Valente—THANK YOU for all of your time and knowledge in helping me retrace my father's routes, encampments, and battlefields during WWII—it was truly A Daughter's Pilgrimage.

And to the many friends over the years who asked how the book was coming along—their continued genuine interest and cheerleading sustained me.

Preface

This riveting account of a medical officer on the frontlines of World War II, responsible for the physical and emotional well-being of traumatized and wounded soldiers, is a unique perspective of war. Engaged in some of North Africa and Italy's bloodiest battles: Kasserine and Fondouk Passes, Hill 609, Monte Pantano, Cassino, and Anzio, Lt. Col./Maj. Arthur L. "Lud" Ludwick, Jr., M.D.'s story is one of devotion and heroism. He earned the Purple Heart in Tunisia and the Silver Star for "gallantry-in-action" on Monte Pantano, Italy, both unusual combat commendations for an unarmed Medical Officer.

Ludwick's keen observations on the landscapes, cultures, and people he encounters are packed into the eloquent love letters written home to his wartime bride. This multifaceted narrative of one man's resolute journey through the minefields of love and war, is also a daughter's discovery of the young man she never knew, before he became her father.

Based on a rich archive of interviews, letters, photos, and military documents, this captivating chronicle of history lends new meaning to notions of true leadership, human character, and the irrational nature of war.

A wide-range of resources was used to provide context for my father's letters and interviews, giving the reader general background knowledge about the North African and Italian campaigns of World War II, including: well researched and scholarly overviews of the Mediterranean Theater; first-person testimonials by veterans who participated in the conflicts there; embedded journalists' reporting; military archives; veterans organizations' newsletters and publications; U.S. Army's "After Action Reports" and related websites; live action film footage of the conflicts in North Africa and Italy, etc. Please refer to the bibliography for more specific information.

This book follows the 133rd and 168th combat regiments of the U.S. Army's celebrated 34th Infantry "Red Bull" Division, the first U.S. troops sent to Europe after the bombing of Pearl Harbor, from early training at Camp Claiborne, Louisiana, to the U.S. entering World War II on December 8, 1941. The Red Bulls spent ten months "secretly" training in Northern Ireland before being deployed to North Africa in Operation TORCH, and on into Italy. All in all, my father's two infantry regiments participated in fourteen major engagements with the German Army, each averaging one to three weeks. The 34th Infantry Division holds the U.S. Army record for most days in combat, over 500, in American military history.

The interviews with my father give a more detailed account of the 34th's orders and outcomes that he could not disclose in his letters home to my mother due to the strict censorship policies of the military. Serving as a companion and lead-in to batches of the chronologically corresponding letters, the interviews showcase my father's modest and matter-of-fact manner. After his death, while researching the North African and Italian campaigns on my own, I learned that he had vastly underreported the danger and grim circumstances of his service.

To provide the reader with some context and a better understanding of World War II's Mediterranean Theater operations, I added my own commentary throughout the narrative with historical references and support material. I tried to keep the footnotes and background information to a minimum in the "Letters" sections, so as not to interrupt the flow of my father's beautifully written accounts.

His letters and interviews reveal a myriad of new details about combat life: his unusual management of soldiers suffering from PTSD; the medical treatment of local villagers, often victims of war's collateral damage; the crucial role of entertainment used to boost his men's morale and build unity; frustration with the Army's "way-of-doing-things"; the challenges of living conditions on the front.

Underscoring the war narrative is the unfolding of a love story between a young wife of only two months and her courageous Medical Officer husband, serving overseas in a horrific war. Desperate to keep the flame of his new marriage burning over their 2½ years of separation, my father was not only fighting for his life and country, but perhaps for his marriage, as well. This more personal glimpse of war's trauma and its potential lingering effects within family relationships, still reverberates amongst our military personnel serving abroad today.

A daughter's discovery of her father as a passionate, courageous, and engaging young man, before becoming her father, is the final layer to this multi-faceted story. It transformed the image of the man she thought she knew, reshaping his legacy in her life. Is it possible to rewrite one's family history? Perhaps.

I never intended to write a book. I merely interviewed my father about his World War II experiences a few years before he died so the stories would not be lost or forgotten. Then, after his death in 2008 and my mother's passing in 2013, I spent three years reading through the 265 typed, eloquent letters Dad had written home during the war. They were so remarkable and such a revelation, I decided to excerpt their most compelling passages. Together, with the interviews' transcript, a book began to take form.

Out of curiosity and motivated to research the specific battles in which my father participated, I gained a better understanding of the details and extreme circumstances of those bloody engagements with the German army. Inserting this historical information into the manuscript provided critical context for the letters and insights into the challenges experienced by the celebrated 34th Infantry Division.

Subsequently, I added a few more personal chapters to flesh out my parents' profiles as individuals and exploration into the emotional trauma of war. As a daughter, I was also led to consider how this new information about my parents as the young, idealistic adults they once were, has given me a better understanding of not only *them*, but of myself, as well. This more subjective layer of the book may resonate with a broader range of readers, giving them a reason to care about the main characters driving the narrative, while also inspiring them to reflect on their own family's complex stories.

There have been many nonfiction books written about World War II over the decades: third-person scholarly narratives focusing on strategies and outcomes of major conflicts and campaigns; anthologies of war letters and diary entries or a specific focus on one soldier's letters home, with little to no context of the locations and specific battles being fought; first-person accounts of veterans' World War II experiences; collections of tributes to World War II veterans and recent interviews with those still living, etc.

But there are very few in-depth personal accounts of war told from the perspective of a regimental surgeon on the frontlines of combat. In addition to this fresh look at war, the underlying love story that develops over a newly married couple's 28-month separation—and a daughter's discovery of the parents she never really knew as the young adults they once were, add new insights into and understanding of history's most enduring themes of love and war. This multi-layered/multi-generational compendium of our country's last "good war," has not yet been seen in one book.

Introduction

My father, Dr. Arthur L. "Lud" Ludwick, Jr., 1913–2008, lived in Wenatchee, Washington, for sixty-three years where he was a beloved family physician. A year before he retired, he was honored by the Washington State Medical Association for practicing medicine in Washington State for over fifty years.

He was a modest and quiet man and most people didn't know of his heroism during World War II. He served on the frontlines from 1942 to 1944 as a Battalion and Regimental Surgeon in fourteen major engagements with the enemy in North Africa and Italy. As part of the 34th Infantry Division (133rd/168th Regiments), he insisted on serving as far forward as possible to ensure that wounded soldiers were quickly treated where they fell and properly evacuated.

As a result, he earned the Purple Heart in Tunisia and was decorated with the Silver Star in Italy, where during the bloody battle of Monte Pantano, the treatment and evacuation of the wounded had been slowed under intense enemy fire. For five days he made frequent trips to the battlefield to not only supervise and coordinate the treatment and evacuation of the heavy casualties, but also to administer aid to the wounded himself. "Due to his initiative and tireless efforts, many lives were saved that otherwise might have been lost," reads the official commendation. "Major Ludwick's courage and bravery were highly meritorious and a credit to the Armed Forces of the United States."

The official "Confidential" Silver Star Commendation reveals the full scope of my father's courage and commitment to the care of his men, even while putting his own life in danger. (See Appendix A: Silver Star Commendation.)

Lud married Jean Katherine Hoyer in Alexandria, Louisiana, on October 11, 1941. Not quite two months later, on December 7, Pearl Harbor was bombed and our country abruptly entered World War II. On New Year's Eve 1941, Lt. Arthur L. Ludwick, Jr., M.D., found himself saying a tearful goodbye to his young wife from whom he would be separated for two and a half years—not an ideal way to begin a marriage.

He and his 34th Infantry Division were headed to Fort Dix, New Jersey, by train, where they boarded the first American troop ship to Europe, destination unknown. Although none of the soldiers knew where they were going, they certainly knew why.

After the bombing of Pearl Harbor by the Japanese in December 1941, Lud's Iowa National Guard unit was immediately federalized and mobilized into action as the 34th Infantry "Red Bull" Division. This major detour in his life plan was unexpected. Eleven months earlier, in January 1941, at the urging of his friends in Waterloo, Iowa, Lud had joined the Iowa National Guard with the promise of a thousand-dollar bonus and a captain's commission after just one year of service. It sounded like a pretty good deal, since he had come to realize he needed to get out of the Midwest fairly soon and find a different part of the country in which to practice medicine. His severe hay fever, an allergy to ragweed in particular, had become almost debilitating. A thousand-dollar check at the end of the year would allow him to take some time off to explore the West and find a place to settle. But, on December 7, 1941, all that changed.

As it turned out, U.S. troops were headed to Northern Ireland to secretly train for ten months before deploying to North Africa to engage with "the Desert Fox," renowned German General Johannes Erwin Eugen Rommel, and his highly trained infantry. President Roosevelt had wanted to establish an early and strong presence in Europe, strategically located in a neutral and low-profile country where American troops would be poised and ready to "take care of business," wherever that happened to be. And if the United States was the first to land in and occupy Northern Ireland, the Germans could not.

Through extensive interviews with my father about his war experiences, his 265 eloquent letters home to my mother during the war, and my own World War II research, I have pieced together one man's resolute journey through the minefields of love and war, and back. What he discovered about himself along the way became its own story, as did my discovery of the young man I never knew—before he became my father.

Lud fervently believed that the love of his wife, doing his job well, and the Providence of God would protect him and allow his safe return. Apparently, they did.

The Interviews

The ingenuity of an American soldier is something to behold.

Using a small hand-held recording device, I interviewed my father during the last few years of his life to capture and document his experiences as a combat medical officer on the frontlines of World War II. I did not want these remarkable stories to be lost or forgotten.

He was never one to embellish or exaggerate, but loved recounting the basic details of what happened. It was only after his death in 2008 and delving deeper into World War II history that I realized Dad almost always minimized and understated the danger and hardship of his circumstances. Through background reading and research on the North African and Italian campaigns, I learned he participated in some of the bloodiest and deadliest battles of the entire war.

Because I lived over two hours away, our interview sessions were sporadic, often with months passing between the conversations. As time progressed, my visits required more focused attention to Dad's chronic and acute health-related issues. Occasionally, when the timing was right, we picked up the interview sessions where we thought we had left off, leading to some sequencing gaps, slight variations of the stories, a few discrepancies, but also new details that Dad would suddenly recall.

Considering that his war experiences had occurred almost 65 years earlier, his memory was remarkable.

Eventually, I patched together and transcribed the disjointed and rambling audio-tape interviews into a forty-page typed document that Dad was able to proofread before he died. In retrospect, I regret not conducting these interviews years earlier and wished I had been better informed about the specific battles and locations to which he referred. A more interactive interview process and asking critical follow-up questions during our sessions could have fleshed out his narrative. But at that point in time, I had not yet taken a serious interest in World War II and certainly had no intentions of writing a book. Nor had I read his 265 war letters home to my mother during the war. As it turned out, time was against us and in the end, it was my father's energy that gave out, not his memory.

The interviews give a more detailed account of the 34th Infantry's orders and outcomes that my father did not disclose in his letters home to my mother. Due to the strict censorship policies of the military, letters from overseas could not contain any sensitive information regarding location, details of battles, combat casualties, or current status—*any* news that might be appropriated by the enemy and used to its advantage.

Censorship of all packages and letters was usually handled by a unit officer and this was one of the many duties assigned to my father—he strictly adhered to the mandatory protocols. He was required to read his enlisted men's mail and black out or cut out anything that might be of interest to the enemy. Dad carefully censored his men's letters and his own, as well. He was not only obeying the army's directives, but more importantly, he did not want to worry or alarm his young wife back home in the U.S. Consequently, his letters contained vague references to his locations and some coded language.

After reading about the specific battles in which my father was engaged, I came to realize that his phrases: "it was very rough/very tough going" and "it was kind of a big deal" *really* meant dangerous engagement with the enemy, extreme conditions, bloody battles, and high casualty rates.

Included in the interviews with my father are quotes and references from a variety of historical resources, as well as expanded information in the footnotes, endnotes, and appendices that provide a better understanding of and context for what he and his 34th Infantry Division soldiers endured. The relentless courage and reliability of those wearing the red cross armband in his regimental medical detachment, often responding to the wounded under fire, was truly extraordinary.

The World War II history and background information I have added are not intended to give a comprehensive overview of the *entire* war, but to provide context for the "Iowa boys" of the 34th Infantry Division's 133rd and 168th Regiments' experiences during my father's service with them.

The interviews, combined with my commentary, serve as a companion and lead-in to the batches of the chronologically corresponding letters. I tried to keep the historical footnotes and background information to a minimum in the "Letters" sections, so as not to interrupt the flow of my father's powerfully written accounts.

Dad loved to tell stories, full of details and with many asides. The words in the interviews are distinctly his—and still resonate in a humble, timeless, and vital way.

The Letters

"Making war on a foreign soil is a curious mixture of almost hysterical excitement and mind-dulling boredom."

Dad was a compulsive saver and record keeper: a grandfather's 1867 Civil War discharge papers, a 29-cent receipt for batteries purchased in 1957, carbon copies of all the typed letters he ever sent, as well as carefully filed correspondence he received throughout his lifetime.

Gray dented filing cabinets lined all four walls of his home office and were jammed with neatly labeled folders of medical journal articles, medical school lecture notes, philosophical ponderings, operating manuals of all the appliances he ever owned, decades-old financial statements and receipts, profiles of interesting patient cases from his residency and early medical practice—all typed, except for a few beautifully handwritten journal entries in fountain pen—always blue ink in his pens and typewriter ribbons.

His rapid-fire, index-fingered, "hunt-and-peck" typing technique was legendary and produced long, detailed and endearing letters to friends, family members, and colleagues. They were filled with snippets of gentle counseling and encouragement, professional medical advice, and invitations to visit the beautiful Wenatchee Valley, and were peppered throughout with a few quick words of dry wit that would make the reader smile.

Blue-ink typed labels and instructions were everywhere in our family home—some discreetly placed on the inside of cabinet doors, others blatantly stuck on a wall above a quirky electrical outlet, a reminder that "The smoke detectors are hard-wired into the house," etc. He made a habit of recording and documenting the details of his life, leaving written reminders or instructions for those who might need what he thought was important information.

Even as a medical officer on the frontlines, Lud lugged a bulky Remington typewriter with him at all times—into Irish peat fields, Tunisian wadis (dry creek beds), and through dangerous river crossings in Italy.*

---

* "Apparently, the War Department scooped up every typewriter they could from the civilian market and pressed them into service. The main brands were Remington, Underwood, and Corona. No typewriters were made during the war years, and the Remington and Underwood factories were converted to war production (Underwood made M1 Carbines). It was illegal for a civilian to purchase a typewriter during WWII as all existing stocks were turned over to the Quartermaster Department. The department also set up typewriter repair schools, which was the most common machine the QM mechanics would repair in WWII. Among the cargos of one of the few ships sunk at Normandy were 20,000 typewriters. That must have put a major crimp in the supply chain." Salvage Sailor, U.S. Navy Specialist and Moderator. U.S. Militaria Forum (online) January 28, 2008. https://www.usmilitariaforum.com/forums/index.php?/topic/11032-wwii-typewriter-question/&tab=comments#comment-99244.

Introduction

18 October 1943; somewhere in Italy (letter excerpt)

> "I'm snatching a moment to write to you and tell you that I'm all O.K. I'm standing in the muddy courtyard of a house in a small town in Italy (censored). The typewriter is setting on the hood of my jeep and artillery shells are whistling both ways overhead."

My brother and I spent over two years sorting through and clearing out my parents' home after my mother's death in 2013. The rich paper trail of my dad's life was a record of what he considered essential—and the sheer volume of it was overwhelming. Yet, once I began, I felt compelled to read through every file, letter, note, journal entry, and photo caption—a form of grieving, I suppose, that grew into a deeper understanding of who my father was, as well as coming to know him in a very different and more mature way. Amidst the trivial were touching and revealing glimpses into his mind and life. I keenly felt his presence and heard his voice through what he had saved and determined was important—I could not seem to part with any of it.

Most revealing were the 265 long, detailed, typed letters my father wrote home to my mother during the war. I'd been aware of these letters for many years, bundled with white cotton string and stored in a shoebox under my parents' bed. But it wasn't until my dad and mom died, in 2008 and 2013, respectively, that I gave myself permission to read them. They murmured softly at first, then beckoned like a siren song.

1942–1944: The box of 265 typed wartime letters Lt. Col./Maj. A.L. "Lud" Ludwick, Jr., M.D., sent home to his wife, Jean.

Over the course of three years, I finally read them all. I was mesmerized. These eloquently written letters were sheer poetry, filled with longing, hope, and despair as well as giving a unique, never-before-seen perspective of war: the daily, multifaceted duties of a combat regimental surgeon responsible for the psychological and physical well-being of his men; keen observations about the landscapes, culture, and people of Northern Ireland, North Africa, and Italy; and insights into true leadership, human character, the irrational nature of war.

They were essentially journal entries, chronicling my father's growing frustration with the Army's bureaucracy and inefficiencies, concerns about the emotional health of his men, and a crucial lifeline to the more "normal" world and life back home in the U.S.

But above all, these were love letters from a homesick medical officer on the frontlines of a horrific war, to his young, beautiful wife of only two months. Dad was desperate to stay connected with her and keep their flame of new love burning over the course of their twenty-eight-month separation. Here was a romantic, clever, engaging new husband and courageous army officer, seemingly different from the father I knew growing up. From 1942 to 1944, he was thousands of miles away and fighting not only for his life and country, but perhaps, for his marriage as well.

Through the prism of World War II, I was surprised and moved by the young man I met in his letters. Learning about the daily operations of a medical detachment and my father's leadership during the bloody incursions of North Africa and Italy, were fascinating discoveries. It became obvious that his quiet and gentle nature were not only a comfort to those soldiers under his command, but that he also possessed an inner strength that commanded respect, admiration and even, inspiration. These personality traits were what also endeared him as a Family Practice physician to his devoted patients over the course of five decades.

Even more intriguing was the intimate glimpse into my parents' courting, romance, new marriage, and their hopes and dreams as a young, idealistic couple. I was astonished to see and contemplate them as individuals, struggling to find their way in tumultuous and uncertain times.

I found these letters so extraordinary, I decided to excerpt portions that felt especially compelling and, in so doing, came to realize I was touching the same keys, in the same order as my father had done almost eighty years earlier. In essence, his words were being "written twice." The hours I spent reading and extracting passages from the letters via the tactile act of re-typing his thoughts and words, were transforming. A deep intimacy developed that reshaped my dad's presence and now, absence in my life. These letters have been both a gift and a revelation. Is it possible to rewrite one's family history? Perhaps.

* * *

Dad's prolific letter writing to my mother during the war was remarkable, especially since he was also corresponding regularly with his elderly widowed mother and 10 to 12 other family members and friends. How did he do it?

Introduction

Over three-quarters of a century later, my father's letters are still surprisingly relevant in revealing what soldiers endure during combat and in separation from their loved ones back home. Their hidden, uncounted casualties of war, the invisible wounds that veterans carry into their postwar lives, can affect families for generations to come.

> "I know that a great many men who are now overseas will be strangers when they return, and their secret need for understanding and companionship will go unheeded. No rough, tough fighting American is going to admit that need, but it'll be there just the same, and its frustration will come to the surface in a variety of actions, reactions, and behaviors. Darling—I'm going to need you very much when I get home." Italy, 1944
>
> —Lt. Col./Maj. Arthur L. Ludwick, M.D.

I've come to believe that my father's almost daily letters from the frontlines of World War II were each a tiny triumph, marking his days and getting him through the indescribable horrors of war. They became his focus, purpose, and ultimately, his salvation—to survive another day, to send another letter and, perhaps, to receive one, as well.

Reading Notes

- An indispensable resource for my learning about the war in North Africa was Pulitzer Prize-winning author and historian Rick Atkinson's book *An Army at Dawn*. I gave this book to my dad for his 93rd birthday, a year before he died in 2008. Even though the book weighed in at almost 700 pages, Dad was able to read this book to the end, leaving many faint underlines in pencil, plus a few notes and stars in the margins. We never had the opportunity to discuss the book, but while researching the North African campaign and reading the book myself several years later, I discovered my dad's markings within its pages. This happy finding was not only touching, but also confirmed some of the locations of my dad's 133rd and 168th regiments—and flagged more extensive details of the specific battles in which he participated.
- My questions to my father in the Interviews are in **bold.** His answers follow.
- The letters are dated and in chronological order. A reminder to the reader that not *all* of my dad's letters have been included in this book, and that most of what appears here are only *excerpts* from the selected letters' full text.
- In some cases, my commentary, providing historical context and references, is set apart from text in the interviews and letters by three asterisks: * * *.
- Brackets [...] indicate information I added for clarification.
- The "Chronology of Events": In the letters, Dad's eloquent descriptions of the North African and Italian landscapes, small remote villages and residents' homes where he and his men spent time, their "rest" and bivouac areas, locations of conflicts and cities visited, all piqued my interest. As a result, I

pieced together a "best guess" chronology of the 133rd and 168th Regiments' movements across North Africa and Italy, gleaning information and clues from World War II military documents, books, old newspaper and magazine articles, and published firsthand accounts. You may refer to this guide while reading the letters to get a better sense of what was *really* happening and where—details of which my father did not and could not reveal in his letters home due to the U.S. Army's strict censorship protocol, and his determined effort to not alarm his young wife. Although I was able to corroborate most of the dates and locations, there are some unnamed locales referenced in the letters where I could only guess the exact village or camp location, based on the evidence at hand. Therefore, there are portions of this chronology where I cannot guarantee absolute accuracy.

Main Cast of Characters

- Jean Hoyer Ludwick: Lud's wife (and eventually my mother) of just two months, when he left on the first U.S. troop ship to Europe after the bombing of Pearl Harbor in December 1941. They were separated during the war for 28 months.
- Lt./Maj. Morris J. Leslie, M.D.: my dad's "Sidekick," Medical Assistant and best friend in the 133rd Regiment, and throughout my dad's 28 months of service during the war. "Les" was a family physician from Brooklyn, New York, married and, at the time, the father of two young daughters. My family and I visited the Leslie family in New York City during the summer of 1956. After my father's death in 2008, Les' daughter, Joyce, and I became email friends and corresponded regularly until her death in 2017.
- Sgt/Corporal Hubert "Hub" Mott, from McKinney, Texas, ran a family dry cleaning and tailoring business. He was Lud's fearless jeep driver and indispensable all-around fixer/procurer. He served with Lud in Northern Ireland and North Africa.
- John "Jack" Vail Hoyer, my mother's younger 23-year-old brother and a sergeant in the 752nd Tank Battalion. Lud was able to meet up with Jack a few times during the war—in North Africa and Italy. Jack was tragically killed near Eboli, Italy, just three weeks after a rendezvous visit with my father.

"Beginnings"

Where *HE* Began

My father was an unassuming and thoughtful man. Born on November 15, 1913, the only child of older parents, he spent each of his first four years of elementary school in a different state. His father, a physician and psychiatrist, served in the U.S. Army during World War I as one of its earliest trained flight surgeons, treating shell-shocked aviators, our nation's first daring pilots. When Dad was in the fifth grade, the family finally settled in Overland Park, Kansas, where his father, after being discharged from the Army, practiced general medicine.

In high school, at 6'1" and weighing 128 pounds, Dad was a gangly, fair-haired boy who was two years younger than his classmates. He was physically late to bloom, socially naïve, and inexperienced in many ways, although his father made sure he learned the manners and practices of a proper Southern gentleman: how to ballroom dance, play a decent game of golf and bridge, and above all, respect women.

In 1930, when his father died unexpectedly of a massive heart attack and left few financial resources, Dad was only sixteen. This sudden and traumatic loss might have been crippling, but he coped by setting himself on a focused course of college and medical school, while also helping support his widowed mother. The demands of his higher education and new role as head-of-household suddenly ratcheted his life into fast forward, forcing him to grow up quickly.

Dad entered the University of Kansas at age sixteen as a freshman, then medical school at eighteen via a special fast-track program for ambitious students coming out of the Great Depression. His mother followed him to Lawrence, Kansas, and operated a boarding house near campus. For a few months, my father lived in the Delta Upsilon fraternity house, enjoying the companionship of "brothers" he'd never had, as well as his first real social experiences. However, he was overcome by guilt at the thought of his elderly mother with high blood pressure shoveling coal into the furnace every night. So, after six months of living the consummate college/fraternity life, Dad moved into his mother's boarding house to help with the daily chores.

As a result, most of my father's life was one of sacrifice and duty with little time for leisure or "fun." Each day presented new challenges requiring a disciplined routine, hard work, and careful choices, all of which eventually brought him a sense of security and satisfaction. Over time, this strict regimen became his own recipe for pleasure and success.

Where *SHE* Began

Jean Katherine Hoyer was born on September 30, 1917, in Virginia, Minnesota, a small town in the Iron Range of northern Minnesota, 90 miles from the Canadian border. She was the oldest of four children and was especially close to her brother, Jack, second oldest and just twenty months younger. She was adventurous and athletic and spent most of her time outdoors with Jack and friends playing golf, swimming in and ice-skating on nearby lakes, skiing on homemade wooden skis, and sledding on the elaborate snow-packed "roller coaster" course built in their backyard lot by her father, Ben.

Winters were long and harsh, prompting Virginia High School to become a competitive force in ice hockey, basketball, and swimming, with an indoor heated pool funded by tax money from the mines. Jean loved being on the school swim team and traveling to neighboring towns for swim meets.

The family spent summers at Lake Esquagama, the highlight being a "Grand" 4th of July community parade with decorated bicycles, wagons, and fireworks.

Jean's father, Ben, was born on July 4, so for many years, she thought all the hoopla was in honor of him.

Jean started driving a car when she was just twelve, walking miles to meet her dad on his way home from work in the evenings so she could drive the rest of the way to their house. By the time she was fourteen, he would send her in the family car to pick up the young miners near Eveleth after their afternoon work shifts for his team's evening hockey practices.

She was as smart as she was naturally beautiful, with classic features, thick dark auburn hair that she cut herself, and a lean yet curvaceous figure. Clothes looked good on her 5'6" frame—but with a nod to her tomboy-ish childhood, she preferred bare legs to hosiery and function vs fashion. Her million-dollar smile dazzled everyone she met.

Where *THEY* Began

Jean and Lud met in 1938 in Waterloo, Iowa—he from Kansas, she from Minnesota. He had taken his first job as a *real* doctor there, joining an older physician's medical practice, Dr. Ivan Powers, on the seventh floor of the Blackhawk Building. She, fresh out of the University of Minnesota's new Medical Technology/Laboratory Science program, had accepted an "internship" at Waterloo's small Presbyterian Hospital for more practical training. However, upon arrival and despite her inexperience, Jean found herself put in charge of the hospital's clinical laboratory, x-ray department, and blood bank, with little to no supervision by the attending pathologist. She was, in fact, the only certified Medical Technologist in sight, on call 24/7, and expected to run all three departments on her own. She had very little bench experience performing the blood and fluids tests that physicians ordered, and when she learned she was required to also make the chemical reagents used for these critical lab tests, she panicked. Her college courses hadn't covered this aspect of higher-level chemistry in an actual clinical lab setting.

But Jean was bright and resourceful, and wanted to be successful at this, her first real professional job. She had taken a huge risk by striking out on her own so far away from home in Duluth, Minnesota. And so, with charm and a practical goal, she approached the new young doctor in town for help. He was Dr. Arthur L. Ludwick, Jr., who was navigating his own challenges as a first-time practicing physician.

She called him "Lud," which was a bit cheeky, but also surprisingly appealing to this socially awkward and serious young man. He was intrigued with the arrangement—a seemingly professional liaison with an exceptionally ambitious, smart, and attractive young woman. She was independent, sporty and tanned, with a tendency to freckle—someone that tested his more conservative and traditional views of the feminine stereotype. My father had never met anyone like her.

When she had a few hours off from her hospital duties, she pedaled her bicycle to the airfield on the outskirts of town and took flying lessons. She was in partnership with four other pilots, all men, in renting a Taylor Light single-engine airplane. After acquiring enough training hours to fly solo, she delivered critical units of blood to outlying rural hospitals, using only the visual landmarks of Iowa's tidy geometric patchwork of corn fields for navigation. One evening, as dusk was falling, her pilot pals were concerned she wasn't yet back from her afternoon delivery flight and lined their cars up on the airport runway with their headlights on so she could find her way home … or so the story goes.

After a somewhat tumultuous courtship of almost three years, Jean and Lud were married in Alexandria, Louisiana, on October 11, 1941, near where Lud had been training in the Iowa National Guard. Almost two months later, Pearl Harbor was bombed and Lud left for two-and-a-half years to serve as a Medical Officer on the frontlines of World War II.

Jean cultivated a full and active life in Waterloo, Iowa, while Lud was serving overseas from 1942 to 1944: working in the hospital and helping out in a few physicians' offices, continuing her flying lessons, getting together with friends and other army wives and generally just managing life on her own. For whatever reasons, she did not write to my father nearly as often as he wrote to her.

Excerpted from an uncle's letter to my dad during the war:

> April 5, 1943
> Kansas City, Missouri
>
> *Dear Doc:*
> *Just a line to tell you that we had the pleasure of meeting your good wife and she made a tremendous hit with every one of us. She is so sweet and charming and has such fine poise and high intelligence. We were delighted with her and the whole family feels highly honored to have her as one of us. You sure are a lucky devil to get a girl like that, so you will have to keep on your P's and Q's to keep her. You certainly are to be congratulated.*

"Sidekick"

Soon after Dad's congestive heart failure was diagnosed in 2006, I brought up the large dusty cardboard box marked "WWII" from the basement and decided it was time to see what was there. Although I had listened to his war stories my entire life, I was coming to realize there might be only weeks or months left to examine the contents of that box, with my father as commentator.

His physical frailty and failing energy were obvious, although his memory and cognition were as clear and precise as ever. As I opened the battered box full of photographs and yellowed, curled military documents, I was stunned by the treasure trove of buried history. It was filled with scores of two-by-three-inch black and white photos from World War II—Northern Ireland, North Africa, and Italy, many with typed captions on the back, as well as detailed records of his daily operations as a medical officer, all perfectly preserved. I immediately understood that *this* was to be the illustrated version of my father's service on the frontlines of World War II.

"Who's this, Dad?" I said, holding up a small black and white photo. He took it and examined it closely as the sun streamed through the family room's window behind him. His large, perfectly shaped bald head practically glistened as he turned the snapshot over and read the typed caption: "Lt. Morris J. Leslie—antics ????"

"That's Leslie," he answered. "Lt. Morris J. Leslie, a physician from Brooklyn, my Medical Assistant and "sidekick"—a swell egg. I think that must have been in Northern Ireland. That guy was a real character. He was the best one of the Brooklyn boys that we got. Excellent sense of humor—we enjoyed each other's company very much. He was quite a clown in many ways and saw the funny side of everything."

The man in the photo was clearly posing for the camera and reveling in the moment. His goofy, outstretched arms and obvious sense of play immediately led me to believe that this guy could be a handful, in sharp contrast to my dad's more serious and formal comportment. As an only child of older parents, coming of age during the Great Depression, and suddenly losing his beloved father to a massive heart attack in high school, my father's sober demeanor was well-earned.

Leslie was seemingly everything my dad was not—a Jewish doctor from Brooklyn with a full head of thick dark hair, black bushy mustache, a "cut-up" and party organizer who made Lud laugh. Alongside my dad's tall, lean, balding, fair-skinned profile, they must have looked like Mutt and Jeff at their medical aid stations—but they complemented each other well and became inseparable.

"Don't you remember him?" my dad continued. "In the summer of 1956, we visited the Leslie family in New York City. You were just seven."

Remnants of that three-week family trip back east had always lingered and became an indelible childhood marker, stored deeply within the drawers of my memory. We had traveled by train and car that hot summer to visit distant relatives in Illinois and Kansas, all the major historic monuments and sites in Washington, D.C., and then on to New York City. Even now, I can feel the sticky summer heat and humidity of Manhattan and vividly recall

1942 Northern Ireland: Lt. Morris J. Leslie, M.D., Ludwick's Medical Assistant in the 133rd Regiment of the 34th Infantry Division.

1942 Northern Ireland: Ludwick's best friend and "sidekick," Lt. Morris J. Leslie.

1942 Castlerock, Northern Ireland: 1st Lt. Arthur L. Ludwick, Jr.

the strange sights and sounds of Central Park: mothers sitting on benches watching their children play and speaking with strange, thick foreign accents; dark-haired olive-skinned babies with pierced ears; old, wrinkled women wearing colorful silk head scarves and shawls; and strange food I had never before seen or smelled.

I had vaguely remembered running across a batch of old family vacation photos in a jammed drawer of my childhood home. A nagging recollection kept surfacing of two black and white photos in particular, taken with another family so many years ago, on top of some tall building in New York City.

Finally, in the years following my parents' deaths, while meticulously sorting through each file, drawer, shelf and closet of their home, I found them—the two sought-after pictures taken almost seven decades earlier of the Morris J.

July 1956, NYC, NY: A happy postwar reunion of Dr. Morris J. Leslie (left) and Dr. Arthur L. Ludwick, Jr., atop the Empire State Building.

Leslie family and mine. Who were these people, how did we know them, and why were these photos so haunting?

After reading my dad's war letters, I found the answer. This was my father's beloved "Leslie," with whom he had spent two and a half years overseas during World War II. Seeing my dad and his "Sidekick" together in these 1956 photos—their affection for one another so obvious, I wept, and vowed to locate the Leslie family and send them this tangible evidence of our fathers' unique bond. I was beginning to more fully understand the "existential cord" that stretches through time and miles, binding soldiers who serve together in battle, for a lifetime.

Prologue

November 2007

Sitting in the passenger seat, he looked the same as always—eyes straight ahead in quiet alert, subdued, smartly dressed. It was late November and he wore his favorite plaid flannel shirt, blue agate bolo tie, a weathered hounds-tooth sport coat with tiny Masonic and Rotary Club stick-pins in the lapel, all topped off by one of his signature wool caps. His look was somewhere between practical and dapper—well-worn, but classic and sensibly composed.

He'd sported a hat for most of his life: a variety of U.S. Army officer service hats and a helmet during World War II, a felt fedora to his office every day and on evenings out, a wool or cotton English driving cap for more casual settings on the weekends, and a broad-brimmed straw Panama hat for protection from the sun during the summer. He wore them all well. Topping his large, smooth bald head, they seemed to "dot-the-i" and smartly finish his poised presence.

I glanced over at him as we approached the bridge spanning the "Mighty Columbia" River in my hometown, Wenatchee, Washington. It was mid-afternoon and we needed to get him settled in before dinner at 5 p.m. He knew, all too well, what was coming. As I reached to squeeze his cool, bony hand, I tried to detect any hint of anger or resentment in his face. His gaze was focused forward, not even glancing at the steel gray ribbon of river underscoring the landscape outside the car window and silently escorting us to, most likely, his final "home." Against that familiar backdrop of water's powerful and timeless flow, I decided his look seemed more determined, than anything else—one I had seen many times before.

"Dad," I began, trying to push through the catch in my throat. "You know what this means. Mom just can't take care of you anymore—it's killing her. You're making the ultimate sacrifice—you're saving her life. I'm just so sorry that it's come to this. You're very brave."

I'd grown up with the framed black and white photo of my dad during World War II, solemnly standing before Lt. Gen. Mark W. Clark as he was decorated with the Silver Star for "Gallantry-in-Action." It was an unusual combat commendation for an unarmed medical officer. He had led squadrons of litter carriers up Monte Pantano, Italy, through a curtain of heavy mortar fire during the winter of 1943. His mission was to treat and evacuate the pin-downed, wounded soldiers from his unit, the 168th Regiment of the 34th "Red Bull" Infantry Division.

March 14, 1944, Benevento, Italy: Official U.S. Army photograph and caption: "Major Arthur L. Ludwick, Jr., M.D., of Waterloo, Iowa, is decorated with the Silver Star by Lt. Gen. Mark W. Clark in a ceremony at Fifth Army Headquarters in Benevento, Italy. A member of the 34th Infantry Division, Major Ludwick was honored for his 'gallantry-in-action' at Mt. Pantano, Italy" (NEA Service, Inc. 461 8th Ave., N.Y. 8 × 10 original).

"Major Ludwick voluntarily and of his own volition, treated, supervised, and led the evacuation of wounded soldiers pinned-down by heavy artillery fire on Mt. Pantano, putting his own life at risk over the course of five days...." reads the official U.S. Army Silver Star Commendation.

He had volunteered to do it—didn't have to, yet made countless trips to retrieve as many wounded men as possible and get them to safety. He would never have ordered someone else to do something he wasn't willing to do himself.

He was resolute. This was his nature. He always did what was necessary, despite the danger, unpleasant circumstances, adversity involved. It became the foundation for his definition of success, a phrase I heard throughout my life: *Success is doing something you don't want to do, and doing it well.*

And now, here I was, driving my 94-year-old father for elective admission to a nursing home. I was, indeed, doing something I didn't want to do and I was going to try to do it well. Was that even possible?

I knew the statistics. Most patients live six months or less in such a facility. Dad's congestive heart failure had become too much for my mother to handle at home. My brother, Jack, and I both lived out of town and after discussing Mom's inability to manage a team of around-the-clock caregivers, we reluctantly agreed that the nursing home was our only option.

Dad flashed me a faint smile, nodding. His deeply veined hands clasped in his lap were covered with a Rorschach of purple and burgundy bruises. As we drove, he compulsively checked his pulse, as he frequently did, and I thought I detected a slight clench in his jaw.

This was to be his Final Front.

1

Camp Claiborne, Louisiana

34th Infantry Division Training, February 1941–December 31, 1941

"I think that my leaving Waterloo and home was a very good thing for me. I had a hunch as to what would happen, and I think I am beginning to grow up—after a very long adolescence."

—27 April 1941, Camp Claiborne, LA

Interviews

PL: How did a young physician from Kansas find himself on the frontlines of World War II?

Dad: I was practicing General (Family) Medicine in Waterloo, Iowa, after my surgical residency at the Hertzler Clinic in Halstead, Kansas. It was my first job as a real doctor. I think it was early December 1940, I decided I had to get out of Waterloo because I was suffering from such severe ragweed hay fever. Honestly, I couldn't even lean over to examine a patient without my runny nose dripping onto the field of treatment.

I proposed to myself that I would join the Iowa National Guard as a Medical Officer. The recruiters told me they would make me a Captain: "C'mon down, Doc, we'll make you a Captain. You'll go down to Louisiana for a year, but the last month, you'll get terminal leave and you'll be discharged after the year's up—and you'll get a thousand bucks." I decided that would be a good way to save up a little money and serve a year in the Army, which, at the time, was really just the Iowa National Guard. I could spend that last month of "leave" looking for a place to settle and practice medicine. At that point in time, the federal government was thinking something about the war in Europe and I was afraid we might eventually get involved in it. But I went ahead and joined the Iowa National Guard, on December 2, 1940, and was commissioned as a First Lieutenant.

The Iowa National Guard became part of the 34th Infantry Division, that was officially federalized on February 10, 1941. America had begun to see that Hitler was extending his cruel reign over much of Europe and Germany was re-arming. In fact, they were about ready to start bombing London. They had declared war and were already at war with the French and the British. They had whipped the French, but because of the large British Navy, they were hemmed in a little bit—but they, the Germans, were building these super battleships. There was a big cataclysm coming up.

In February 1941, I left Waterloo, Iowa, when we were shipped by train to Camp Claiborne, Louisiana, which was about ten to fifteen miles southwest of Alexandria, Louisiana, in the center of the state—I think it was on the Red River.*

I paid a corporal in the medical detachment to drive my '39 Oldsmobile Coupe down there—I had to go with the troops on the train in case one of them got sick or injured. We found Camp Claiborne to be a Tent City—it was a tent camp of about 6,000 tents for the enlisted men and about 750 tents for officers. There were some buildings—every company had a mess hall, a wooden building on a concrete foundation with running water. And then there were the latrines, which were also wooden buildings. There was also a hospital, two service clubs and a theater. But all the

February 1941, Camp Claiborne, Louisiana: "Tent City." Site of the 34th Infantry Division's basic training and the Louisiana Maneuvers, prior to U.S. entering World War II in December 1941. [Lud's caption in quotation marks.]

* "The grounds were a sea of red, sticky mud; ... this tent city served about 25,000 men over about five square miles. The drenching downpours of rain that prevailed throughout the spring and summer months [were] followed always by the boiling Louisiana sun and a stifling humidity ..." Sgt. Milo L. Green, *Brickbats from F Company,* Capt. Paul S. Gauthier, ed. Grosse Pointe, Michigan: Gauthier Publishing Co., 1982. 19–22. [Hereafter cited as *Brickbats*]. The first Brickbats column was published in late March 1941 by Sgt. Green who throughout the war continued to send a steady stream of "Brickbats" columns back to his hometown newspapers in Iowa.

living quarters were canvas—tents on a solid wood foundation. They must have had at least 30,000 troops there.*

PL: What did you do there?
Dad: I was a Battalion Surgeon there. I came in as a First Lieutenant, expecting to be quickly promoted to Captain, but the Division Surgeon who made all the medical promotions was Colonel Fourt from Des Moines, Iowa—that was the headquarters of the Division, I think. He had already promoted a bunch in order to enlist his friends and get doctors to go into this not very popular deal, to go into the Army at that time. I was willing to do it for a year because I was promised a Captain's salary. The guys that promised me that thought they knew what they were talking about—I didn't blame them, but I didn't get the promotion I had expected that whole year.

I took care of men in four companies, with about 150 men in a company, a total of about 500 to 600 men. We had a little aid station and we had sick call every day—and anything that was serious, we sent to the station hospital, which was another wooden building with covered walkways. The station hospital was staffed by other doctors—so I didn't get to follow those I sent there. I didn't know all these things at the time, you see—I was a little naïve.

I had a battalion section of the medical detachment—about 125 officers and enlisted men—I had a First Sergeant and other enlisted men under me—and I had an Assistant Battalion Surgeon that was a

Summer 1941, Camp Claiborne, Louisiana: 1st Lt. A.L. Ludwick, Jr., M.D., MC; "On maneuvers in Central La" (Lud's caption).

---

*In 1941, prior to the United States declaring war, the camp, located just north of the tiny town of Forest Hill, was used as part of the Louisiana Maneuvers, a 400,000-man training exercise involving two imaginary countries fighting each other. In these simulated "war games," the two armies faced each other across the Red River and vast expanses of forest in rural Louisiana. Near the end of the war, German prisoners of war (POWs) were held at the camp. "Camp Claiborne," *Wikipedia*. https://en.wikipedia.org/wiki/Camp_Claiborne.

dentist. All Assistant Surgeons were dentists—they took care of the men's teeth, simple things like fillings and extractions.

We went on maneuvers in June or July 1941 over at Fort/Camp Polk, which was west of us about twenty-five miles. We were in the Louisiana forest near there for the maneuvers. Because I was a Medical Officer I didn't have much to do—I just had to run sick call every morning.

One unpleasant experience was I discovered they have real bad chiggers down in Louisiana, which are tiny little red mites. One time I had about eighty-five bites on

1941, Waterloo, Iowa: Jean Hoyer and Lud behind Presbyterian Hospital where Jean worked.

me—these little itchy pimples—they're bad. So, I went to the Five & Dime store and got a large kitchen salt-shaker and filled it up with powdered sulfur. I'd shake this powdered sulfur from the waist down all over me and spread it around. The chiggers didn't like the sulfur—it acted like a repellant. I smelled a little like rotten eggs, I guess, but I didn't care what it smelled like as long as I didn't get those darn chiggers. I got so lonesome for Jean before and during maneuvers, in the spring and at other times, I would drive my '39 Oldsmobile about 1,200 miles north—had to drive all day and part of the night to Waterloo, Iowa, to see her. I went up there probably three or four times.

Letters: April 2–September 6, 1941

2 April 1941; Iowa

… This afternoon, Lt. [Glenn] Smith and I got in my car and started out about 2:30 p.m. for a ride through the "back country" behind the camp. It sure was a lot of fun. We passed through several little villages and back woods settlements, picked some wild flowers, and otherwise conducted ourselves as befit the advent of Spring. The farmhouses down here all follow the same pattern. About 90% of them are unpainted and consist of two clapboard rooms with an open passageway between, all under the same roof. There are also quite a few log cabins, and a few Model-A Fords, and a few houn'dawgs.

I certainly would like to get you down in this country. You could let your hair grow long, braid it, go bare-footed, and wear gingham dresses. When I came home from work with a satisfying chew of tobacco in my mouth, you could light up your pipe and come out to the stile (lots of places don't use gates) and meet me. There is much less strife and hurry and worry in this country than up Nawth. This life of quiet contemplation of the phenomena of nature transpiring not over 10 feet away, or 25 feet, if you trouble to turn your head, really looks good to me. I am thinking of joining the citizens of Dogpatch.

17 April 1941; Camp Claiborne, Louisiana

… The "Old Sol" is really beating down on the camp now, and the rains are letting up so that we now have our meals "a la red grit" from the fine red dust that blows across the camp in large gusts. It is impossible to keep clothes clean, etc., unless you lock them up in an airtight container, but I don't mind. In fact, I am beginning to enjoy camp life more and more except that my missing you is getting worse and worse and I can't always sleep at night for thinking of you.

You ought to see our infirmary now. We have purchased window shades for eight of the windows and brown and orange striped awnings for two more. We are now calling the place the "Westchester Beagle Club" as we are now very snazzy and do not always speak to just anyone that we may see. The only hitch is that some general will probably drive by in a day or two, take one look at our beaooootiful awnings and order that we paint them olive drab (O.D.).

We are now having litter drill and practice in the field. This morning another officer and I took the detachment in three trucks and an ambulance out into the woods and set up a first aid station, camouflaged, about 300 yards back of the line of fire and had the boys go out with litters and pick up the wounded men that we had placed. We then shuttled the loaded litters back to a collecting point where we loaded them in an ambulance and then began all over again.

Our day is full here, from 5:30 a.m. until 5:00 p.m.—something is happening most every minute during the day. Most of the men are kind of like children and have to be herded around by someone, which is me part of the time.

27 April 1941; Camp Claiborne, Louisiana

… Your letter came Friday. Everything stops when your letters come and I feel very good for about five minutes, but then I get more lonesome than ever.

I think that my leaving Waterloo and home was a very good thing for me. I had a hunch as to what would happen, and I think I am beginning to grow up—after a very long adolescence. I was pretty much of a little boy in some ways in Waterloo. Some of the things that I said and did astound me now, they were about such trivial things. The fact that you were always so patient with me, I can never remember you railing back at my tirades, (it would be all right with me if you had wanted to), but you always listened quietly, sometimes with a funny look in your eye—and you *did* let me come back to you when I would again approach a lucid interval. All these things are the only hope that I have that maybe you cared a little and might sometime let me grow up and marry you. Of course, I don't have much to offer you in comparison to all the other boys that flock around, but I can absolutely guarantee that there'll be no *monotony*. The most important thing of all is that I love you more than anything else in the world even though we'll probably be separated in the next (don't look at me like that).

If we could get married (I'm sorry, but this typewriter gets stuck and keeps writing the same words over again) when you come down in May, I could get a week or so's leave and we could go down to New Orleans or wherever you want to go (Mexico?) and catch up a little on the very first installment of our honeymoon. Then we could get a furnished room nearby for a little while, while you watched me work hard for you and the U.S.A. and then during the June maneuvers, you could go North again and try to explain your big mistake to your folks.

In any event, let me know when you are coming so that I can have things organized. You MUST come, Jean, whether you think you want to make the big jump or not, because I must see you and talk to you. If you don't come, I'll go A.W.O.L. and come up to see you and then they'll throw me in the guardhouse when I get back and we'll lose the war, if it ever comes. Seriously, I don't think we'll be in the war to any great extent, but it's true, as you said, that I may be in the army for a little longer than one year, but if we wait until utopia has come to get married, I'm afraid the rest of my teeth will be loose and I'll have only four hairs on my head instead of six.

... I must close and get this to the post office. You'll be sorry in later years if you let down Uncle Sam now. Consider yourself drafted.

I love you, Lud

8 May 1941; Camp Claiborne, Louisiana

... I was somewhat surprised by your flying lessons, but don't mind if it really is necessary to your happiness. There may come a time, however, when your responsibilities to someone else will prevent you from flying, at least for a time, but you will probably recognize that before I will, anyway. Of course, if I had my "druthers," you wouldn't fly alone very much as flying IS a little more dangerous than walking (even the best get killed occasionally, also auto drivers, and bath tub accidents) and I am selfish enough to worry about you and wouldn't like it if anything were to happen to you. If you are going to learn to fly you ought to do it the best way. You should have a careful physical and neurological exam by a competent flight surgeon, preferably an army flight surgeon to see if your head, particularly your semicircular canals are o.k. I have sent to Washington for some works on aviation medicine, which will explain to you why a competent exam is quite necessary. You know, my dad was a Flight Surgeon in the service for some time and in a way, I was exposed to the early beginnings of aviation medicine. Most of the tests now in use have been standardized and found necessary after years of painful experience of losing the investment of several thousand dollars in pilot and plane when one or the other would go wrong.

In addition to the exam, you should become a competent navigator, as you will probably find out after you solo that it is very easy for you to get lost in the air. If you are really serious about flying much you really ought to get a license, private or L.C. and pass the exam from the C.A.A., etc., but we'll talk about that when you come down.

3 June 1941; Camp Claiborne, Louisiana

Jean, darling, I am very happy that you are going to marry me. On my way in to Alexandria yesterday it almost seemed that I was out practicing again and with the knowledge that you would be with me, I was walking on air. You know, I think I'll be a whiz-bang when I get out of the service, if I have you to balance me properly and develop me a little more along some lines. I'm not marrying you for a "tutor," however. The main reason is something that I don't know "whether I ever told you about." I am very much in love with you. I can wait until October if you think best, but I wish you could come down here and marry me before then.

14 August 1941; Camp Claiborne, Louisiana

… Well, here we are encamped in a "grassy meadow" about a mile east of the town of Dequincy, La. There are thousands of troops in this area. Our whole division, 18,000 men, is placed between us and the town and we saw large bodies of troops under canvas on our way in here from the east. They say that the town of Dequincy (about 4,000 pop.) is swamped with soldiers and that all the stores are sold out.

Oh, for the life of a soldier. It is so dagnabbed hot down here that my shirt is wet all the time. Baths are going to be "somewhat restricted" unless we can find a private creek somewhere that several thousand other soldiers haven't spotted at the same time. The army engineer corps are setting up field showers several miles down the highway, so I guess we'll get an honest to goodness bath once in awhile. As for me, I'm getting used to the smell. You'll get used to me, darling. After all, don't you want your man to be strong??

17 August 1941; In bivouac, near Merryville, Louisiana

… So far, the maneuver has been quite enjoyable although there are some rough spots, as was to be expected. The mess has been surprisingly good for being on the move and we can usually "cadge" a small piece of ice from one of the kitchens to put in the portable water cooler that I brought along with me and thus get one drink of ice water daily. Otherwise the water gets pretty hot in the iron cans, although it is not quite hot enough to shave in comfortably.

One thing that amazes me, however, is the excitability of the higher-ranking officers. They are very susceptible to rumors. They hear a rumor that we are going to pull out at 2 p.m., say, and issue a lot of orders: "mess at 11:30 a.m., have all packs rolled, get kitchens loaded and heavy tentage down, etc." Then a half an hour later another order will come through that it's not yet necessary to take down the big tents (by this time they are already down), and finally, after sitting around for several hours, or maybe all day, in a great state of preparedness, we leisurely move out. They act like a young doctor with his first obstetrical case, i.e., sitting bug-eyed by the bedside. Sometimes we get 5 or 6 contradictory orders within the space of half an hour. Thanks be that I "was once a physician" and am inured to the little crises of life.

Last night being Saturday night and since I had for the first time in my life worn the same shirt and pair of trousers for 5 days (wasn't able to get my laundry on schedule), with no bath except two quick swims in a creek, I walked over to a farm house on the edge of the wooded pasture where we are camping. The house was a typical Louisiana farmhouse with a large open hallway or passageway running through the house from front to back. Two men and two barefoot girls, one of them pretty fair, were seated on the front "porch." I asked them if they would let me use a tub and let me have some water for a bath around behind the barn. They said they would be glad to, so I set off to get my clothes.

I returned about 20 min. later and they washed out a galvanized tub for me and filled it full of water from the well pump in the front yard and then insisted on placing it in a little room behind one of the back bedrooms. I protested that I expected to use the woodshed but they would have none of it, saying that they always used that room for bathing, etc. So I had my bath in style.

The young husband of the house, a young fellow about 26 or 27 years old, lounged on the bed while I bathed and we had quite a conversation. He wanted to know about the army and I wanted to know about farming in Louisiana. After I had completed my bath, I sat on the front steps for a short while. Soon an elderly (65?) man came into the yard dressed in overalls and barefoot. He had a rag around a sore toe. Apparently, the young man was his son as he told him that I was a doctor, so I offered to look at his toe, which I did, giving him some of my very best professional advice.

20 August 1941; In bivouac, between Evans and Caney, Louisiana

… Yesterday ended the first phase of the first maneuver. We advanced rapidly all day; I moved my aid station forward four or five times. Once, just after we had put a Thomas splint on a simulated fracture leg and had the man on a litter waiting for the ambulance to evacuate him, the umpires planted an artillery flag a short distance away and we had to slam our equipment into the weapons carriers that we use for trucks and make a hasty retreat. Evidently, the enemy had spotted the area of vehicular concentration of which we were a small part and began to lay down an artillery barrage. The barrage, not real of course, is represented by a red flag with a white center. Whenever this flag goes up, everything within one hundred yards of the flag must clear out within about two minutes or they will be "ruled out" as destroyed.

There are all kinds of soldiers down here in large numbers now. Several days ago a large group of horse cavalry passed near our bivouac area, must have been a regiment at least as it took 10 or 15 minutes for them to pass double file. Yesterday, a "dive bomber" swooped directly over me and later in the afternoon five bombers wheeled (banked) to the right around the regimental command post. The "boys" seem to like the maneuvers very much. There is much less "griping" when we are in action as it gives them something interesting to do and they go for it in a big way. It also cuts way down on the sick call, although there is always an expected percentage of actual illnesses that we have to evacuate in addition to the simulated casualties.

Today we are resting, and will continue to do so for another three days. We are camped about a mile from a clear creek and small waterfall. The regiment has installed its portable showerhead, which is fed by a small centrifugal pump on a gasoline engine. Believe me, it's pretty nice to get a shower out in the brush after being in your clothes constantly for several days at a time. No doubt these letters will be quite interesting a generation from now, if you ever save them, as our grandchildren will get the impression that our courtship consisted mainly in letters from me to you telling you how many baths I took this week and what kind. However, the reason I write about them is the fact that I am getting more and more primitive every day and a bath takes on more and more significance all the time. You had better hurry up and get down here or I'll be running around in a cloud and eating with my fingers and snarling at some of my friends.

24 August 1941; In bivouac, 3 miles south of DeRidder, Louisiana

… You should certainly appreciate this letter; I walked about half a mile through the bush tonight in order to get to one of the few typewriters in the regiment and am now seated at a field table with a kerosene lantern perched on top of the typewriter case, in a grove of pine trees in the land that the Lord just barely remembered.

I went in to the great town of DeRidder this afternoon and encountered the usual madhouse when several hundred thousand soldiers camp near a Louisiana town of about 3,500 population. These towns look just like something had hit it, a cross between a carnival and a cyclone. The townspeople all look a little tired and bewildered. Most of the stores are sold out of staple and standard products.

In addition to the townspeople and the soldiers are the "camp followers" who peddle ice cream, pop, and other goods of varying nature to the soldiers. Last night the M.P.s hauled three truckloads of drunken soldiers out of the town. That is one thing that the army should be given credit for—they try to take care of the soldier when he needs it most. Not all of the boys are picked up, however, and some of the stories are pretty wild about what goes on. After being in the army for 6 months, however, I don't believe half of what I hear.

Tonight, just as I was turning into the bivouac area in the truck I had ridden from DeRidder, we were met by one of my weapons carriers being driven at breakneck speed. We stopped them and my sergeant, who was on the carrier, breathlessly informed me that he had a seriously injured man in the carrier. I went around to the back and found a man stretched out on a litter. He had been wrestling with another soldier and "they" had heard something pop in the back of his neck and they were all pretty sure that he had a broken neck. The soldier was stretched out on his back and did not respond at all when I tried to question him. I blew on his eyelids and he blinked them (the old give away) and I picked up his pulse and it was slow and regular and of good quality. I tried to get him to talk to me again, but he wouldn't open his eyes until I quietly convinced him I was on to his game by repeating the eye blowing. I got him to move both hands and feet O.K. and then took him back to my aid station. He slowly "recovered" over a half hour period and was soon asking for a cigarette and sitting up. The next time I look to see where he was, he was gone. There was quite a gang of scared looking boys around the station when we brought him back. Talk about hysteria; it only takes an audience of about three men to convince any of these boys that they are almost dead. Of course, I "cautioned" him very seriously about "taking it easy" for several days and that he had a very severe "sprained neck," etc., etc., so he went on his way satisfied. The poor boy that had been wrestling with him was much relieved that he wasn't going to die.

Jean, I'm not surprised that some people think we won't get along well together. As usual, all they see are the externals. You know, it's a little unusual for two "unique" people to team up together. I wouldn't be for throwing any bouquets at ourselves, but I think I'm not laying it on too much when I say that we are both quite a little above the average intelligence. We are both ambitious (usually one just tags along), and neither one of us is afraid of much. It's true that we do have some ideas that don't quite jibe together, and we are also independent enough to express them and live by them until a compromise or merger is effected. I imagine that we'll be the topic of a great many conversations all during our married life because the dumb clucks won't be able to see the spark that draws us together. Neither one of us can define it, Jean, but there certainly is something that makes us overlook all the scraps we've had; something that cools me off and makes me want to see you and make love to you; something that makes you forgive me and accept me.

I'm very much in love with you, Jean, and I promise you that I'll always take care of you—it's practically a gilt-edged accident policy—you can't lose.

6 September 1941; In bivouac on training maneuvers near Camp Claiborne, Louisiana

... We pulled out of our DeRidder bivouac area Thursday afternoon after the usual 4-hour wait, all packed up. Thursday night we caught a few winks' sleep in a temporary bivouac and then Friday afternoon, we went into action. We had the usual 8:30 p.m. supper near the front lines under cover of darkness. It certainly helps to know exactly where your mouth is when eating in the dark. The boys went out on the line immediately after eating and then were pulled back in relays for breakfast at 3:30 a.m.

About the time dawn broke, the action began to get pretty hot. Altogether, the Colonel was unusually well-pleased with our battalion's performance as "we" captured almost a whole battalion of the enemy together with 56 of their trucks. They were parked bumper to bumper on a road (strictly against tactical teaching) and were so tired out that it was difficult to arouse some of the drivers. I didn't get in on the capture as I have to stay back with my aid station about 500 yards behind the front, just where you can't see much but get most of the wild bullets.

This afternoon I had a very fine swim at Lake Valentine, which is in the Kisatchie National Forest about 3 miles from our present bivouac. This is the only honest to G—lake I have seen in this country. It is about a mile long and a quarter wide and the water is fairly clean. There were no civilians around and so the five or six hundred soldiers that went in made quite a scene as the army does not include bathing trunks as an article of issue. I found an old scow and paddled across the lake with a board and entertained myself muchly and finally came home (get that "home" business) as tired as I have been for a long time. I would say at the present that my odor is a cross between sun perch and Camay.

Interviews

PL: When did you start to think the U.S. would be pulled into World War II?

Dad: Well, Jean finally consented to marry me and she came down to Louisiana and we were married on the Eleventh of October 1941, in Alexandria, Louisiana, in the Episcopal Church. I had arrived in Waterloo in 1938—and Jean and I had known each other about three years. We courted off and on—at times it was kind of stormy—but we reconciled our differences. She had been raised a Catholic and I was pleased that she was willing to become a Protestant. Her father was a Protestant—he was a Mason and a Lutheran, in name anyway. And so, we were married in the early afternoon in the Episcopal Church by the regimental chaplain who was the Episcopalian rector/minister. Jean's younger brother, Jack, was at the wedding. He was about 22 years old and Jean was 24. Then, we got in our car, which was all packed, and took off on a two-week honeymoon—first stop was Baton Rouge, then New Orleans, and along the Gulf Coast to Biloxi, Mississippi.

When we got back to Louisiana, we found a place to live in Oakdale, La., a little

December 7, 1941, Oakdale, La.: On a Sunday afternoon, Lud and Jean playing golf on Pearl Harbor Day a few hours prior to being called back to Camp Claiborne and readying for immediate deployment.

town of about 1,200, about ten or twelve miles south of camp. We rented an upstairs bedroom with a bath in a boarding house and had kitchen privileges. I had to get up early every morning and drive the ten or twelve miles to camp and eat breakfast in the officers' mess.

It was pretty much routine from the twenty-fifth of October 1941 to the twenty-fifth of November—but twelve days after that, on December 7, 1941, the Japanese betrayed me and all of America by bombing Pearl Harbor. It was such a shock, this unprovoked attack without warning. So, we declared war on the Japanese and, of course, they were allies of Germany and Italy, and so we really had to declare war on all three nations.

That "Day of Infamy" was on a Sunday, and Jean and I were out playing golf in Oakdale, Louisiana. They had a little golf course there with oiled and sanded greens, not the more typical grass greens. You had to drag them with a little hand rake to make a smooth putting surface. We were out playing golf and it started to shower a little bit. We had a picnic lunch with us and we were with three engineering officers and their wives—there were about eight of us, I guess—two foursomes. And it had just sprinkled a little bit—it looked pretty cloudy and it was going to rain, so we decided to abandon our golf game and took our picnic lunch to one of the engineering officer's house. He had a bigger place than us, not just a single room in a boarding house. And as soon as we arrived at the house, boy, the phone started ringing: "Where have you guys been—we've been huntin' for you for hours. The Japs have bombed Pearl Harbor and you're to report to camp right away!"

And so, we had to report to camp immediately and, as I recall, I then went back to Oakdale to make some arrangements. We soon got orders that the whole regiment was going to go to New Orleans. We all loaded up our six-by-six trucks, everything—three battalions—and two or three days later, we headed down to New Orleans.

I told Jean, "It looks like we're going to be here guarding the port, I hope." A lot of people had died—the Arizona battleship had been sunk, and a lot of planes destroyed. President Roosevelt addressed Congress and called this momentous day the "Day of Infamy"—and that was true.

Jean came down to New Orleans a few days later and we looked for an apartment. But after about a week, we were ordered back to camp. What that was, was a shakedown exercise, to see how fast we could load up a convoy of trucks and move out.

PL: It sounds like a hectic time. Did you feel ready to go to war?

Dad: Well, after Pearl Harbor was bombed, things happened fast. We received orders to board a troop train on New Year's Eve, December 31, 1941. The Iowa National Guard, which I was part of, had suddenly become federalized and was now the 34th Infantry "Red Bull" Division.

I was a medical officer in the 34th, which was a combat division of three regiments, what is called a triangular division, comprised of the 133rd, 168th, and the 135th infantries. Most of the boys I served with were National Guard units from Iowa and Minnesota.

The 34th Infantry's nickname, "Red Bull," originated back to the Mexican War in

1917, when Marvin Cone, of Cedar Rapids, Iowa, and a member of the Iowa National Guard, saw Indian jars and steer skulls during desert training in New Mexico. The Red Bull shoulder patch that I wore on all my uniforms was a red bovine skull on a black Mexican water jug. It was easily recognizable.

My battalion was loaded on the troop train in New Orleans with all of our personal luggage. The other stuff was sent by baggage train, I guess—a lot of our equipment. We were sent to a tent camp in New Jersey, Fort Dix, and there was six inches of snow on the ground, and muddy boardwalks. It was pretty terrible, at least compared to what we were used to. We were there about two weeks.

What I didn't know at the time was that President Roosevelt wanted to show the world that America was prepared and establish an early presence of combat troops in Europe—so, the federalized Iowa National Guard/34th Infantry Division was the first combat unit overseas. We didn't know where we were going until we got on the ship and were out to sea in the middle of the North Atlantic. I left your mother on December 31, 1941, and I didn't get back from the war to see her again until two or three days before Memorial Day, 1944, 28 months later.*

PL: Did you not know what the plans were or where you were going?
Dad: No, that was all secret. I had finally decided before we left the U.S. that we were going to Norway. They were fighting in Norway and this Norwegian guy, Quisling, was a politician and officer who favored the Nazis. He actually held the office of Prime Minister of Norway while the elected leaders were in exile. He was later considered to be one of the biggest traitors in World War II and was shot by a firing squad after the war.†

But the guerrillas, the Norwegian patriots, were opposing him. I think the British had tried to land there but had been repulsed by the Germans. I had figured we were going to Norway and that it was going to be cold and I wanted to be prepared. So, I bought some winter long underwear (they hadn't issued us any) and about $15 worth of vitamins because I figured we weren't going to have much sunshine, citrus fruits, or tomatoes to prevent scurvy. And so, on January 15, 1941, my unit, the 133rd

---

* "The 34th Infantry Division was selected over all standing regular Army divisions to go overseas on the Atlantic side as the first American troops to set foot on European soil. First committed to combat, the 34th Division compiled an incredible record of over 500 days of frontline combat ... the most of any U.S. Division that fought in the European Theater." *A Short History of the 'Red Bull' 34th Infantry Division During WWII*. 34th Infantry Division Association Newsletter (Summer 2010) [Hereafter cited as *34th Inf Div Assoc*]. http://www.34ida.org/association/newsletters.html.

† Quisling's pro-Nazi puppet government, known as the Quisling Regime, participated in Germany's genocidal Final Solution. Quisling was put on trial during the legal purge in Norway after WWII. He was found guilty of charges, including embezzlement, murder, and high treason against the Norwegian state, and was sentenced to death by firing squad. The word "quisling" became a byword for "collaborator" or "traitor" in several languages, reflecting the contempt with which Quisling's conduct has been regarded, both at the time and since his death. "Quisling," *Wikipedia*: https://en.wikipedia.org/wiki/Quisling.

Infantry Regiment, part of the 34th Infantry Division, boarded the *Strathaird*, which was about a 17,000 tonnage British passenger ship that had been used to go down through the Suez Canal to India and back before the war. It was a real high ship—had a high freeboard because they didn't have many storms in the Eastern Atlantic, Mediterranean, and Indian Oceans. And later on in the voyage, we experienced how poorly designed it was for Atlantic Ocean storms.

Most of the men on that ship were from the Midwest and had never seen an ocean before. Many thought they were embarking on some grand adventure, which they were, but had not considered the reality of hostile submarines looking for us every inch of the way.

We were loaded onto that former British luxury liner that had been converted to a troop-carrier, and quickly discovered that in an ordinary state room, they had put a triple bunk bed. There were three of us officers in that one small room. The other men were down on the lower decks and some of them were in hammocks.

We sailed off, but we didn't know where we were going until we were about eight days out, or so, and learned we were headed to Northern Ireland, to Belfast. President Roosevelt wanted to show the world that we were ready, that we had a full division overseas by the twenty-second of January [1942] after Pearl Harbor was bombed on the seventh of December [1941]. He was determined to get American ground forces into combat with the Germans as soon as possible. At first, we were escorted by the battleship *Texas* and two destroyers. The U.S. was sending these two destroyers to Britain because they were considered out of date. They were four-stackers and belched black smoke constantly. We had two troop ships with about five thousand men between us and basic transportation equipment of jeeps, trucks, ambulances, etc. After a while, the battleship *Texas* turned off to Iceland and left us with just these two little destroyers.

Towards the end of the voyage, we were hit with a real North Atlantic storm with 13 to 17 foot waves and which the ship could barely tolerate. We would look out on the two destroyers escorting us, one on either flank watching for subs, and those four-stackers would disappear from view, and then suddenly re-appear and we'd see them again. The waves were that high. The ship would list 13 or more degrees one way or another. The men had to be very careful going to the bathroom just to stay upright. A lot of them were seasick—but I wasn't. There was nothing you could do about the seasickness. I didn't treat any of them because we didn't have any drugs. I don't know what we would have used, maybe bromides or phenobarbital—there just wasn't any way that we knew of to treat seasickness.

Most of my time was spent with sick call, inspecting the ship for general hygiene and cleanliness of the men's sleeping quarters, toilets, kitchen, etc. The food was pretty fair, but it was so rough, you didn't go outside—the cold water would spray constantly. There was a lot of gambling that went on, poker and craps going all the time to pass the time away.

PL: When did you find out where you being sent?

Dad: Not until we were in the middle of the Atlantic. We ended up in Northern Ireland, a neutral country that had no army of its own, where we could train in secret and establish a foothold in the European theater. Roosevelt wanted to make sure the Germans didn't land their troops there first. It would be undefended, which is the reason we wanted to have an American division in North Ireland, so that if the Germans landed there, we could turn and attack them immediately, as early as possible. Because we had a whole division there, it would take maybe a week or two to get a division of Germans in there.

We were landed by lighters, the boats that come right up alongside the ship, and we climbed down ladders, got on board, and they took us in to the port of Belfast.

November 1942, Northern Ireland: Note the World War I "shallow" helmet (and equipment) issued to the 34th Infantry Division upon its rapid deployment to Europe after the bombing of Pearl Harbor.

We marched from where we were landed to a train in Belfast—and we had the band playing and everything.* We were almost hailed as conquering heroes, but, of course, we had not conquered anything, yet. In fact, we had not even been tested.

We heard later that the British had been through a lot: the bombing of London, kicked out of France where they were pushed off by the Germans at Dunkirk, etc. Apparently we, the U.S. Army, were the "shot-in-the-arm" that the British needed after having faced Germany's increasing aggression, on their own.

After we'd been in Northern Ireland a few months, these British colonels and staff officers were asked, what was their opinion of the American soldiers? And they said, well, they're very well equipped, but poorly trained. And they were right—the best training is experience—actual

---

* The soldiers of the 1st Battalion of the 133rd Regiment of the 34th Infantry Division were the first U.S. troops to set foot on foreign soil in WWII. The 34th was almost exclusively a division of soldiers from Iowa and Minnesota. Two of the regiments, the 133rd and 168th Regiments, were primarily Iowa National Guard outfits. Contingent strength on arrival in Northern Ireland was 4,058—medical personnel consisted of a total of 41 officers, 42 nurses, and 322 enlisted men." Col. Walden S. Lewis, *History of 133rd Infantry, 34th Infantry Division* (Gorizia, Italy, September 29, 1945), 1–13. http://34thinfantry.com/history/history-133rd.html, http://www.34ida.org/. [Hereafter cited as *133rd History*.]

combat. And even though we trained using live ammunition, at times, in Northern Ireland prior to landing in North Africa, we were not really ready for combat. In Louisiana we had practiced marksmanship using a variety of weapons. We knew how to fire rifles, machine guns, and artillery shells, we had spotting planes, and we had pretty good training with the equipment. But actually, we were not very well trained because America had never experienced any true, modern, efficient troops like the Germans had developed.

In Ireland, we learned how to transport troops and supplies, manage logistics, set up medical hospitals under canvas. And we knew how to move a kitchen and an aid station, where to put an aid station—relocate behind something so direct fire wouldn't hit it. Most battalion aid stations were about a quarter to half-mile behind the front. We had learned a lot, but were very young, inexperienced, and ill equipped for actual live engagement with the highly trained troops of the German army.

In fact, our troops had been so quickly deployed to Europe after Pearl Harbor was bombed, the only gear and uniforms available were the outdated World War I uniforms and equipment that the army had on hand. Our machine guns were still in their World War I storage packaging; we had little ammunition; our anti-tank weapons were outdated and not even capable of stopping a jeep, much less a modern German tank. However, despite all of this, I must say, that the ingenuity of the American soldier is something to behold.*

Actually, we'd been contaminated a bit by Hollywood and the many inaccurate war films that we had seen. When finally engaging with the enemy in North Africa, we discovered that the Germans were a very tough adversary. When we got up with our tanks and cannon and beat our chests, we kind of expected them to fold and run—but they didn't. They dug in and it was very tough going.

---

*"The U.S. Army Quartermaster was unable to supply these newly mobilized divisions adequately. At first, the uniforms were leftovers from WWI. The men wore WWI helmets and carried their belts, WWI entrenching tools, packs, canteens, and mess kits. The only article of clothing the soldiers liked was the campaign hat that was thought to look pretty sharp cocked rakishly forward atop close-cropped hair … Some of the crew's weapons were wooden training dummies and stovepipes for mortars. The rifle companies were issued .30-caliber 1903 A3 Springfield bolt-action rifles, Browning automatic rifles and Colt .45 pistols, which was understandable when one considers that the units had just emerged from the Depression, during which period the entire military budget wouldn't buy a modern-day bomber … The division would suffer from lack of extensive combined arms training with tanks and artillery." *34th Inf Div Assoc* (Summer 2010). *History of the Iowa National Guard: The 34th Infantry Division in WWII*, 3–4. [Hereafter cited as *History of IA Nat'l Guard*.] https://www.iowanationalguard.com/History/History/Pages/World-War-II.aspx.

2

Northern Ireland

First U.S. Troops to Europe,
January 26–December 20, 1942

"...Your letters do more than anything else to keep me believing that there is some order and reasonableness in this world after all. I have a two-pound candy box full of [your] letters now, but have to throw one off the bottom of the pile occasionally. Boy, if I'm ever captured, which I certainly don't anticipate, they'll know what I'm fighting for."

—24 July 1942, Northern Ireland

Letters: January 27–October 31, 1942

27 January 1942

[handwritten w/ fountain pen; due to strict censorship protocol, Lud could not disclose his location, Castlerock, Northern Ireland.*]

... We have finally arrived all safe and sound at our destination after a sea voyage and have connected with some sort of postal service via our own forces.

I enjoyed the trip in many ways. There were some interesting people on board from various parts of the world. I shared a cabin with Lt. Lupton. There was quite a little sea-sickness among some of the men and some of the officers. I supposed that I would be very sick, but it didn't bother me at all. Part of the voyage was very rough, although we were never in danger.

We officers are quartered in an old house, fairly comfortable except for rather rudimentary heating arrangements, at least to an American. Tonight we

---

* Castlerock was a small seaside village of ~ 200 year-round residents on the north Atlantic shore of Northern Ireland and was very popular with summer tourists. It is situated five miles west of Coleraine, in County Londonderry, about 52 miles north of Belfast. This is where the 3rd Battalion of the 133rd Regiment first set up camp in January, 1942, taking over all the vacated private homes, rooms, and buildings for about three months. The native villagers welcomed these U.S. troops of about 1,000 men, but their previously quiet main street quickly became a bedlam of army jeeps, squad cars, weapons carriers, trucks, and even tanks.

have our "living room" warm enough for the first time so that I can sit down without an overcoat on.

This afternoon I went downtown to a hospital to make arrangements for evacuation of any of my patients, although none have needed it so far. The people here are quite congenial and very cooperative and the countryside is beautiful although it is my opinion that the people here have very little idea how to live. They certainly are behind the times. One of the chief forms of transportation is the bicycle. I wish I had yours here.

If you are pretty sure that you might know or think you know where I am, write Mother and tell her that you've heard from me. Write her anyway, if you can.

12 February 1942

Dearest Jean:

Two or three days ago I received the first letter that I wrote to you—returned from the base censor here. Apparently, I was a little careless and allowed some forbidden information to creep in. The censor marked the objectionable part and I have cut it out of the letter and so will try again.

5 March 1942; Northern Ireland

… I am up to my neck moving into a new building, getting sick call organized, getting a place to live, checking water and milk sources, issuing sanitation and hygiene orders, advising the newly arrived officers, trying to get supplies, running the medics canteen, inspecting mess halls and kitchens, making reports of sick and well, ad infinitum. (other two medical sections confined and not working).

I received the letter you wrote January 26. Believe me, it's like receiving a gift from heaven to get a letter from you. I have read and reread all four letters and will wear them out as I guess it will be about a month before I get any more. You were a little mad at me in the last letter addressed to the States; I don't blame you, darling. As things have turned out, our finances ARE in a mess. We'll come out all right in the end, though. We have always played for a little higher stakes than we should have, maybe too high. I always knew we would have some tough sledding but always thought I would be with you to do the heavy. You mustn't take everything on your own shoulders. Your job sounds very interesting and I am very proud of you that you can go right out and land a job paying you $90 a month (with board!), but your father is absolutely right about your working too hard. Jean, dearest, it just isn't worth it if you work so hard that you might get sick. Sell the car if you need cash.

During the last two weeks when I was able to get a little time for myself, I looked around a bit. One night the Naval officers were there and we gave a dance. The Navy provided the roast turkey, American potato chips, and coffee and we furnished the American beer. The regimental orchestra (it came with us in the first contingent) played and we certainly had a good time, but I was lonesome

January 1942, Castlerock, Northern Ireland: "The medical detachment & 'medical aid station' were set up in the house second from left 'on the beach.'"

for you. The Irish women are all right I guess, but they're not in the same class as American girls and you know where you stand there.

We are getting canteen supplies more regularly now. In addition to my many other duties, I am now a cigarette, candy, soap and beer salesman. I am getting pretty quick on the English money now. It's "a bit of a choah, riahlly old thing" to keep all the accounts straight, especially when the section is split up and moved around, but I like it.

Yesterday we received a two weeks ration of canteen supplies: 12 cans of beer, one carton cigarettes (70 cents a carton), 6 candy bars, 1 cigar, 1 pkg gum, 1/2 can tobacco, 4 rolls Life Savers per man for the two weeks. When you consider that all those things or most of them are very hard to buy (English) over here, that is pretty good. We are like children when such things are issued to us. It's funny how the war changes your attitudes and some of your ideas. Who would ever have thought that a candy bar would be a big event in my life?

Before I left the other place, I did another operation in the British hospital. Some stuff! The Americans are taking over this week, however, so my surgery days are over for awhile. I enjoyed my stay in the first location very much.

16 March 1942; Northern Ireland

… Things are settling down pretty well here in the new place. Lt. Leslie is with me now, came several days ago, replacing Lt. Horowitz. Somehow, I am beginning to get a little restless, haven't made a move now for about two weeks. (Hah, Hah, Hah).

Lt. Leslie and I are living together in the officer's mess building. We have the nicest accommodations that we have struck yet and are going to remain as quiet about it as possible. We live on the third floor of an old Victorian style house, have a bedroom all to ourselves. It has a fireplace in it and—believe it or not, a lavatory with hot and cold running water right in the room. I finally managed to wrangle some folding canvas camp cots from the supply depot for the boys so they are now off the British board beds for the first time since we arrived, and incidentally, got one for myself so that we are really living in fine style. There are no closets, of course, so we hang our clothes on nails stuck around at various picturesque and appropriate spots in the wall.

Leslie is the best one of the Brooklyn boys that we got in December. He has an excellent sense of humor and we enjoy each other's company very much. He was with me about three weeks down at the other place and we played the British Hospital hot and heavy while the going was good. The Americans have taken over there now, and all we get now is a polite and very cold stare when we do finally manage to get down there instead of an invitation to do a little operating that we had from the British. I can't help but grin a little to myself. Maybe I am losing what little sense I ever had, but I am getting to be quite an optimist about shifting for myself over here. Maybe I am too cocky (you know me) but it tickles me how we moved right into the open arms of the British (who were certainly VERY nice to us) while a large number of other medical officers were cooling their heels and incidentally, sitting on their fannies waiting for a rainbow.

You had better write the insurance company and have the policy reinstated if you still have the car. That's the trouble with doing business by mail—it's my fault, but things were in such a mess as we left that I couldn't check on it. If we had just had three days' warning, or better, two weeks' warning so that we could have done all the things back at Claiborne that we had to do at Fort Dix, such as drawing equipment, inventorying stocks (many times over and over), etc., we would have had a little time to try to straighten out our own personal affairs. I guess I'll just have to quit talking about it as it won't do any good and it's almost impossible to explain without a few cuss words. I'll tell you about it some time. I think I understand why so many in the last war refused to talk about their army experiences very much.

We are far better off than any other army, though—don't get me wrong. In the hustle to get going into high gear, *the American way is to push through*, to hell with the consequences, for which I am very glad.

31 March 1942; Northern Ireland

... For several days last week, I was on a "sightseeing" trip through Ireland. Actually, it was not that, but censorship forbids my mentioning what we are doing any of the time, but believe you can figure it out, as we have done it before at home. The trip was most interesting, wish I could describe it to you. As usual, Lt. Leslie and I were the first medical officers to go; seems as though we're the pioneers. That suits us O.K. as we are getting to be pretty tough eggs by now and actually enjoy ourselves most of the time. Of course, all the trip was within the six northern counties of Ireland which comprise the section known as Ulster as we are forbidden to enter the Free State at any time.

Our canteen supplies are coming through quite regularly now and we went on American rations the other day. The American rations sure make a difference. We have jam, and apples, and oranges, and butter, and peas, and many other things that the people over here can't get and which I hadn't seen since I left the States. I am eating like a horse, as usual.

Jean, darling, I sure do get lonesome for you. Sometimes the uncertainty of the future is pretty hard to think about. If I could just see you once in a while, it wouldn't be so bad. To know that you're waiting to take up where we left off is the heaven that keeps me from going a little nutty at times.

4 April 1942; "Swamp Island"

… About a week ago I suddenly noticed some enlarged and slightly sore lymph glands in the back of my neck and behind my right ear. I couldn't quite figure out where they came from; they popped out so suddenly, without a sore throat or toothache, etc. I got my answer Thursday when I broke out with German Measles. We had been having a few cases and so, of course, I had to get it. I was evacuated back to the hospital, but didn't run any temperature so only stayed two nights and a day and was released this morning. The German Measles are also called the "three day" measles so if you haven't had them, you'd better wash your hands after reading this letter and then burn the letter. You'd better pass a hot iron over the pictures.

At the present moment I am a very unpopular officer at the officers' mess because due to my measles, the after-Easter dance had to be called off. The whole officers' mess is

April 1942 Castlerock, Northern Ireland: The Dance Cancellation poster, due to Ludwick's measles infection and subsequent quarantine of the entire regiment.

in quarantine (working quarantine) which allows them to work O.K. but curtails their socializing a little. Of course, they aren't really mad at me, but spread it on pretty thick. I feel fine and have made a rapid recovery, so don't worry about me. It's funny that I've never had them before, having been exposed many times. Of course, I'll admit my ideas are getting younger every day. You know we officers have to censor all the letters written by the enlisted men. Occasionally the letters are pretty funny. The other day one of the officers said that some soldier, in describing the girl he had had a date with said she could have passed for Scarlet O'Horror. After seeing some of the Irish girls, I am inclined to agree, although occasionally one sees one that is not bad looking. They do not compare with the American kind, however, so don't worry.

17 April 1942; Northern Ireland

… Leslie and I walked along the beach to the next town [Port Stewart?] which is about 4 miles away. It is a beautiful town, quite a bit larger than ours which is only a hamlet. There was a large promenade along the seashore. We have a "promenade" too, but it is just sand along the beach. In one place on our walk we had to cross a river by getting some workmen to row us across, as they wouldn't lend us the boat. This must have inspired Leslie quite a little as today he went in to town (to the still larger town back from the seacoast where we shop) and bought a fish line and sinker and is going to go "deep sea fishing" (with about 10 ft of line) when he can get a boat. He is quite the clown in many ways and sees the funny side of many situations. The quarantine occasioned by my "German measles" is off now. I guess the boys will be going about more now. Last week we had a traveling vaudeville show (British variety) and are having another one tonight. We are also having our own movie about twice a week. In the little village here, there is an "Orange Hall," apparently some sort of lodge over here, which we use as an auditorium, etc. We have our own portable sound projector and have had such pictures as Dorothy Lamour ("Our Favorite!!") and Bing Crosby & Bob Hope in "The Road to Singapore." Last night we had Spencer Tracy in "Edison, the Man," so you can see that we are right in there swinging when it comes to the latest in entertainment. Just because the swing was late is no reason to call it a strike.

Censorship prohibits our even "guessing" or surmising what is in the future as far as military movements are concerned.

We are now receiving some baseball equipment and are holding baseball practice pretty regular now. The outfit also received an electric radio with record player attachment and about 20 hot records, so guess we'll all be able to remember we're Americans, at least for awhile.

I've had four dates since being here. Had a good time, I guess, but the trouble is that I always think of you. They were always just "dates" to large group parties, so don't worry. I love you more than anything else in the world and it gets "more and more" as the days pass by. Keep your chin up and I'll be back to you soon.

23 April 1942; Northern Ireland

… Yesterday Leslie and I did a "Hebrew amputation" [circumcision] at our aid station, unbeknownst to the Major. We also have been carding our boys that need tonsillectomies (I have established a card history system for all patients seen on sick call) and yesterday sent five of them down to the hospital. This afternoon we went down and each did one tonsillectomy under local anesthesia, the other three cases being done by medical officers in the hospital. They are just as anxious as we are to do something so they "split fees" with us: that is, let us do some of the work on a portion of the patients that we send in. At least that's better than we were able to do back in the States, but of course is all on the Q.T. because of regulations, etc. It still seems funny, though, that a licensed M.D., who has been out in practice some time, has to "beg" or "engineer" deals in order to practice his profession for which he is trained, but that's the army for you. Leslie thinks I am a whiz at making contacts with the right people, but he is quite a leg puller so that I don't swallow all he feeds me.

Before we left the States, I wrote your father that we might be separated for a long time and that I certainly didn't want you to live the life of a morbid recluse. You can't just stay at home and mope because I am going to need a girl with plenty on the ball (like you've always had) when I get back and we start all over again. So, use your own judgment, remembering that it is very easy for any male to quickly become temporarily unbalanced in your presence if you give him half a chance. Look at all the competition I had to get you, and I'm not through yet, dearest, because you deserve one of the "better boys."

Must close and get to bed. You keep me awake nights and then I meet you again, after I've gone to sleep.

April 1942 Northern Ireland: "Leslie—the strike-out king." The 133rd Infantry Regiment finally receives some sports equipment.

30 April 1942; Northern Ireland

... I must close and save something for next time. Lt. Leslie was in this room using another typewriter and then went out about an hour and a half ago. He just came back and looked at the 5 pages of this letter and said, "Good night, how do you do it? What chapter are you on now?" I'm on the last chapter of this one, which is the best because I can tell you that I love you more than anything else in the world, and am coming back to you just the way you want me to.

12 May 1942; Somewhere in Northern Ireland

[George Leslet Gallaher was the older brother of Lud's mother, Margaret (Peggy) Gallaher Ludwick]

"The following letter was written to George L. Gallaher, former Sigourney, Iowa, resident, by his nephew, a physician, now with the expeditionary force in Northern Ireland. The letter is so unusually interesting that the Review was very glad to have the privilege of printing it."

—The Sigourney News Review

Dear Uncle George:

Yesterday I received your good letter, written April 17th and post marked the next day. A month is about the usual time that it takes for mail to reach us from the States.

I suppose you heard from Mother and Maine and Gail about "Northern Ireland" from my earlier letters to them. This is quite an island, very picturesque and possessing many beautiful views and landscapes. The land is not as fertile as ours in the middle west of the U.S., however, and the climate precludes the growing of many crops that we have there. The main crops are potatoes (incidentally, you know that the so-called "Irish Potato" was introduced from the New World—Peru, I think it was), stock beets or turnips, oats, flax. There is quite a bit of grazing land along the low mountains where cattle, sheep, and goats are raised. About the only thing that I have seen that compares favorably with a "United States Product" is the Irish horse. The draft horses here are numerous, large boned, well proportioned, and are really beautiful animals. I have had some difficulty in explaining to myself how the boney framework of the horses is so well developed and yet, the teeth of the natives here are so poor. It is not unusual at all to see snags in the mouth of people in their early twenties or thirties over here. Apparently, the answer is a lack of care on the part of the humans, which is consistent with the general retardation of customs and ways of doing things as compared to the average standard of living in the U.S.

I think it is quite safe to say that the people and customs over here are 50 years behind the times or maybe more, although there are a few modern inconsistencies that surprise one occasionally. There is also another difference in the people that is partially indefinable. I have thought a great deal about it at odd times, and am not sure that I have reached the answer yet, but believe that it springs from the "Freedom" that we have in the U.S. As I was growing up, I heard a great deal about the "heritage" from Fourth of July and other political speeches of the spellbinders, as every youngster does. I heard so much about "Liberty," in fact, that familiarity made it lose part of its significance and led me to take it as a matter of course along with the central heating, hot and cold running water, and other common commodities. Another point that may have a great deal of influence on the attitude of the people is the lack of "frontier" that we have always had in the U.S., a gift from nature, it is true, but which I believe we can continually recreate under the auspices of Freedom.

The people over here seem to lack a great deal of confidence in their ability to surmount the environment or strata into which they were thrust in this world. They lack the imagination of a man reasonably confident that his future depends to a large extent on his own efforts. All this, of course, is closely linked with their backwardness. They don't miss air-conditioned theaters because they've never seen them. They don't know that their houses are cold all the time because they have been raised in them and are ignorant of central heating for the masses (coal is all imported). They trudge behind a walking plow because they think that to ride would be cruel to the horse, instead of getting two horses and trying to acquire a larger farm. Several months ago, I read an editorial in a newspaper extolling the virtues of spaded ground over plowed ground, saying that the country was going to the dogs because the young people were not being trained to spade the ground at home on the farms, but were flitting after the more modern methods of farming which the writer warned would lead to destruction.

Some time ago, we were out in the country for a few days. My outfit stopped awhile in a farmyard and my Iowa farm boys all gathered around to talk to a white haired and practically toothless farmer. His buildings were all of stone and built right next to each other, the cows living in one room at one end and his house being at the other end of the row of buildings. He owned 35 acres of land, had been born in his same thatch roofed cottage where his father lived before him. He tilled about 15 acres, as his father had before him. He mentioned that it was only a generation or so back that the land had been taken away from the "landlords" and parceled out to the people. Over here, they don't know what our corn is. They call all small grain, "corn," so he was pop-eyed when my boys told him about corn 14 ft. high with ears a foot long. He could not conceive of a farm large enough to raise 250 or 300 hogs. He couldn't understand a government that paid farmers to kill hogs (he wasn't entirely isolated in this respect) and of course the conversation about combines, manure spreaders, etc. left him puzzled. My boys "spread it on," of course, about the Utopia in the U.S. and at times were gleeful in their tall stories about the ways back home.

For some time now I have been stationed in a small hamlet [Castlerock] on the seashore. In peace times it is a favorite resort in the summer. It is quite a beautiful place but wouldn't have much favor in the U.S. due to the temperature. Today it got up to around 68 degrees. Another medical officer [Leslie] and myself room together on the third floor of an old house. We have the nicest accommodations we have struck, yet, without a fireplace in the room or a lavatory with hot and cold running water. A few miles from us there is a nice little town of about 6 or 7 thousand people. The natives are very nice to us here, although no doubt think that we are a bunch of crazy galoots much of the time. There are several theaters in town that show American films from 1 to 3 years old. Much of what the natives know about the U.S. is influenced a great deal by the Hollywood films that come out, so it is sometimes difficult for them to understand an American, especially if he elaborates any on the way we do things.

I can't tell you much of what we are doing due to censorship. We are forbidden (and rightly so) to discuss our location, our daily program or state of supply, detailed weather reports, etc., which might be of value to the enemy. I cannot refrain, however, from wondering if Hitler's victories have come at the expense of people who live like the Irish. If they have, there is very good reason for us to be greatly encouraged.

There are a great many Presbyterian churches over here, as it is the prevailing denomination in Northern Ireland. I attend church fairly regularly. The sermons, to an American, are rather austere; but the big difference is in the hymns. The hymns have absolutely no tune to them. We sang "Rock of Ages" one Sunday not long ago and it was unrecognizable. Secretly I would like very much to get up an American quartet and sing that hymn for them as we do at home. Compared to the hymn here, though, they would probably accuse us of bringing "swing" or "jazz" into the church. I never realized before that the way we sing carries an almost "lilting" tune. I can't remember of seeing anyone laugh in church; that is, before the services, as we sometimes do quietly while talking to our neighbor. After services we solemnly file out and go our way. Maybe I am hypercritical (as I know I am), but there is a grimness about it all that seems unnecessary. I expect that the poverty of the land through the centuries, together with the restricted amount of land that each farmer can have, due to population, is a big factor in their attitude. The war, of course, has distorted the true picture a great deal also. There are fewer young people present to balance the picture. It is also true, certainly, that after I have been through the mill in this war, that I may not be as effervescent as I am now, although I hope that I may retain a cheerful outlook on this life.

I must close as it is getting late. The days are long here; we have sunlight until about 10:30 pm. It is now 9:30 pm and I am typing beside a window without the use of electric lights. Just saw two Irish girls pedal by on their bicycles.

In looking back over this letter, I can certainly pick holes in myself at my attitude toward the people and customs here. It makes me realize that God has been very good to us in America, and, I think, very good to me. I hope that I can realize fully, as I think I'm beginning to, of His great generosity, and that someway I may be able to deserve even a small portion of what I have already received.

Lot of love to all, and write soon. A.L.
Lt. A.L. Ludwick,
Med. Det. 133rd Inf.

15 May 1942; Northern Ireland

… Jean, darling, don't worry about me. I'll come through this O.K. I've always had a feeling that faith in a kindly Providence, and together with a little native wit from the same source, will do the trick. I detest war because of all the misery and suffering it causes to innocent people; but if it can't be settled any other way, I'm for getting started. I guess I'm getting impatient, but the sooner things start popping, the better. I certainly am going to be plenty cautious about running risks, but I think there is going to be quite a little excitement when things do break loose and I'll have a grandstand seat, maybe.

20 May 1942; Northern Ireland

Dearest Jean:

I have received only one letter from you in the last two weeks or so, that letter being the one written April 15. Am hoping to get a bunch of letters in a few days as another "shipment" or convoy has arrived and there should be some mail on it.

Although I think I manage to conceal it now better than I did back home, I surely am burned and disgusted with the promotion deal and many things in general. I guess there's no use talking about it as most "talk" is interpreted as "excuses," which I don't relish; but it seems peculiar the way one is "allowed" to hold down the job of both a Capt. and a 1st Lt. (Bn. Surg. and Asst. Bn. Surg.) for 10 months, shipped out first on every job to get things rolling O.K.; repeatedly told what "good work" you're doing and then be passed over on the promotion end with the explanation that they have made so many new captains that the quota is filled (even though the vacancy for the rank still exists).

Believe me, darling, I am certainly learning some lessons in life, some of which I guess I needed pretty badly. I hate it doubly so for your sake because it is tough on you, too. All I can say is that it all adds to my knowledge and will make me more and more difficult to fool in the years to come. I am going to be a three-headed hydra when I get out of this army. To you first, and then to my patients, I'll always preserve a warm and gentle attitude; but for the "business men," I am going to do very little talking and they are going to do most of the writing on paper. I hope I don't sound too bitter about it, because actually, I'll survive O.K. and still be the same guy you married. Things will eventually turn out better and I'll feel better; in fact, will probably have to watch myself to be sure that I don't forget the lessons learned now.

30 May 1942; Northern Ireland

[Tynan Abbey]

… Hey, beautiful, remember me: I'm the guy you had that romance with, does the light begin to flicker? I believe you've broken your arm or something. The last letter I received from you was postmarked April 16 and that's a long, long time.

Thursday, day before yesterday, we moved again. We knew about a week ahead of time but weren't supposed to say anything about it. We are now about 77 miles from our old place at the seashore [Castlerock], although of course we are still in Northern Ireland. I moved down a day early to check into the water supply and sanitary facilities, which are not as good as the camp we left, but are better than some I've seen here and can be put in good shape with a few weeks' work on them, I think. The country around here is beautiful. There are a great many more trees in this part of Ulster than there were at the seashore; the first "big" trees like we have in Iowa & Minnesota that I have seen in Ireland. The farming country and towns also look a bit more prosperous and the girls are a little better looking.

The camp is situated about a half mile from a little farming village of about 75 people (three churches, two or three general stores, a telephone office, a police station and about 15 or 20 houses). We are really out in the sticks. The camp is on a knoll with grassy slopes and quite a few large trees under which the tin huts nestle. Across the small valley, there is an old Abbey with beautiful grounds surrounding it. About two miles away is a village of about 200 population. And ten miles away there is a town of about 10,000. This larger town is pretty good looking, has more merchandise in the shops than the town near our old camp. There are two "cinemas" in the town 10 miles away. Last night, some of us went in to the show, saw Errol Flynn and Fred MacMurray in "Dive Bomber."

Apparently, we are the first American troops to be stationed around here as we are quite the center of attention and many people stop on the streets and stare when we walk or ride past. They are very friendly and rather curious about us.

Jean, darling, it sure must be tough on you to go through this war business with me. Don't think for a moment that I don't realize what it is for you to go back to the old hometown [Duluth] after 2 1/2 months of married life, and carry on. It takes a lot more courage than I'll ever have to put out over here. I wonder how you are getting along: if you're happy at least part of the time, if you have any fun with the old gang, as you ought to. I want you to do anything you want to because I know that there is something between us (and us alone) that will burn on forever. The happiest days of my life, those days with you in La. are so close to me, they seem like yesterday, although in another way, it seems ages since we sat together in the rain in the Olds at camp. Those were brave words I said that night about it being a long time. I didn't even begin to know how long the time could seem. I love you very, very much, Dear, and you are the only girl for me. I'll come back to you if I have to swim, stow away, fly, or walk.

1 June 1942; Northern Ireland

… It is now 9:40 p.m. and I am sitting at the typewriter without any light burning in the room. The sun is still above the horizon. Many of the days are pleasant and it is slowly warming up, although it apparently won't get as warm as at home. The weather here now reminds me of the first week in April in Iowa. The wind gets pretty cold at times and I am still wearing my short overcoat.

Must close and go down to the dispensary to see a soldier's hand that has a spreading cellulitis near the base of the thumb from a thorn prick. He is waiting there now, one of my boys just came in and told me. Am including some pictures that might be interesting.

3 June 1942; Northern Ireland

… This is one of the nicest days that we've had since we've been over here. It is warm and balmy and the sun is shining brightly through the leafy trees in our "place of abode." This morning is one of those rare ones that I was able to sleep late; in fact, didn't get up until about 11:00 a.m., when I leisurely shaved in our room using our new private hot water system and then went down to the basement and had a shower. This afternoon my boys have just gone over to Glenn's place to play his outfit a kitten ball [softball] game. I sort of wanted to go along, but inasmuch as I had let Leslie do all the "work" of running sick call this morning, I am staying home to watch the dog while he chaperones the boys. I'm not going to stay inside very long, though, just long enough to write you a note.

I don't believe I told you about our private hot water system in our new Officers' Mess. As I told you in my last letter, we've moved, a good-many-miles from the seashore. The Officers' Mess is now situated in a country rectory which is in reality a large country farmhouse with three stories. The village rector and wife and maid live in three of four of the rooms that are sort of blocked off from the rest, which we occupy.

There is only one toilet and one lavatory in the whole building for our use and they are tacked onto the entry hall downstairs, apparently as an afterthought. There are four showers downstairs in the basement, which seem to be O.K. In order to have hot water for shaving in our room, Leslie and I have rigged up a hot water tank in our room on the third floor. I bought a faucet in town and he installed it in a "petrol tin" which is a five-gallon square tin used a great deal by the British. The whole thing sets on an electric hot plate that we just acquired and it works very well. In about 20 minutes the water gets quite hot and we use my old grey wash pan on a washstand. For a drain we have another petrol tin with a funnel in it. We plan to improve the whole setup soon by installing a built-in sink as soon as we can circulate around some plumbing shops and pick up the needed gadgets. I'll send you a picture of it when and if we get it finished and I can get the camera and film.

The water for the Officers' Mess building is furnished by a 100 ft. well in the back yard. The water is lifted to tanks in the pantry by a large wheel type hand pump that looks like an old hand-turned coffee mill, if you've ever seen one. The British, when they were here, had the tanks filled twice daily by having "details" of soldiers come up from the area and turn the pump by hand for two hours each time. Our boys tried it for a few minutes and then someone conceived the idea of jacking up the right wheel of one of the jeeps and stringing a belt from the front wheel drive to the pump. This was accomplished in short order and soon the jeep

2. Northern Ireland 53

June 3, 1942, Northern Ireland: "Yankee ingenuity at its best." The 133rd Infantry Regiment using a jeep's 4 four-wheel drive transmission to pump water from a well in just minutes that previously took the British many hours to pump manually.

was pumping away filling the tanks. One of the British officers who stayed behind to help us move in was amazed at the setup and said, "None of us would ever have thought of such an idea," which is 100 % correct. Look at the expressions on the faces: rapt attention. Compared to other nationalities, Americans are fascinated by machinery. And, I might add, the ingenuity of an American soldier is something to behold.

As you know, Glenn [Smith] is located only about two miles from me now. Several evenings ago Leslie and I walked over to their Officers' Mess and saw him. (daughter born, wife "Mid") The Officers' Mess where Glenn lives is a veritable wonderland. It is the mansion and estate of an Earl and is really some place. It will take a whole letter to describe it—also, it bears some more exploring. There are tunnels and passageways, formal gardens, live peacocks and deer, a lion cage, a stable three stories high and a half a block square, a private fire wagon (horse drawn), and many other features. Glenn lives up on about the fifth floor of the mansion in the servants' quarters. Several whole floors of the house are full of furniture and locked up. There is supposed to be quite a collection of paintings there. The flower gardens and landscaping, as well as the Greek statuary in the surrounding grounds, are beautiful. All this, and only two bath tubs available, which is typical.

The news over the radio about the war certainly sounds encouraging. Yesterday they announced the 1,000-plane bombing raid on Cologne and stated that there would be more and that the U.S. Air Force in G.B. would soon equal the British. I think the bulk of the people in the States are too optimistic, but there is certain evidence that the pendulum is swinging. It will still cost a great deal of blood and tears, but at least I think we're on our way.

18 June 1942; Northern Ireland

... I'm enclosing some pictures that may be of interest to you. Lt. Leslie has a "dollar" box camera that he paid a little over two dollars for as it was slightly rusty in places. It is a rather cumbersome thing and will only take snapshots under good light (or time exposures inside) but it does pretty good work. He has extra prints made for me on some of the pictures and these are what I'm sending.

Picture No. 1 is of one end of "our" room on the third floor of the old rectory that now serves as our Officers' mess. We (Leslie & I) live in a large "closet" with one window. It was pretty much of a mess when Leslie snapped the picture. Note the shoe kit that I got for Christmas under my cot on the left. Incidentally, I sleep like a king. I have Hefty's air mattress and on top of that I have the mattress from camp.

Picture No. 2 shows the other end of our room which is occupied by our "hot running water" wash stand. The tank to the left contains the cold water. We haven't been able to get a faucet for it yet and have to pour it out by hand. The tank and funnel are our drain. Note paper towels and

June 1942, Tynan Abbey, Northern Ireland: The hot water system that Ludwick and Leslie rigged up in their room using discarded "petrol tins" and a hot plate.

June 1942, Tynan Abbey, Northern Ireland: The village rectory building that served as Officers' Mess for Ludwick's 133rd Regiment's Medical Detachment. Ludwick's and Leslie's room was on the third floor, left window of the building.

"coke" bottles in the "chest" below tanks. At first the photographer wouldn't print this negative because he thought the contraption was some kind of a "wireless" machine or set. Boy, these Irish!!!

Picture No. 3 shows the outside of the building. The little addition tacked onto the left side of the front entryway is the only bathroom in the place although there are showers in the basement. Our well, that furnishes the water for the place, went dry this week so we have to take our baths at camp which is some distance away, as I have mentioned in other letters. After I finish this tonight I am going down to the "shower house" near headquarters where I am writing this, for a hot shower, if there's any hot water left. My room is the left-hand window on the third floor of the building. Note the large number of chimneys which is characteristic of houses over here; fireplace in every room, but no central heating! A couple of feet from the fireplace and it's just as cold as if there were no fire at all.

Must close and get my bath and to bed. If we would get more rain the well would contain more water and we wouldn't have so far to go to bathe. Some people are never satisfied, I guess.

24 July 1942; Ulster, Northern Ireland

… Your letters do more than anything else to keep me believing that there is some order and reasonableness in this world after all.

In your letter of July 4, you asked me if I remembered last July 4. How could I ever forget it! I still have your letter to me at camp written July 2, 1941, from

Waterloo. I guess I'm getting to be a softy but I got it out and looked at it. I don't have the room to carry all your letters around, but I'll never throw that one away. I have a two-pound candy box full of letters now, but have to throw one off the bottom of the pile occasionally. Boy, if I'm ever captured, which I certainly don't anticipate, they'll know what I'm fighting for.

On the way home from the meeting with Glenn, we passed through some beautiful scenic parts of Ulster. Some of the broad valleys, all patch worked with hedge fenced fields, were beautiful to see from the heights. I took a picture of an old Irish farmer riding along in his little donkey cart. Once as we were rolling along the road, I saw a white-haired old farmer cutting wheat with a scythe while a young woman in a red bandana snood worked beside him gathering up the grain—quite primitive to an American.

Sherman was certainly right—it isn't the fighting that's hell, it's the waiting.*

1942 NI: "Modern Ireland! A rather common sight in Ireland. They are on their way to market."

I hope that we won't be tied down in a foreign country for awhile after the war is over. The day that peace is declared I'll be ready to come home, but of course it'll take some months, maybe longer, for us all to get back. I pray that we may be together soon. I have never wanted anything as much before in my life.

26 June 1942; Northern Ireland

... I'm enclosing the note that Joan sent me. I think it's a peach of a letter from an 11-year-old girl and it pleased me very much, especially the salutation ("Dear

---

* William Tecumseh Sherman (February 8, 1820–February 14, 1891) was an American soldier, businessman, educator, and author. He served as a general in the Union Army during the American Civil War (1861–65).

Ludwick"). I'm a little awed at the realization that at last, I have a "sister." I think she'll do all right in this world. I think her style is pretty good, what do you think?*

I'm also enclosing a few more snapshots. That guy in bed with Hedy LaMarr [*Life* magazine cover] is a friend of mine. His wife wrote him that she'd trust him with Hedy LaMarr. I believe she's right, as he doesn't look very enthusiastic or amorous. She must know her man pretty well, I'd say. She must really be something to make him take Hedy so casually.

20 July 1942; Northern Ireland

… We both know down deep inside just what we both feel for each other. Maybe I'm too "melodramatic" about it all, but I feel it very intensely, Jean. We'll have to plan our happiness together, both now and for the future. The one thing that makes me calm in my despair at being separated from you is the knowledge that we two possess something very rare in this world, something that we instinctively felt in each other ever since we've been together. We tried it many times before we were married, and it always proved that it had the strength of steel. I know that whatever happens, however long we may be separated, I'll be able to walk up to you one day and look into your eyes and say "Hi, kid," and kiss you, and take you in my arms and the world will be heaven again. You'll know, and I'll know that this is why we were born.

Well, I must close and go to bed, to think and dream of you. It's funny how many things in my past life are slipping slowly out of my consciousness, but you burn on forever. Hold on, Kid, I'm coming. I live for you.

6 August 1942; Belfast, Northern Ireland

… It is now 10:00 p.m. and I have just arrived back at our little country camp from a 24-hour pass in Belfast. I rode in on the ambulance that was taking a suspected acute appendicitis in last night and stayed over last night and today. I took a few pictures while there, although the day was overcast and they may not be good.

Maybe I don't realize or experience the full significance of the deprivations of the war on the people over here, but Belfast is certainly a dud to an American. There is practically nothing to do there and every time I go, I wonder why I ever went. There are about three good "cinemas" in town, but usually long queues of waiting people makes one wait a half hour or so before you can get a seat. I've never been that interested in going. I stayed at the "Midland Hotel Officers'

---

* Joan Vail Hoyer was Jean's almost fourteen-years younger sister. She was about 11 when she sent her letter to "Lud" overseas. She had never met her sister's new husband and must have assumed his first name was "Ludwick" since Jean referred to him as "Lud." Lud was an only child of older parents and had always yearned for a sibling.

Club" which is located in one of the railroad stations there. It has recently been refinished as a "Club" for American officers and was a pleasant surprise. I had a nice room, thick mattress, hot and cold running water (but no bath) for 13 shillings ($2.60).

After I deposited my "duffle" in the hotel, I sallied forth to the "Embassy Club" where several of the other officers who were in Belfast from our outfit, were going. I'd heard a great deal about this club during the months I've been in Ireland but had never been there. It was described to me as the only decent place to go, etc., by several American officers. When I got there, I found that the admission charge was "two and six" (two shillings, six pence, or 50¢) and then entered the ballroom. The dance floor consisted of a ballroom about 120 ft. by 35 ft. with a "fair" Irish orchestra dressed in "soup & fish" at one end. All of the orchestra were white except the bass fiddle player who was a typical American Negro, Cab Calloway style. Along both sides of the floor were small tables, without table cloths, where were sitting numerous American officers, a few enlisted men, a few British officers, etc. In one corner of the room were about 15 girls, about 18 to ?, well dressed and neat appearing in sports spectator and afternoon dresses, etc. There were also many girls sitting with the "parties" at the tables. No liquor was served in the place, but the setups were and most of the patrons had brought their own. I found that the custom was to walk up to a girl and ask her to dance and then, if you both felt like it, to introduce yourself, which I did.

The orchestra was fair, and of course the girls danced well, etc. Apparently, all the girls stag it, paying their own way in order to have an evening of dancing. Soon the boys and girls began pairing off and by the time the place closed at 1:30 a.m. most of the girls had escorts home via the few taxis waiting downstairs at the front door. Of course, what the place really is, is a fairly good "taxi dance" hall, run respectably enough, but it certainly was a surprise to me as I thought I was entering the best night club in the Ulster metropolis. One of the girls I danced with said that things were a lot more lively now than before the war. She said that before the war all the dances closed about 10:30 p.m. No wonder there are so many "black-out babies" which is what we call the great numbers of children from one to three years old that are seen on the streets of the towns all over Ireland. I sometime wonder if the war planning commission, or whatever controls such things as black-outs, remember to order a few hundred thousand extra perambulators as necessary adjuncts to the black paint, curtains, and other materials used in black-outs.

I slept until 1:30 p.m. in my luxurious bed in the hotel and then got up for lunch and strolled around some, got a haircut, and then called up the blonde that I met up on the seashore and whom I hadn't seen to talk to for two months. My train back to camp left at 7:15 p.m. so we didn't have much time to go around much. I met her at her office at 5:15 and we had "dinner" together before I left. "Dinner" consisted of everything that they'd let me order: sausage (part sawdust) and bacon and mushrooms, "chips" (French Fries), a lettuce salad with about three whole slices of tomatoes in it, and tea. I asked for a dessert, but the waitress said my bill was already "5 shillings" worth and the ration bureau has prohibited meals that cost more than 5 shillings. When I got home this evening, I dug a candy bar out of my trunk and drank a coke and I think I'll go downstairs to the kitchen and eat a couple of slices of bread and jam before going to bed. Incidentally, you know, white bread is no longer available to the people here, and the American soldiers are the only ones that eat white bread. Leslie and I were lucky last week and managed to get a whole case of Coca Cola through the post exchange.

I just read the above paragraph to Leslie as he knows my prodigious appetite and thought he would enjoy knowing what I had to eat at Belfast. He said that now he understood why I dived for the candy bar as soon as I got into our room and then proceeded to give me a lecture about writing home about my doings in Belfast. He said the only thing your wife will remember in that whole paragraph is the one word: "blonde," that after this letter has traveled 3,000 miles it will sound entirely different, etc., that it is VERY undiplomatic and wondered how long we'd been married, etc., although he already knows. He has been married 13 years and has two little girls back in Brooklyn. Of course, his whole tirade was in a jocular manner as we kid each other a great deal, but I think he was serious underneath and wouldn't do the same as I did, i.e., write home about it. Either I am an unsophisticated dumbbell or he has missed something that we have, and you and I know it's the latter. I love you and only you and there never could be anyone to take your place, nor will there ever be. I'm just killing time and trying to maintain some sort of balance until the great day comes when I can return to you.

Some months ago, the outfit received a shipment of athletic goods and several days ago one of the officers dug out a badminton set of racquets and shuttlecocks. Night before last we had quite a game over the volleyball net behind the Officers' mess. I'm willing to concede that I'm an expert already and will be able to move amongst the elite of the playboys when I get home with my experience in ping pong and badminton. What I can't understand is who it was that thought rough and tough American soldiers on foreign service would relish a game of badminton. I wouldn't be surprised if a croquet set shows up next.

9 August 1942; Northern Ireland

… Tell Hefty and the gang hello for me when you get to Waterloo. Tell Hefty I sleep on the best bed in the whole army. I have put his rubber air mattress on my army cot and then a camp cotton mattress on top of that and believe me, it can't be beat (over here).

Also remember me to your father and family. Being an only child, I sometimes forget that I'm not writing to all my family directly. I'll always remember the letter that he wrote to me just before we sailed in answer to my hurried and I'm afraid garbled attempt to explain the insurance setup at that time. His answer was a model of the understanding that characterizes him. If I can be as good to our kids as he has been to you and to us, I'll count myself a perfect success in this world.

I still don't want anything but you for Christmas. Why don't you step on the scales at the post office and find out how much it would cost for you to come by airmail?

Last night was "quite a night." I rode into town with several other officers who were going to "celebrate" a promotion. They wanted me to start in with them, but I detached myself from them at first and went to the show alone. Saw "Skylark" with Claudette Colbert, Ray Milland, and Brian Ahern. It was pretty good. The sight of a snappy Cadillac sport roadster in the picture brought loud sighs from the American soldiers in the audience.

It's remarkable how well we are fed. Today at supper we had "stew" (beef, string beans, carrots, peas), fresh sliced tomatoes, sliced beets, bread, butter and jam, coffee and doughnuts, freshly baked. I'm sure that most of it did not originate in Ireland, especially the tomatoes. Several weeks ago, we had fried chicken. The chickens arrived whole and frozen and bore the trademark of a large packinghouse in the Midwest. I'll bet the British never get anything like that.

21 August 1942; Somewhere in the Peat Bogs of Northern Ireland

[handwritten]

… Jean, I wish I could tell you something of what is going on over here—sometimes things happen pretty fast as the momentum of this war gathers speed. I don't know anything definite at all as far as the ultimate question is concerned, but there are signs and rumblings of things taking shape for the big event. Personally, it can't happen too soon for me. I'm anxious to get going. I guess I ought to have some fears about it, but I think about you a great deal more than I do about the war. Each day in combat will mean to me only that you and I are not together. The days then will be counted just as they are now.

The point is, though, that if you should suddenly stop receiving letters from me for a while—you'll know that it's only because it's humanly impossible to write—not because I don't want to.

P.S. Wrote a letter to Hefty last week about my promotion. Does he know a congressman? Some of us are getting a royal run-around over here and I've realized that there needs to be a few firecrackers lit. Am going to write Cousin Frank in Washington—but no favors will be asked. I've been recommended for promotion 6 times over here. Actually, the few years I'm in the army it won't make much difference—but to others it does.

9 September 1942; Northern Ireland

… Next to being with you, I am in the nearest thing to Heaven this side of the Atlantic. Friday, I came up to the 5th General Hospital on two weeks' exchange temporary duty and boy, oh boy—it sure is wonderful. I'm practicing medicine again! This hospital is staffed from Harvard and Mass. General Hospital—they certainly are a swell bunch. I have charge of a surgical ward while one of the officers is on leave. I've assisted on some surgeries and have done some minor surgery on my own in an American operating room, put on a plaster cast, looked at x-rays, made ward rounds, etc., just like old times. These boys are plenty good up here and I find that I'm a little rusty—but not nearly so much as I thought I'd be. Things come back to me pretty fast. I'd give my right arm to stay here and maybe I can work it—later; at least I'm going to do all I can, but secretly believe that it will be a tough and maybe impossible job to swing. They certainly are friendly to us here. Lupton and two other officers from the "field" are here with me.

Leslie missed the party—gone on leave. When he returns to the outfit tomorrow and finds a strange officer in my place, he'll have a fit until he learns the setup, as this temporary duty deal materialized rather suddenly.

28 September 1942; Northern Ireland

... Leslie and I have had quite a time the past week. We both went up to higher headquarters and asked for transfers. I had Maj. Gittler's approval and also the acting C.O. of the regiments and Col. Clark was the acting commander of the higher unit for a few days when we went up there. He was very sympathetic, etc., and friendly but when he called in a Lt. Col. who is on the regular staff and I told him that there was a vacancy at the hospital, he jumped right down my throat and gave me a terrific bawling out, etc., and flatly refused, so of course, Col. Clark couldn't do anything. I can't mention all the details or my opinion of the whole deal as the profanity might shock you. It'll just have to wait until I get home. I'm certainly getting good training for the cold cruel world, to follow the war, believe me, kid. This war will be over some day and when it is, your husband is going to be a pretty smooth gent in the handling of his affairs. If the world should happen to drop out from under me anytime in the future, I'll probably open one eye and grin and start looking for a new world. I'll bet the Lt. Col. thought he had finished me for good by his little speech. I'll bide my time cheerfully. In the meantime, young and recently commissioned medical officers who probably have never had any field experience will get the vacancies that I sought.

Leslie is very much depressed today. Today, he went up to see the medical officer in a higher unit and got told off. You'd be astounded at what this officer told Leslie. I'd like to read the Declaration of Independence to that guy (the Med. Officer up above). There isn't a whiter guy in the army than Leslie. In spite of his being several years older than I, he's always pitched in to the things I wanted him to do, and has never in any way even implied jealousy or ill feeling.

I don't think I may need the car for a few months after I get home. Recently I ticked off a 37-mile walk through the "emerald landscape" in one day and felt pretty chipper when I finished. I'm getting so tough both in mind and body that

I'm thinking of trading my Gillette in for a Blow Torch. I think I could shave quicker with it and it'd save water.

I just heard that one of the boys in the outfit received a metal recording of his mother's voice speaking to him. He played it on one of the portable Victrolas we have. Boy, I sure would like to hear yours. Could you make a pretty speech to me and send it along sometime? That'd be the best Christmas present I could ever have. I was just kidding about the "pretty speech," just say anything you want to, as if I were sitting there with you. Do you think you could?

31 October 1942; Northern Ireland

... This letter was just interrupted by the moving of another officer into our room. We've been living like kings, Leslie, Barone, and I, in the largest room in the house, on the third floor and have had much junk spread all over the place, but now we'll have to crowd up a bit to let in the newcomer. As you know, we run most of the rackets in the outfit from this room, and have all the fancy gadgets (such as private water system, etc.). We have moved some time ago from the little "closet" that I sent you the picture of. It is the most comfortable room in the whole place.

By "rackets," I meant that we are the promoters of the outfit. Barone is canteen officer and unit bootlegger, I have the cleaning shop and other small businesses such as laundry, etc., and Leslie is engineering the party this time for the medical detachment. I guess I've never told you, but my medical section has had a full-fledged cleaning and pressing shop for some months now. One of the boys was interested, so I gave him part of a hut partitioned off and he works much of the time cleaning things American style. He does very good work at reasonable prices and gets the clothes back to the owners in about two days whereas the best the Irish can do is a week and they are liable to wash them in water, the way they did mine when we first came over. About a month ago we got a new man who used to run a cleaners' and tailors' shop in Texas, [Mott] so he also works some in the shop and we do quite a big business. Of course, there is no profit to me, but I have the cleaners kick in 25% of their income from the shop to the unit canteen fund because there are times when some of the other boys do extra work on account of the cleaner being busy in his shop and not taking his turn in all the chores that are to be done.

While I was away on the trip (to London), the boys clamored for another party so loud and lustily that Leslie started working on one and when I returned, found the plans practically completed. It will be similar to the first one we had that I wrote you about, except that it will be held in a different hall. Leslie has arranged for hamburgers, ice cream, cake, and imitation orangeade and the music will be made by that well-known Swing Band, the "Rhythm Majors." That band is the best I've ever heard over here. They are really smooth. All of the girls in the 7,000-person town where the dance is to be given, are clamoring for tickets. That's a little unusual as many of the better girls don't come to all the soldiers' dances due to the "cosmopolitan" character of the gathering. We'll have the cream of the town, as usual. We always have to have help from a few men in other units, such as cooks, guards for the motor park, etc., and the boys have been pestering our fellows to death to get the odd jobs associated with the party. We need a hat-check girl, one that can dazzle all the boys as they come in, so I'm sending you the ticket. Don't be late for work or you won't get in on the next one.

Interviews

PL: Were you getting anxious to see some action—to actually get into combat?

Dad: Well, yes—we'd been training in Northern Ireland for ten months and finally, around Christmas of '42, we were shipped down to North Africa where we then engaged with the enemy for the first time—German Field Marshal Erwin Rommel, the infamous "Desert Fox" and his highly trained Afrika Korps. He'd been beaten in one or two battles by British General Montgomery, but he was still trying to save the day for the Germans in North Africa.

But right before that, in November 1942, I had just been promoted to Captain, *finally*. I was sent to the London School of Hygiene and Tropical Medicine for a week's training in tropical medicine, which I thought was rather strange. I thought maybe they thought we'd end up in a tropical country sometime. A couple of other medical officers and I stayed at a little hotel across from a big famous hotel—can't recall the name right now, in downtown London. And we went to the University and we had a very famous tropical medicine professor, who was old, but was well-known and had a wonderful reputation.

We then went back to Ireland and in early December the entire 133rd Infantry Regiment, where I was a battalion surgeon in the 3rd Battalion—was ordered to go to Northwich, England, which is an interior, small city up the river from Liverpool, about 25 miles east and a little south of Liverpool. Liverpool is on the Mersey River—it's an excellent port—one of the best ports in the British Isles. In Northwich, we re-vaccinated everybody and got ready to ship out—we did not know where. I had previously had this week's training at the University of London in tropical medicine, so we thought maybe we were going to a tropical country, which, we found out later, was not the case.

While there in Northwich, I had some time off after we got the vaccinations done—and nobody was real sick, and I had someone else to run sick call, so I took the train for London. And, I kind of knew my way around London a little bit because I had just been there for a week taking that tropical medicine course. I looked around and really enjoyed myself. The bombing of London had ceased—many of the German planes had been shot down—so it was fairly peaceful.

And when it came time for me to go back to Northwich after a day or two on the train, I went down to the station to buy a ticket. The ticket seller saw that I was a Captain in the American army, and she said, "Captain, the train is going to leave in about 20 minutes and there's a private state room on the train (they have 1st, 2nd, and 3rd class accommodations on British trains, which are very good trains). There's a private state room always reserved for the King's Courier—so if he doesn't show up, you can ride in that." So, I stuck around and I got on the train in the King's Courier's private state-room and rode back to Northwich in style. That was real nice. It had two upper and lower berths facing each other because the corridor on a British train runs along the side—it doesn't go down the middle the way it does in this country. And it was the full width of the car less the narrow corridor, which is about two feet wide. The windows are at the far end of each lower berth.

Finally, we (division headquarters) boarded a ship, the *Empress of Australia*, in Liverpool, England about December 20, 1942. Again, we had no idea where we were going. As I recall, we were on the high seas for Christmas. We only learned well after leaving England that we were going to North Africa. It took us about two weeks to get there. We landed at Oran, Algeria, and subsequently worked our way across North Africa to Algiers, then into Tunisia, which positioned us to move in to Italy.

North Africa is very much like the eastern part of Washington State. It's kind of an irrigated desert—there's nothing tropical about it. But some higher-up in the Army thought that Africa meant tropics and that was the reason they sent me to study tropical medicine in London for a few weeks. I did learn something about malaria and they did have some Malaria in North Africa and Italy.

Letters

Christmas Day 1942; Aboard the Good Ship (Censored)

[entire letter]

Dearest Jean:

Hello, darling. Well, here we are on a troop transport bound for a destination that I can't mention now, but one which you will probably know within certain limits sometime in the future. We are now coasting along in quiet waters; the sun has recently broken through the clouds for the first time in several days and most of the troops are up on the decks watching the water, the sea gulls, and other things. It's all pretty exciting and very interesting and I'm certainly glad that at long last we are now on the road to possible business. It certainly doesn't seem like Christmas, though.

It's funny, but when things get a little exciting like this I'm always glad I'm here and "in on the party" and wouldn't miss it for anything, and yet, it's at these same times that I get the most lonesome for you. Of course, I'm glad that you're not on this ship at the present time, but I sure do wish we could share the excitement together. You certainly would enjoy it, that is, the pleasant aspects of it, and everything has certainly been smooth sailing so far. We'll have to take a trip on a steamship together sometime, as there's nothing quite like it, as you probably know from your lake trip.

Yesterday morning I had charge of the sick call for the entire ship, but today

Leslie did it while I helped Major Kelso make a sanitary inspection of half the ship. We found everything shipshape. The men are quartered and fed much better than on the "tub" that we came over on originally. This ship is about the same size, but is much cleaner in every way. It's actually a re-outfitted luxury cruise ship, which suits us fine.

Today at luncheon, the dance orchestra, made up from our band (The Rhythm Majors), the one that played for our dances back on the island (Northern Ireland) sat on the balcony in the main dining salon and played sweet and smooth during the meal. The service and "cuisine" are excellent as many of the civilian steward staff are still on board. The tablecloths and silver are spotless. It certainly doesn't seem like a troopship in wartime, more like a nice hotel or nightclub in the States. We are going off in "style." I feel great, except for being very lonesome for you.

Right at this moment, over the loud speakers in the corridor outside the cabin, King George VI is speaking to his loyal subjects and allies. I can't quite make out all that he says from here, but his slow, measured, and deliberate choice of words well befits a monarch's speech. His speech is much more cheerful, as it should be, than it has been in past years. Things are certainly looking up for the Allies lately, aren't they? The Russians are going to town again and it looks like things may soon be brought to a decision in Africa.

We are going to have a picture show on board ship this afternoon and a meeting of some of the officers this afternoon, and I must grab a quick shave, so I'll close. Of course, this letter will be sent on its way after we've arrived at our destination, but I couldn't resist writing on this Christmas Day, when I love you so and want to see you so much. Keep writing.

3

North Africa

Operation TORCH and Meeting the Desert Fox, January 3–September 22, 1943

"The Medical Officer always has plenty to do. In a theater of operations, I think the M.O. takes on some of the duties performed by home and mother."

—16 March 1942, North Africa

"Some of the 'glamour' that has been dished up to us from Hollywood during the last few years fades to superficiality when you are crouched in a foxhole with the earth vibrating to the crash of incoming artillery, and shrapnel is buzzing over your head."

—13 April 1943, North Africa

In 1940, within months after World War II began, France fell and a French government under German domination was set up in the spa town of Vichy in southern France. The French colonies in North Africa—French Morocco, Algeria, and Tunisia, remained under the control of this puppet Vichy government, which was now technically allied with Germany.

President Roosevelt made the decision to invade and seize North Africa, specifically Tunisia, as a launching site for Allied troops to more easily gain access to Sicily and southern Italy. Engaging with the Germans in North Africa was also a delay and diversion tactic to give Allied Forces more time to prepare for their eventual D-Day invasion of Normandy in June of 1944.

The North African incursion was called "Operation TORCH." Historian Rick Atkinson, author of the consummate account of the North African campaign, *An Army at Dawn: The War in North Africa, 1942–1943*, notes that "No large operation in WWII surpassed the invasion of North Africa in complexity, daring, or risk...." The North African campaign became a pivotal point in Allied forces defeating the Germans in World War II and in America's military history.*

The very real drama of war was about to unfold in North Africa for the 34th

---

* "Two great armadas would carry more than 100,000 troops to the invasion beaches. One fleet would sail more than 2,880 miles from Britain to Algeria, with mostly British ships ferrying mostly American soldiers." Rick Atkinson, *An Army at Dawn* (New York: Henry Holt and Company, 2002), 22. [Hereafter cited as *Army at Dawn*].

December 1942: Map of the *Empress of Australia's* sailing route from Liverpool, England, to Oran, Algeria for Operation TORCH. Not to scale. (Invisible Ink Corporation)

Infantry Division. Even though the 133rd and 168th regiments had trained in Northern Ireland for ten months, they were untested in live combat and at a disadvantage with outdated, World War I era equipment: weaponry, communications systems, and clothing.

In his book, *Meeting the Fox,* author Orr Kelly notes: "Their imaginations did not prepare them for reality: high mountains, snow, cold, torrential rains, and mud so thick it would swallow trucks, jeeps, airplanes, and even tanks." These inexperienced National Guardsmen from the middle of Iowa, were amongst the first American troops to engage with Germany's highly trained *Afrika Korps* army and its double threat of panzer attacks and dive-bombing Stukas. As the 34th Infantry Division moved eastward across North Africa to Tunisia, they learned hard-fought, costly lessons. These were some of the bloodiest and most intense battles of the entire North African campaign but eventually, both the 133rd and 168th regiments became fine-tuned combat machines against a backdrop of brilliant poppy fields and cactus patches.

Interviews: January 3, 1943–February 1943

PL: When and where did you land in North Africa—and what happened next?

Dad: I think we got to our final destination, the Port of Oran, Algiers, around the third of January 1943. From Britain, we went down the entire coast of France and Spain and through the Straits of Gibraltar. But of course, at night, we had no lights burning. We were in a convoy—and we would zig for a mile or two, then zag for a mile or two. There were no lights showing—and there was a 5,000-ton Dutch ship on our flank that was supposed to zig when we zigged, and zag when we zagged and it didn't, and they accidentally rammed us. I was in our stateroom with the triple bunk beds—I think I was in the top bed. We all went to bed with our clothes on. We didn't have pajamas—you don't have those in combat; but I had a full canteen—you never know what's going to happen.

We got rammed by one of our own Allied ships that tore a big ten-foot gash in our side, about four feet high and partly below the water line, and we started to list, and we started to tilt more and more. I didn't know how much more we were going to tilt, so I ran out on the upper side of the deck with my full canteen, ready to jump, if necessary. The ship listed about fifteen degrees, and then it quit. It had water-tight holds and doors which they shut and sealed. I think they had to evacuate some of the enlisted men on the lower decks, but a lot of us got out on the deck, just in case—and we were able to continue on under our own power because the propellers were still under water. But we had to slow down to about two to three knots an hour.

We finally pulled in to Oran at Mers El Kabir on January 3, 1943, which is actually down in the dock area of Oran. Again, we were lightered ashore by fairly large lighters [shallow draft barge-like boats used for carrying "light loads" in amphibious landings] that held 50 or 100 men. We were part of the "Operation TORCH" landings, which were intended to bring a quick end to the North African war and serve as a diversion to German troops and buy time until the odds for a cross Channel invasion improved. I guess it was a huge gamble. Our mission was to press eastwards across North Africa as quickly as possible towards Tunis—both sides were building up forces in a battle for control of Tunisia—the launching point for movement into Italy.

After being taken ashore in Oran, we marched to Assi Ben Okba, about ten miles southeast of Oran and were billeted, or camped out, in tents for about a week—in the farmland, I guess, but it was actually kind of a brush desert. That's where we first encountered British rations. We were out there in tents and were fed these British rations that were sustaining, I guess, but not to an American taste. We had a lot of tea, stale chocolate cookies, and lamb, which they call mutton. That's the first time we didn't have American rations—and we didn't know we'd miss them so much.

Then we were moved into a barracks building in central Oran, which had been occupied by some Black Senegalese French troops who wore red fezzes as part of their uniform. Their quarters was a sort of fort, half way up a big hill and had a commanding view of the city of Oran—but the sanitary conditions were deplorable. These troops were moved out because the French Navy had begun to defect from France. The Americans were there now, with a stronger military presence. And so, a lot of the French captains and admirals renounced their command. I think the Germans came in just before we arrived and sank about ten French warships in the harbor of Oran. That's the reason we couldn't get up to the dock when we were landing. They had just been shelled with artillery and were blocking our access. The Allies were realizing that with part of the French Navy down in North Africa, there was no German Navy in the Mediterranean, except for submarines. And so the French were going to defect—and I think the Germans sunk those ships, but maybe it was the British that did it, those trying to be loyal to the cause.*

Soon after landing in North Africa, Allied troops seized the French Vichy Government capital, which led to the end of French resistance in North Africa. So, we were moved into this barracks, and brought our own cots and bedrolls with us because the whole place was riddled with millions of bed bugs in the cracks of the walls. They kind of looked like a little sheath of wheat or something, and they were everywhere. I don't know whether those troops from Southern Morocco were immune to the bed bugs—they must've been. But at least we had running water and latrines and transportation. None of us stuck around in the building much except to sleep at night—and we slept in our own bedding and bedrolls, so fortunately most of us did not get bitten.

---

* "... it was the hope that the French in North Africa, who would be inclined to resist the British, might welcome Americans. Although the British and the French had been allies at the time of the German invasion of France, their relationship had turned sour after the French capitulation and especially after the British attacked units of the French fleet at the port of Oran." Orr Kelly, *Meeting the Fox: The Allied Invasion of Africa, From Operation TORCH to Kasserine Pass to Victory in Tunisia*. (New York: John Wiley & Sons, Inc. 2002), 20. [Hereafter cited as *Meeting the Fox*].

We were there in Oran about a month and then we got orders to go by motor convoy—truck and automobile—east. It took us about three or four days. We ultimately wanted to get to Tunisia, for positioning into Italy.

From Oran, we went through Relezane, Midea, Sétif, Sucaras, and finally at El Kef (French: Le Kef, we called it) we turned south toward the road that ran from Tebessa to Kairouane where about midway between, we came upon Fondouk Pass in Tunisia. There, we deployed into defensive position, because that's where the enemy was—up on the high ground of Fondouk Pass with entrenched artillery and some ground troops to defend the artillery that they had in place. And then we attacked, a few days later, at Fondouk.

January 1943 Oran, Algeria: "Ambulance: ½ horsepower." The 133rd was waiting to move east across North Africa and engagement with the enemy in Tunisia.

We fought the Germans for about a year, moving across the northern coast of Africa to its east coast, and then went in to Italy. The Red Bull 34th Infantry Division fought with great distinction in the Italian Campaign, although prior to that, we were finally able to prove ourselves in North Africa with the Battle of Hill 609.*

The 34th Infantry Division's narrative history sums up the North African campaign in this way:

---

* In his book, *The Breakthrough Battalion: Battles of Company C of the 133rd Infantry Regiment; Tunisia and Italy, 1943–1945,* Col. Richard F. Wilkinson noted that in its rush after Pearl Harbor to establish an early presence in Europe, the 34th Division had not been issued the newest anti-tank weapons, such as the bazooka. Nor had they received modern radio equipment at the levels of platoon to battalion. One reason for this deficiency was that other U.S. divisions in Tunisia, which had later been deployed *directly* from the United States, brought this equipment with them. However, the 34th came from their 10-month training in Northern Ireland, where modern equipment was not available for issue. In fact, the 34th did not get these items until April 1943, well into the North African campaign. Col. Richard F. Wilkinson, *The Breakthrough Battalion: Battles of Company C of the 133rd Infantry Regiment; Tunisia and Italy, 1943–1945* (self-published, 2005), 10. [Hereafter cited as *Breakthrough Bn*].

3. North Africa

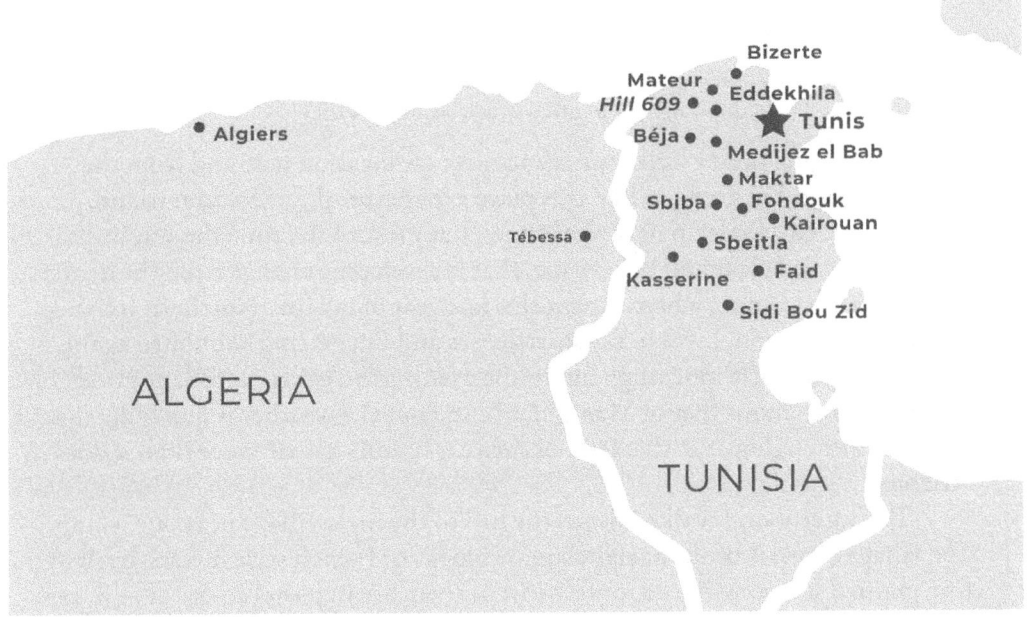

February–May 1943, Tunisia, North Africa: The major locations where Lud's 133rd and 168th's Infantry Regiments camped, staged attacks, and/or engaged with the enemy. Not to scale. (Invisible Ink Corporation)

After landing in Oran, the 34th [Infantry Division], joining with other Allied forces, pushed eastward into Tunisia. Stiff opposition by reinforced German troops was encountered in Tunisia. Many of the battles were for possession of mountain passes leading eastward, and particularly fierce fighting took place in February 1943. Engagements at Faid Pass, where an entire battalion [of the 168th Regiment: 106 officers and 1,747 enlisted men] was taken prisoner.

A powerful German attack near Kasserine Pass inflicted heavy casualties, but Germany's failure to follow-up enabled the Allies to recover and resume their offensive.

The critical task of taking Hill 609 was given to the 34th. An attack began early on April 29, 1943, when the 3rd Battalion, 135th Infantry moved to the base of the hill and captured a small village. From there the 34th began an all-out assault under intense fire.

After two days the bastion was finally taken, and with Hill 609 in American hands, the German Army's defense line collapsed. It was a momentous victory and fitting revenge for the division's setbacks at Faid, Kasserine, and Fondouk. Two weeks later, on May 15, 1943, the enemy surrendered and the battle for North Africa was over.

The now tough, combat-hardened men of the 34th Infantry Division were justifiably proud of what they had accomplished, but they were acutely aware of the price they had paid: total battle casualties of the 34th in the Tunisian Campaign numbered 4,049, of which half were missing in action.

Letters: January 6–February 5, 1943

6 January 1943; Somewhere in North Africa

[in pup tents on the side of a small mountain,
looking 30–40 miles over a beautiful valley]

… We are getting pretty well adjusted to our new location here and from the looks of things, I'm going to like this place a lot better than "Swamp Island." It has sprinkled a little on us several times, but most of the time the sun shines down bright and clear and believe me, that is a welcome change from the dreary cloudiness of the place where I spent this last year of my life [Northern Ireland]. Today, around noon, I was in my shirtsleeves and I'm getting a sunburn again, although in the early mornings and in the evenings an overcoat feels comfortable. Our latitude is about that of Memphis, Tenn., but the weather is more like that of Arizona, although just at this time of the year it rains a little more than it does in Arizona.

This afternoon I walked down the hill to the little village near our "camp." The village consists of about eight square blocks of French style houses, built of fine-grained stucco with tile roofs. Most of them are in pastel colors of buff, tan, pale green or greyish blue, although all of the roofs are of an "orange-ish" color. There is much iron grill and fancy work along the eaves, and in several places there are French style "compounds," that is, there is a high wall along the sidewalk with a roofed large gate through which you catch a glimpse of a very pretty inner courtyard with flowers, etc., and maybe a farm cart or two. The blocks of houses are "solid," that is, one house is built right up against the next house or courtyard wall. All of the street windows of the houses have wooden shutters, which were closed against the afternoon sun. It all reminded me very much of New Orleans. Several of the houses in town looked new and were of "modernistic" architecture, looked just like some of the newest modern "Hollywood" type homes with round windows, flat roofs, etc. It's a surprisingly clean town, but strangely enough I didn't notice any stores in town. The land around the village in the valley is all farmed neatly, part of it irrigated from wells. It may be that the village is a "collective" group of homes for some large ranch or estate, I don't know. I certainly am "crazy" to learn French so that I can find out a lot of things I want to know about.

16 January 1943; North Africa

[probably in the Tlemcen region, Algeria; training for a few weeks;
the war in Tunisia, ~ 700 to 800 miles away, was at a standstill.]

… When I last wrote (6 Jan.) we were parked in pup tents on the side of a small mountain, but great changes have taken place since then. We are now living in a place that overlooks the blue Mediterranean, in buildings that are certainly different from pup tents. It is just as though we had engaged a villa for the winter season. Leslie, "Ace" Balliet (dentist) and I have a front room from the windows of which, one can look down on a beautiful panorama of sea, cliffs, and town. This spot would bring a high price for a place to put a summer home.

... The sun is warm, but not too hot yet. I wear BVDs, wool shirt, and usually a field jacket most of the time. Gosh, it's different from the rainy raw days in you know where I used to be. [Northern Ireland]

... The move has kept us all pretty busy the last few days getting our new place cleaned up. It certainly was filthy when we moved in and I have been raring back on my heels and "hollering" at all the other staff officers and the company commanders for some time, as is the medical officer's responsibility to get things sanitary and keep them that way. I'm a fairly hardboiled inspector, and things are coming up out of the dirt at last. Oh, yes. I forgot to mention that this last move split up the "larger unit" (from home) [133rd] and I have been separated from the Major again, am back with Leslie in the outfit I left in Nov. Leslie had carried on alone after I left, and had done very well, but Col. Clark thought that the unit should have its regular (2) number of medical officers with it when it split off. I talked Maj. G. into letting me take one of the dentists also, so we really have a nice set-up now. Everybody likes it very much, although I don't think it will last too long. At present the Major [Gittler] and Col. Clark and Duggan, etc., are 80 miles away in the "sticks." I went out there yesterday in a ton & a half truck. It certainly was a ride, believe me. I saw so many things I can't remember all of it and haven't digested it yet; but I'll get it all to you in a little while.

January 1943: "Ludwick takes a bath, African style."

21 January 1943; In Sunny North Africa

The "ration book" you sent on January 4 arrived here last night. It sure is the nuts, all right, but I like it very much. I thought about sending in my first two coupons with this letter, but decided that I'd better save them to collect all that's coming to me in person over the counter, and Baby, am I going to catch up!!! I haven't been "saving myself" for nothing. We'll hang a "measles" sign on the front door and the neighbors can send in a hot covered dish or something once in awhile during the first few months of my convalescence.

... The "ration book" arrived just before I went to our first party here. It seems that the young bucks amongst the officers have been agitating for a party for some time and apparently had everything pretty well arranged when it was announced two days ago. They arranged for some nurses from a hospital about eight miles away to attend, ... for the "Rhythm Majors" to furnish the music, and hired a hillside restaurant for the evening. The party began about 7 P.M. as the girls had to be home by 10 P.M. The girls arrived in trucks before we did and so when we came, we mingled with them getting acquainted, etc., and whom should I meet but Wagner; you remember the nurse that used to work out at the Allen? I thought her face was vaguely familiar, but she didn't register until she came up to me and asked if I weren't from Waterloo. She and her outfit haven't been here much longer than we have, but of course they didn't come here from where we did. She had a date with one of the Military Police officers that live at the same place that we do and whom of course we invited to the party. She invited me out to see her outfit, a general hospital unit from Chicago. I might go some time, if I ever get the time and the transportation....

The party didn't last until 10 P.M. It was suddenly broken up about 9 P.M. and the girls were hurriedly bundled into their trucks and we tore out for our post to be with our men. I can't tell you what caused all the commotion, but you might guess. Nothing came of it, although we saw some pretty colors in the air. I think the girls will remember that evening as short, but exciting.

... Tonight, the moonlight is very bright. We have the brightest moonlight here I've ever seen, almost as light as day. We certainly are enjoying the weather here, and also the oranges. As I've written before, we can get great big oranges, weighing about a pound each, for about 3 or 4 Francs. I've eaten three of them today and I'm about ready to "bust." I took several pictures of the very juicy and surprisingly sweet oranges a couple of days ago.

28 January 1943; Somewhere in North Africa

... In your letter of Nov. 25th, you asked me what I thought I wanted to do when I came back home. For the first time in my life, Jean, I don't exactly know. Always before, as you know, I've been a long-range planner, but this army business and the war have put such a dent in my plans and have altered my outlook on things in general so much that my plans have not crystallized into anything definite yet. All I know is, that I'm not worried a bit about the future. When the time comes, I'll be able to step into something that we both will want and like and will do O.K.

 I've never broached the subject before, but, Jean, I've changed somewhat since we parted. I'm sure that when we are together again that you'll notice some things about me that are different from what you remembered. There is one thing that has not changed in the least bit, and that is my love for you. I'm just as much in love with you as I ever was which was "all out" after our first kiss. That will never change. Most of the change in me, I think, is an increase in tolerance of other people's ways, and also the realization that I'm going to take more time for fun and not take myself so blamed seriously all the time. You'll probably be shocked when you see me again, although seriously, I don't think a stranger would notice the change. Hope you like the new model.

 … The weather continues to be balmy and there is plenty of sunshine, which we like very much. There isn't a great deal to do in town at night and besides, all military personnel have to be off the streets by 10:00 P.M. There IS a fairly good "variety" show in town. I've seen it twice now. It's essentially a French vaudeville show, and some very good acts. It's a clean show and it's always packed with American soldiers. Of course, most of the songs are in French, but we occasionally get a "ziss and zatt" English (???) song sung for us and of course we enjoy the dog tricks and the magician, etc.… Another thing worthy of remark is the grace of the French actresses on the stage. They certainly know their business all right. There are movies also, but I haven't been to any yet. The boys say that most of them are in French, although most are produced in Hollywood. Some of them have English diction and French subtitles.

 I think I've commented before on the great variety of native costumes here. The French have not worried so much about the "color line" as we Americans do, and of course as a result, there has been much more intermarriage with the natives than there would be in a corresponding city in America. As a result, each "shade" of mixed coupling wears a different combination of modern (French) and native clothes. I could take pictures all day and still get different "outfits" to show you. The common head gear is either the red Fez or a white or yellow turban (male), sometimes both. I don't know whether I described the standard article of dress for the native male below the waist or not, but it consists of a baggy pair of bloomers with a crotch cut quite low, usually below the knees. This makes a sort of "bag" of excess material that swings along between the man's knees. I don't know whether he carries his extra rations there or not. In one small town that I was in recently, I saw a native man wearing a pair of jodhpur-like breeches that were (believe it or not) a bright pink color. Where he got them, I don't know. Some of the boys have seen natives walking down the street wearing a pair of G.I. woolen underwear pants as an external garment. I think I wrote you about the kid that cut two holes in the bottom of a barracks bag and tied the drawstring about this waist.…

 … Must close as my candle has gone out and the ceiling electric light is too dim to see with ease.…

2 February 1943; Somewhere in North Africa

Dearest Jean, Darling:

Yesterday was quite a day … the arrival of the biggest batch of mail that we've ever received. I received 50 pieces of mail—all at once. There were 37 "letters," including two cables and several Christmas cards, etc. There were THIRTEEN LETTERS FROM YOU!!!, as well as three from Mother and two from your father. The mail came in the evening, and I stayed up until 1:30 A.M. this morning reading it all.

… You mentioned your "brainstorm" about working for an aviation concern. I don't think that's so crazy. You're right about the important future of aviation. If you take it up seriously, though, I wish you'd work on the medical angle if possible, because I want you to be near me at all times and not interested in a branch of aviation too divergent from our bread and butter….

… And Jean, you must never worry about me. We really have the easy job of it over here. Everything that the whole nation does is just for our benefit. We have the best to eat, we have the finest equipment (too darn much of it to carry around at times). There aren't as many casualties in a war as there are from automobile riding in peace times, and even those are only a small percentage of the large numbers engaged in being soldiers. On the other hand, you at home are subject to rumors and fears and uncertainties, and a lonesomeness that maybe sometimes gets a little panicky. Our lonesomeness here, as long as we know that you love us, is the dull, heavy kind that never leaves, but yet one that you can "see through," because there is no doubt on earth in my mind but what we'll be together some one of these days and everything will be O.K.

…Yesterday, being payday, I went downtown and bought you a "Berber" rug. These rugs are hand made out of natural colored wool (no dye used) by native Arab women and I think you'll like the one I sent. It has a thick, soft wooly nap, something like the inside of a sheep skin coat, and I sent it for you to put beside your bed for you to hop out on every morning. The rug is mostly cream colored with grey, brown and black oriental patterns. You can wash it or clean it any way you would ever want to without fear of fading, etc., as the pattern is worked in by hand with different colored wools from different colored sheep.

… It's after 1:00 A.M. and I must hit the hay. J'ai faim pour vous, ma petite fraise.

4 February 1943; North Africa

… We moved again yesterday. It came sort of suddenly and we hated to give up our "villa" on the blue waters, but orders are orders so we are about 10 miles inland, very near to the place where we spent the first week here. We are living in pup tents again. It certainly is different from living in a place equipped with hot showers and electric lights, but none of the boys seem to mind. You ought to see the rig up that I'm sitting under now writing this letter. They don't allow the officers as much tentage as they once did in the army (Even some Lt. Col.s are in pup tents now), so I had our orderly pitch a canvas top of a truck on stilts in such a way that I have a "hut" that I can stand up in and don't have to get down on my knees to get into my tent. I took a picture of it this afternoon but don't know when I'll ever get this roll developed. It may be weeks....*

5 February 1943; North Africa

... Now about joining the WAACS or the EAVES this spring. [he was actually referring to the newly formed Women Air Force Service Pilots, or WASPs.]

Jean, you're your own boss and I'll be for you 100 % no matter what you do; but darling, from what I know of the women's services you definitely wouldn't like it. You could make the grade, all right, and probably would crawl right up the ladder. But darling, I definitely don't want a worn-out wife on my hands when I get home. You mentioned Marion as making a lot of speeches, etc. I'd much rather have you wait until you're through with your family raising to run around the country. However, I realize that the problem is yours, as you say, and I know that busy hands make the time pass more quickly. I DO KNOW one thing, though, that you would hate the discipline after the first six weeks. You'd have to run your life exactly the way some other woman wanted you to. You'd probably (nine cases out of ten) wind up in a job much less interesting and more boring than the one you're in now—but, do as you like. I think you'll be a little shocked at some of the moral aspects of the women's services, but, of course, that won't bother you as it's up to each individual to live his or her own life as they see fit. Let me know what your thoughts are on this. I won't mention this to anyone, don't worry. You say you feel like a 1A posing as a 4F! You're crazy!! It's every woman's job FIRST to keep her man fighting fit, and that's just what you're doing. I couldn't go on without your letters, and what you tell me about what goes on back home. I love you, darling....

* * *

In 1941, Jean Hoyer was an adventurous and independent young woman. She was not yet engaged or married to her "boyfriend," Dr. Arthur L. Ludwick, Jr., who was then in Louisiana with the Iowa National Guard on training maneuvers. While working as a Laboratory Medical Technologist at the small Presbyterian Hospital in Waterloo, she decided to take flying lessons, riding her bicycle to the airfield on the outskirts of town after work and on days off.

After marrying Lud in October 1941 and his unexpected deployment to Europe

---

*The entire remaining Division was on the move—about 12,000 men and their equipment in almost 1,000 vehicles of various kinds. They were headed for Tunisia and combat. This move covered almost 800 miles and crossed the Atlas Mountains. It was bitterly cold all along the way, especially at night, where the temperature dropped below freezing with snow and blizzards.

when war was declared in December, she focused on obtaining her pilot's license in Waterloo. In partnership with four other pilots, all men, she rented a small Taylorcraft Light, single-engine plane. To maximize her flying opportunities when rationed airplane fuel was available, she delivered critically needed units of blood to outlying rural community hospitals around Waterloo. She navigated by looking out the window of her plane at familiar landmarks and the patchwork geometry of Iowa's corn fields below. Apparently, she was not yet trained to use instrument navigation.

After war was declared in December 1941, Jacqueline Cochran, a pioneer in the field of aviation, traveled throughout the U.S. recruiting qualified women to join the newly formed Women Air Force Service Pilots (WASP) branch of the U.S. Army. Due to the demands of the war, there was a shortage of trained pilots to ferry critical war supplies and airplanes throughout the U.S.

From August 1943 to December 1944, Cochran, as director of the WASPs, supervised the training of hundreds of women pilots at the former Avenger Field in Sweetwater, Texas. With Lud serving overseas, Jean was very interested in this unique opportunity to fly and contribute to the war effort—and even traveled to the training facility in Sweetwater, Texas, to check things out. However, at that time in history, in order to join the WASPs, a married woman needed to have her husband's written permission. When this official paperwork finally caught up with Lud somewhere in Italy, he refused to sign the request. His rationale was twofold: he didn't want his wife flying into dangerous combat scenarios; and, he felt certain he would be rotated back to the U.S. at any time. After being separated for more than two years, he wanted Jean to "be there" for him when he finally did return home. He didn't know at the time that in actuality, the WASPs only ferried supplies and airplanes within the continental U.S. and parts of Canada, and were never purposefully subjected to risky aeronautical missions.

Interviews: February 14–15, 1943: The Battle of the Kasserine/Faid Pass Area, Tunisia, North Africa

Col. Richard F. Wilkinson, in his book, *The Breakthrough Battalion,* describes the landscape and importance of the area where the Battle of Kasserine Pass was fought: "… it is desert, with little vegetation, bare valley and mountains, and resembling the surface of the moon. Both on the east and west sides lie mountain ranges—and the two passes in the west, Kasserine Pass and Sbiba Gap, were the key to all military movements of all forces" (5). The Battle of Kasserine Pass was actually a series of smaller skirmishes where German Field Marshal Erwin Rommel's well-trained *Africa Korps* dealt the inexperienced American troops a stunning setback.

PL: When and where did you first engage with German troops?
Dad: My first contact with the enemy was south of Fondouk Pass about ten to fifteen miles in the Hajeb el Aioun/Kasserine/Faid Pass area. I was with the 133rd

3. North Africa

Infantry Division then—had trained with them in Northern Ireland for ten months and then was deployed with them to North Africa.

We were in a somewhat minor skirmish off to one side of the main battle, with only a few casualties. Kasserine Pass was about ten to fifteen miles south of us, and was where the Germans had captured about a thousand Americans from the 168th Infantry Regiment, our Iowa boys and sister regiment of our 133rd. The German tanks had come in and surrounded this butte where the Americans were up on top and thought the tanks couldn't get to them. But the tanks surrounded the butte and started to bombard them with a lot of 88 cannons, and they had no shelter. They were losing men right and left, so they surrendered.

This included the regimental surgeon, Major Fred Beaumont, and most of the regimental headquarters, which is the reason I was later transferred from the 133rd Infantry Regiment to the 168th as their Regimental Surgeon. Apparently, Beaumont's medical battalion was out of touch with the movements of its regiment and advanced too quickly, ahead of the fighting troops. They were all captured, along with a good part of the 168th Regiment. Author Rick Atkinson, in his book *An Army at Dawn*, describes the grim scene:

> The debacle was complete. Burial details combed the battlefield to collect the dead before looters stripped them; grave robbers had become so bold that chaplains carried carbines.... [the remaining soldiers] stacked the dead, wrapped in white mattress covers in a mass grave, then joined the column of American prisoners stretching east as far as the eye could see. For all military intents and purposes, the 168th Infantry Regiment—Iowa's finest—had been obliterated [357].

At that point, our American officers and staff were not very well trained for or experienced in live combat. They were ignorant of the logistics and how to coordinate an operation. The communications were poor, there was lots of confusion, and it was a flawed plan.*

* * *

In a U.S. Army "After Action Report," Colonel Thomas D. Drake, former commander of the 168th Infantry Regiment, summed up the Kasserine Pass disaster in these few words: "You know the problem—good fighting men but inexperienced and only partially trained."

—April 11, 1945

Dad (cont'd): I can remember after the battle was over, I was walking up to one of these 88 guns—they were so fast with their high 34-pound trajectory shells. Previously, most artillery shells, up until the Germans got this "88" cannon, were shot from about five miles away and we could hear them land. Those were the French 75s that the

---

* "Weapons, too, were woefully lacking. Col. Drake made insistent and repeated demands for bazookas, the best infantry weapon against armored vehicles and tanks. When some bazookas finally arrived on the night of the 12th of February, just before the Faid Debacle, it was too late to instruct the men in their use." *Breakthrough Bn*, 96.

Germans had captured. But these 88s—boy, they'd shoot straight, and had such high velocity, you couldn't tell they were coming. You could hear an incoming shell from a 75, and they'd land near you. But these 88s, their trajectory was just flat and they didn't make much noise because they came so fast, and the huge 34-pound shell was ahead of the noise.*

Well, I came upon this body of an American soldier and he was right in front of where there had been an 88 cannon. I guess they had pulled the 88 out and taken it with them, because it wasn't there anymore. But they'd had an 88 right in that position, and the top of this soldier's head was just gone. The top of his skull—it was clean—it looked like some pathologist had lifted out the brain because you could just see the base of the skull. And he had his left hand in his pocket. I think he was reaching for a hand grenade, and he was going to throw it at the squad that was tending this 88-cannon. But he got in front of the gun and stood up and they had it loaded, and they just pulled the trigger or the lanyard when he stood up and shot the top of his head off, just clean. He had his dog tags on, so I wrote an EMT tag.†

I wrote his name and unit and so forth, and listed him as a KIA. The body collectors would come along and put his body into a mattress cover, a white sack about six feet long, about three feet wide, and about four or five inches thick. That's what they'd put the bodies in and ship them back to someplace where they'd be buried temporarily in rows, like they did in France, and eventually would be evacuated to America. The losses were terrible, as well as nearly two thousand Iowa men on their way to German and Italian prison camps. The 34th's self-esteem and reputation had certainly been tarnished by the setbacks at Kasserine/Faid Pass and the subsequent failure of the first attack at Fondouk.

After the Kasserine/Faid fiasco, they had to reorganize the 168th Infantry because they had lost so many men—killed, seriously wounded, or captured, including Major Beaumont, who was their regimental surgeon.‡ And that's when, around the end of February 1943 or so, I was asked, "Ludwick, do you want to go over and be the new Regimental Surgeon of the 168th Infantry?" That's a Major's position. If I transferred from the 133rd Infantry, where I was a Battalion Surgeon and a Captain, to the 168th Infantry, becoming their Regimental Surgeon, I would eventually be promoted to a Major. So, I definitely said yes, and was transferred.

---

* "The German '88' was a much-feared, high velocity, hard-hitting large-bore rifle with great superiority to any such weapon in the American arsenal. It would hit with great devastation, immobilizing an American tank. Two or three rounds would demolish a two to three-story building." *Breakthrough Bn,* 36–37.

† "Every medic, whether enlisted man, noncommissioned officer, or officer, carried an EMT (Emergency Medical Tag) book in one of his canvas pouches. The tag was attached to the casualty's clothing, usually over the breast, or as near as possible to it for ease of reading by medical personnel." WW2 U.S. Medical Research Centre: The WW2 Medical Detachment, [Hereafter cited as Med Research Ctr]. https://www.med-dept.com/articles/the-ww2-emergency-medical-tag/.

‡ "Total losses for the 168th Infantry Regiment included 109 officers and 1,797 enlisted men, including most of the medical detachment and the collecting company and 10 physicians. *Army at Dawn,* 397.

That's when I first encountered Colonel Frederic B. Butler. The 168th Infantry was now commanded by Col. Butler, which had lost its commander, Colonel Drake, and two of its battalions in the disaster at Sidi Bou Zid [Kasserine/Faid Pass]. He was a wonderful man—well trained, tall, mature—about 55 or 60 years old. Butler was a Colonel in the Corps of Engineers, which meant that he was in the upper ten percent of his class at West Point. He had silver hair and piercing blue eyes—we all referred to him, privately, as "The Great White Father" (TGWF). I liked him very much, and he called me "Doc." He was kind of like a father figure to me, as I had lost my own beloved father at the tender age of sixteen.

I think Colonel Butler liked the fact that I didn't get too excited about anything. Most of the guys lost their appetite before combat, you know, but I got hungry. I guess I was nervous, and it made my stomach more active and I'd want to eat.*

Letters: February 13–26, 1943

13 February 1943; North Africa

[east of Sbiba, Tunisia]

… This is the first chance I've had to write since Feb. 5, because your husband has been really covering the ground during that time. I'm about eight or nine hundred miles from where I last wrote, and believe me, this part of Africa is entirely different from the description of the part that we left. I feel just like I was in western Montana. The country is rough and sort of mountainous, the ground being covered with various types of low brush and small evergreen trees. The wind blows all the time. Several times during the last few days we have had snow.

The whole jaunt has been extremely interesting and, in some cases, thrilling. I wish I could talk to you about it, but you know that any great attention to details is forbidden by the censorship. However, it's a small thrill to zoom around mountain curves in the dead of night without driving lights, feeling your way along as best you can with a whole bunch of friends behind you. I realize that these things are not exactly the duties of a medical officer, but then when Johnny Jones gets a little lost or confused by directions and sleepy drivers are worried about slipping off the ledge, sometimes it pays to follow the advice of "your physician."

… The funniest thing happened last night. We were "rolling along" without a care in the world and suddenly passed a sign board along the road in the dark. Leslie, who was in another part of the outfit, got out to read the sign and I guess his hair really stood on end. Talk about U-turns, we can really make them over

---

* "Company cooks were the last to eat, and like mother at home, there always was the thought of the next meal. Efforts and achievements of kitchen crews in the field during combat constituted one of the great accomplishments of World War II. Under severe and dangerous conditions, they managed to get the troops fed. Veterans would particularly remember F Company cooks carrying marmite cans with hot food up the treacherous climb of Mt. Pantano in Italy." *Breakthrough Bn*, 151.

here and there are no traffic cops to hinder you. However, to turn around an Infantry Battalion of approximately 1,000 men and over 100 trucks (we used 2 ½ ton, 6-wheeled vehicles, called 6x6s, not including jeeps and command vehicles) that is spread out more than six miles, is no small feat.*

It sure is fun to see the sights over here, also the signs. The signs sometimes remind me of the Burma Shave ads. We've all laughed a great deal over the whole thing as it's hard in some ways for us to get serious about some phases of this war.

Another interesting thing about our trip was the fact that every kid in North Africa, or at least every one that could walk, I think, stood beside the road as we went by. I'll bet I saw a thousand kids a day and each one of them yelled "Commarod, segahrett, showkalait, shoongom, buzzkwit, bombom, or sooveneir?" ["Comrad, cigarette, chocolate, chewing gum, biscuit, bon bon, souvenir"] at the top of his lungs. Whenever we stopped, some Arab would appear out of the bushes with a basket or bucket of eggs, which he would peddle to the boys. The boys don't really need them, but they make nice snacks and are perfectly safe when hardboiled so I guess the Arabs did quite a business. While we were still in the orange country, we were also able to buy a lot of delicious and juicy oranges.

I must close as I have many household duties to perform. Must air my blankets and get situated. Sure wish I could spot a bath somewhere as it's been quite a while since I've had one. I don't notice the smell, though, so guess I'm O.K. for society yet, as my nose is pretty sensitive. I'm sitting in the front seat of an ambulance writing this as it's the only place that I can get "inside" out of the wind. I have no idea when this letter will ever get on its way, but will leave sometime, I guess. I'm enclosing pictures that I can't carry around anymore as Uncle Hoiman [the Germans/Hitler] wouldn't understand them if he looked at them and it would bore me to tears to try to explain them to him....

... P.S. I wrote your dad a letter about a week or ten days ago. I received two from him in that last big batch of mail. His answer to my frantic letter written just before we left the States, relieved me very very much. I want him to know how much I appreciated it. I enjoy his letters very much. I think he's a swell guy, Jean. I hope I can be as good a dad to our kids as he has been to his family.

16 February 1943; North Africa

... We have moved out of the "villa" where we lived in luxury for about three weeks and are now in entirely different type of country—we aren't kidding any more.

---

* Something was very wrong, indeed. The 133rd Infantry Regiment was obviously lost. When Leslie's jeep left the convoy to investigate, he came upon a cross-road sign with an arrow pointing in the direction they were going: 'Tunis, 10 km' it said. If they had continued towards Tunis, it would have been a disaster. They would have driven directly into enemy hands and either suffered heavy casualties and/or been captured by the Germans. It was later learned that the 3rd Battalion of the 133rd Infantry had been declared missing and presumed lost and search parties were scouring the roads looking for them for miles around.

... I sure wish I could have gotten some shots of the drama that unfolded in the skies over us yesterday, but the movement was too widespread and the principals too tiny to get a good shot. There was a thrilling climax with two silken balls of white appearing in the air immediately preceding the appearance of a descending mass of flame. I don't know if I should write about such things, but they are very interesting and exciting.

... I sure am getting tired of being away from you. You are wasting the best years of your life on a paper romance ... but, we have a job to do over here, and none of us would leave until the job is finished, if we have any say in the matter.

Well, guess I'd better close so this won't weigh too much. The wind blows a lot out here and it sure gets cold in the evenings. The temperature changes between noon and midnight are usually extreme.

24 February 1943; somewhere in North Africa

[hand written; in Rohia area]

... There has certainly been a great many things happen since I last wrote you—but there is very little that I can say anything about. I am now with the 1st Bn.—having moved over to help Lt. Rudoy out as Lupton went to the hospital before we started east and so is missing the party. We have made arrangements for him to return to us, but he hasn't shown up yet so presume I'll stay with this outfit until he does.

Haven't seen the Major for several days, but have telephone communication with him.... Sure hope Leslie shows up soon as he is carrying a two man load (with many of our well trained assistants, of course ...)

26 February 1943; North Africa

... Your letter written on Feb. 5 arrived here this morning. That's the best service that we've received over here, and considering our general situation way out in the eastern grounds, it sure was welcome. I think that every letter I receive from you is the best I've ever read, and then along comes the next one, better yet.

The country has a strange beauty about it, although it's rather barren. It's very much like western Texas and eastern New Mexico, around El Paso.

... There are so many things about you that make a man want to sit beside you forever, even if he can't hold your hand.

* * *

After their first major skirmish in North Africa with German troops, many American soldiers suffered from "combat fatigue," now referred to as Post Traumatic Stress Disorder or PTSD. Although American troops had trained in Northern Ireland for ten months prior to engaging with the enemy in North Africa, they were very young, inexperienced, and ill-equipped for actual live combat.

My dad employed an unusual treatment method to deal with these psychological casualties of war. His own father, Major Arthur L. Ludwick, Sr., M.D., had been a psychiatrist during World War I and treated shell-shocked aviators, our nation's first daring pilots. He pioneered the use of a new and somewhat controversial treatment approach referred to as "psycho-drama," where the traumatized aviators wrote, staged, and performed in short plays about their frightening and dangerous flight experiences. I can't help but think that my father's family stories related to this "talk/group therapy" technique, laid the foundation for his own compassionate and effective rehabilitation of young, terrified soldiers on the frontlines of World War II.

Interviews: "The Magic of Oatmeal"

PL: Tell me about your unusual treatment of soldiers with "combat fatigue," what we now refer to as PTSD?

Dad: Well, we experienced our first heavy casualties at Faid/Kasserine Pass area in Tunisia, North Africa. And, as I've mentioned before, at that time I was a battalion surgeon in the 133rd Infantry Regiment. There, we deployed into a defensive position, because that's where the enemy was—up on high ground with entrenched artillery and some ground troops to defend their position. When we attacked a few days later, it was really rough going because the Germans were so well trained and well situated. This was the first major contact we had with the enemy, and it was a disaster.*

We had many medical casualties, and also the condition known as "combat fatigue"—which they gave different names to in earlier wars—when the men would get the shakes and couldn't take it anymore. Well, they became a real medical problem. In World War I, it was called "shell-shock," and in previous wars, it was said that they were "yellow" or cowards. In World War II, it was called combat fatigue and is now referred to as Post Traumatic Stress Disorder, or PTSD. A lot of them were just evacuated.†

The rumor was that when General George Patton was inspecting an army field hospital in North Africa, he came upon a whole ward of these guys who had been diagnosed with combat fatigue. I think he actually slapped one of them.

He didn't like the fact that they had been evacuated as medical casualties, because that becomes contagious. These guys that don't want to fight or are afraid to fight, they'd say, "Well, if you get the shakes, they'll take you out and put you in a hospital,

---

* "The 34th Division, in its rush to Europe in January 1942, had missed large-scale maneuvers in Louisiana and the Carolinas that benefitted many other U.S. units." *Army at Dawn,* 34.

† "Psychiatric reactions were responsible for 20 percent of all battlefield evacuations, and could even run as high as 34 percent." Albert E. Cowdrey, *Fighting for Life: American Military Medicine in World War II.* New York, N.Y.: The Free Press (Macmillan, Inc., 1998), 137–140 [Hereafter cited as *Fighting for Life*].

you'll get fed three hot meals a day, and the nurses will take care of you." Patton didn't like that, and frankly, neither did we.*

My commanding officer was Colonel Ray Fountain, a former federal bankruptcy referee in Des Moines who now commanded the 133rd Infantry and was an officer in the Iowa National Guard. He didn't want to have a high casualty rate on his record—it wouldn't look good, and if a good portion of these were actually psychiatric casualties, these guys who got the shakes in battle and would have to be evacuated, well, he wanted to avoid that. And so he said, "Doc, see what you can do with these guys."

So, I took four to six of them at a time back to my regimental aid station, which was about three-quarters of a mile behind the frontline down in a wadi (a dry stream bed) where I had a camouflaged tent/aid station.

I got some pup tents and put the men there, around the aid station, and I kept them for two or three days—sometimes four days—and I fed them hot homemade oatmeal every morning, with raisins, if I could get them, and canned milk, and then I'd talk to them. And I'd say, "You know, I'm just scared to death I'm going to be killed. Fear is not uncommon or a bad thing—it's the normal reaction in battle and to this terrible danger we face every day. But we've all got to do it. And we can't give up, and say 'I just can't make it,' because I know you can do it—you're an American soldier."

I'd talk to them from a psychiatric standpoint and in a gentle voice, and after about three or four days of being on oatmeal and talking about what they were feeling, a modified form of group therapy, I guess, they often went back to their unit—and were not counted as an evacuated casualty.

Well, my commander, Colonel Fountain, really liked that and thought I was some kind of miracle worker, and what I was doing was the right way to treat it. These young guys just needed to know that it was normal to be scared to death in combat and they could get through it.†

Anyway, after heavy fighting, we finally repulsed the enemy and their counter attacks and caused them to withdraw. They were ordered back because we were attacking them, and we took it that we had pushed them out. They were just sitting up on the perimeters to protect their troops behind them. If they had hit us with a lot of strength, they would've pushed us back with a lot of casualties. Instead, we kept on pushing forward. Maybe it was a combination of the two—neither of us knowing exactly what the true situation really was.

As it turned out, this was our first big test and we learned a lot about how to fight a war. We had accomplished our mission, even though they had the advantage of

---

* "On August 3, 1943, Patton paid a visit to the 15th Evacuation Hospital near Nicosia. When he asked a private what was wrong with him, the private replied miserably, 'I guess I can't take it.' At this response, the general lost his own self-control and berated the man, slapped his face with his gloves, seized him, and threw him out of the tent." *Breakthrough Bn,* 138–139.

† My father ate a bowl of homemade hot oatmeal with raisins almost every day of his life and regularly touted its health benefits to anyone who would listen. He insisted that hot oatmeal "stuck-to-your-ribs" and would "get-you-through" ... to lunch, and beyond. Little did I know of its power to comfort and transform young, frightened soldiers during combat and, dare I suggest, help win a war?

higher ground. This battle at Fondouk was over a month after we had arrived in North Africa.*

PL: What were your duties as a Battalion/Regimental Surgeon?

Dad: In the 133rd Regiment, I was the senior Medical Officer in the Battalion Medical Section and in command of and responsible for all decisions and plans concerning the Aid Station. I could delegate some of my duties to my Medical Assistant (MAC Officer), who was often a dentist or another licensed physician, depending on the needs and circumstances at the time. Dr. Morris J. Leslie, "Les," was my MAC Officer in the 133rd. We also had an NCO (non-commissioned officer) who was trained in a variety of administrative duties as well as adequate emergency treatment. I supervised the enlisted personnel and their procurement of supplies and made all assignments of duties in the Aid Station. My Assistant usually treated the slightly wounded and, if necessary, prepared them for evacuation, assisted by a Corporal.

Enlisted trained Medics received the casualties, treated the slightly wounded, sterilized instruments, gave hypodermic medications and set up IVs, treated shock, and were responsible for setting up and moving the Aid Station's equipment. We fully examined all the wounded and gave the necessary emergency treatment, either to enable them to return to duty, or to prepare them for further evacuation. Basic first line treatment was usually limited to controlling and stopping bleeding, splinting fractures, treating superficial wounds with sterile dressings, administration of tetanus toxoid and of morphine, and treatment of shock.†

I saw quite a bit of fighting, because I thought it was my duty to be up there on the front and make sure that the medical enlisted men were doing their job evacuating

---

* There's some discrepancy of dates and locations in my dad's interviews and letters regarding his treatment for "combat fatigue." He was with the 133rd Regiment until ~ March 1, 1943, then was transferred to the 168th as its Regimental Surgeon. The two battles at Fondouk occurred in *late* March/early April, when he would have been with the 168th and under the command of Col. Fred Butler. In one interview, Dad stated that his 133rd Regiment's first encounter with the enemy was *south* of Fondouk, in the Faid/Kasserine Pass area, in a somewhat minor skirmish off to one side. This was most likely at Hajeb el Aioun. His "Magic of Oatmeal Story" and the fact that at the time, his commanding officer was Col. Ray Fountain, coincides with dates of the Hajeb skirmish, *not* Fondouk. Although my father may have mixed up the actual dates/locations of this account during our interviews, the essential content of the story remains true.

† "During WW2, Medical Detachments were "attached" to each Infantry Regiment. Their mission was to help conserve the strength of the Regiment by taking the necessary preventive and sanitary measures, and provide the full spectrum of medical care (dental, surgical) to personnel within its parent unit." Officers and Enlisted Men [EM] were adequately trained in medical and other skills. EM were not only trained for different duties such as: Dental—Medical—Sanitary and Surgical Technicians, but also as Record Clerks, Litter Bearers, Podiatrists, and Light Truck Drivers. Detachments were responsible for first echelon medical service in combat situations, including emergency medical treatment in the field, removal of battle casualties, and establishment of Aid Stations for the reception, triage, temporary care, and treatment of casualties."
https://www.med-dept.com/articles/the-ww2-medical-detachment-infantry-regiment/

the wounded, and to otherwise see to the men's health and injuries. I was in 14 major engagements with the enemy that lasted up to a week or two at a time. I saw a lot of "boom-boom."*

There were a lot of casualties and a lot of wounded, and some pretty gruesome sights. The worst, I think, were the mine fields, where the infantry regiment had to jump off a truck in the dark at night, go across a field, and accidentally step on a mine, blowing off a foot or other body parts. I could have stayed back, a half-mile behind the front where the aid stations were usually situated; but I didn't, because I wanted to be sure that everything was going okay.

I was responsible for all decisions and plans concerning the Aid Station and the treatment and evacuation of the wounded. I also saw to the general hygiene and psychological, emotional, and physical well-being of the soldiers under my command, as well as the sanitation of all camp sites, procurement of supplies, and access to a clean, safe water supply.†

PL: What was the procedure for treating and evacuating the wounded out in the field?

Dad: The first field hospitals were five to ten miles behind the frontlines. They were in big circus tents and we evacuated our seriously wounded to them. We had a medical battalion behind us, and that consisted of collecting companies. We picked up the wounded on litters, carried them back a half-mile or so and turned them over to the collecting company. They then either pushed them on bicycle wheels or put them in ambulances and took them back to the clearing station, which was the first hospital. There, they could be given a blood transfusion and plasma, and undergo any emergency surgeries—things like that. Then these wounded would be sent further back to the general hospital, maybe 30 or 40 miles behind the frontlines. This system ensured that the forward medical stations were cleared as rapidly as possible so as to be ready for

---

* Ludwick applied for the Combat Medical Badge (CMB) and was approved for his service with the 1st Battalion 133rd Infantry Regiment—in combat Feb 15, 1943–Feb 28, 1943, in vicinity of Sbiba, near Sbeitla, Tunisia, in Defense of Sbiba Gap. At the time, medical personnel could only apply for and receive one CMB. Subsequently, those rules were changed and Lud could have applied for at least four more. The Combat Medical Badge is an award of the U.S. Army, which was first created in January 1945 (retroactive to 1941). Any member of the Army Medical Department, at the rank of Colonel or below, who is assigned or attached to a ground combat arms unit of brigade or smaller size which provides medical support during any period in which the unit was engaged in ground combat, is eligible for the CMB. According to the award criterion, the individual must be performing medical duties while simultaneously being engaged by the enemy. *Wikipedia.* https://en.wikipedia.org/wiki/Combat_Medical_Badge

† "… In order to perform this job, the regimental surgeon must have in his control all the litter bearers normally assigned to the collecting company, plus whatever additional litter bearers he can obtain. He must make a thorough study of the tactical situation and an accurate estimate of what will be needed and then act accordingly; and he must do this not after the casualties occur, but many hours before." *Med Research Ctr:* https://www.med-dept.com -/articles/the-ww2-medical-detachment-infantry-regiment/

new arrivals. Our Battalion Aid Station was the place where casualties were received and treated, and where they could await further evacuation.

Italy was another story.*

Letters: March 3–19, 1943

3 March 1943; North Africa

> ["The 168th was possibly in the little deserted town of Sbiba, where the regiment set up its headquarters for over three weeks during the lull in battle caused by a stretch of rain and mud which made activity on either side virtually impossible"—*Brickbats* 152].

... Well, the surprise that I mentioned in my last letter written on 26 Feb. has come to pass, even sooner than expected. I have a new address. I've been transferred to the Med. Det. 168th Inf. as Regimental Surgeon and commanding officer of the medical detachment, in other words, the same job that Gittler holds back in the old outfit. I'm not sure that the job is permanent yet, so maybe you'd better be pretty conservative on the announcements, etc.

There is certainly a mountain of work to be done here in the time allotted. I've never been so busy in my life. I wish I could requisition some thirty-hour days. I sure do need them now. There are a thousand and one details to do and my new commanding officer, the Colonel [Fred Butler] of the regiment, is right on my fanny all the time to have me produce the results ... and he'll sure get them if it's humanly possible. The trouble is, though, that there are a few things beyond my control that will influence the outcome. Anyway, you can tell the folks that I had fun trying. You know me.

I'm still pretty much in a daze as to why I was selected for this job. I thought that there were many more favored officers (medical) in the higher unit that Col. Fourt would assign the job to, but here I am. I thought I'd made everyone sore at me at the higher unit because I've raised so much hell at one time or another about many different subjects, but guess they've slipped-up there or something and need a course in "memory." If I'm able to make good on this job, it'll mean some Major leaves for me sometime "soon," whenever that is. I don't believe you'd better say anything about it though, until it comes to pass as I'm sort of superstitious about such things. Someone is liable to get mad and kick me clear out into the next country if I talk about it. I don't know who will treat his broken leg if he does.

---

* In the 34th Division's "Lessons Learned" report [hereafter cited as *Lessons Learned*], First Lt. Roy L. Bates, MAC, 133rd Infantry, noted that: "It is a definite morale factor to infantry troops to know as they go into combat that if they are wounded, they will not have to lay out on the field of battle for a long period of time. The average infantryman has a fear of this which is so strong within him, that the minute he is wounded, he thinks only of yelling 'medics' or 'litter squad.'" https://archive.org/stream/LessonsLearnedInCombatBy34thInfantryDivision-nsia/LessonsLearnedInCombatBy34thInfantryDivision_djvu.txt.

3. North Africa 89

7 March 1943; North Africa

… This 168th Regiment is a very good outfit I'm in. I inherited a fine bunch of sergeants and men. I'll have quite a family when we all get together. I was very much flattered just before I left the old outfit [the 133rd] when several of the men stepped up to me quietly and asked if they could come over to this outfit with me. Don't say anything about this or I'll be getting a swelled head.

12 March 1943; North Africa [most likely Sbiba]

… My aid station is now under a roof, the first time it has been so situated for a long time. We are located in a small Arab town and the aid station is in the building formerly occupied by something like a "justice of the peace" court. In several of the rooms there are shelves containing many printed forms, most printed in Arabic, or a combination of Arabic and French. Very interesting.

There are also quite a few old Roman ruins around here. These consist mainly in portions of stone buildings that are still standing and have defied the effects of time. The buildings are constructed of fairly smooth cut yellow stone, the blocks being about 3 ft. long, 2 ft. wide, and 2 ft. high. The stones are put together "dry"—that is, I can't see any mortar or cement holding them together, but each block has been carefully fitted to its mate. In some of the ruins, the archways still stand and occasionally, one can see a carved stone pillar. I'm not just sure from when these ruins date, but believe that they were built after Rome overcame Carthage (the ancient city of Carthage is a few miles from the modern city of Tunis), which I recall as being several hundred years before Christ. You might look up a little Roman history for me and give me the dope on this as I'm much interested and can't find any reference books out here in the bush.

My aid station is working up quite a practice amongst the Arabs. This morning we put a young Arab to sleep under general anesthesia and drained an infected wound in his arm near his shoulder. Sometimes the Arabs are very careless where they walk and how they expose themselves. You'd think they'd learn, but they are frequently in trouble. I certainly feel sorry for them. I've seen them living in caves, under haystacks, in low stone and adobe shacks with no windows, straw roofs, no chimney. You can't stand up inside, the smoke from the fire just "disperses" out through the roof, etc. Our patient this morning had fleas all over the course cotton "gown" that he wore. What a life. It seems to me that many of the poorest in our country have a higher standard of living, compared to the African Arab, at least around these parts. I wonder if any of them have ever experienced any real joy. I imagine that it's all pretty fundamental and primitive, but I don't really know.

One Arab custom that drives me almost nuts is their frequent handshaking. This morning, one of our dentists pulled a tooth for an Arab, his name was Sahed ben Marhi (Sahed, the son of Marhi). After the extraction the Arab insisted on shaking hands with everyone in sight and murmured his gratitude

March 1943, Sbiba, Tunisia: "Capt. Schiffrin, one of our dentists, pulling an Arab's tooth in front of our aid station at Sbiba, Tunisia, during a quiet time." Many Medical Assistants were dentists.

each time. Their hands are always greasy and no one knows what they had it in last. And yet, if you try to avoid the handshake, they stand there with a happy and uncomprehending grin on their face and keep offering their hand. Ye Gods, what a country. In our little village there are stationed some French native troops. They wear a sky blue (or a little darker) suit of wool, looks like flannel. Can't remember the coat very well, but the trousers are "pantaloons-ish" and over these they wear a large woolen cape or cloak of the same material. On the head is a red fez, and altogether their costume is very colorful. Boots, too, as I remember.

Yesterday, some Arab parked a camel (dromedary) right across the street from our place. The camel is certainly a remarkable animal. They seem very intelligent and are so deliberate and unhurried in their movements that it's amusing. If you bang his rear he will slowly swing his neck and head around and then bring it to a stop and blink his eyes a couple of times while he solemnly surveys you, then he swings his neck and head back to the forward position to think it over. They certainly have a weird cry. I thought someone was beating the H out of some poor fellow the first time I heard the cry of a camel. Sounds like someone in great pain.

I think I've told you before about the fine-looking Arab horses they have over here. All the horses look well, better than the people, but it's only the fairly well-to-do who can own a horse. The common Arab rides his burro, of which there are large numbers. Some of them are quite small, but their size seems to have no influence on the size of their load or rider. Frequently one sees a burro, not over 3 ft. tall, carrying a 160 lb. man on his back. You can tell it's a heavy load as the animal walks stiff legged at that time. Of course, the larger animals carry their loads easily. The burro corresponds to the "Ford" in America. Being over here and seeing some of these things makes one understand the Bible a little better, I believe. I always thought that Jesus' entry into Jerusalem on an "ass" was the sign of abject humility, but I believe now that it was the sign that He was just a "common man." I think it is comparable to FDR or some other personage driving into a city in a Ford. Many other characteristics of the country customs and people around here, remind one of the pictures one used to see in Sunday School. Herds of sheep and goats are frequently seen cropping the sparse vegetation close to the dusty highway, and they are always attended by an Arab in his "draperies," frequently accompanied by a dog.

The Arab language is a guttural, yet somewhat liquid sounding tongue. They yell at each other quite a bit, because, of course, they've never heard of such crazy ideas as to "modulate" one's voice. They roll their "r's" a lot. When several are standing in a group talking, it makes quite a sound.

I thought about you for an hour last night before I went to sleep. I wish you wouldn't have such a pretty memory in my mind, maybe I'd get more rest and relaxation.

16 March 1943; North Africa; V-Mail

... Was much interested in your comment about Jack possibly coming this way. I really hope he gets to stay in the States, but if he does come over here, I certainly want to know as many of the details as you can send, as it's quite possible that I could look him up. Send me his mail address, and I can use that as a starter. If I can locate his A.P.O. I can locate him. He'll probably think his brother-in-law is bats when I see him as I'll most likely have to restrain myself a little from throwing my arms around him. Gosh, it sure has been a long time since I've seen you, Darling, and there is naturally some "transfer" of affections to anything or anyone associated with you. Let me know if he is over here. I sure would like to see him.

Things are pretty quiet around here now, although the medical officer always has plenty to do. In a theater of operations, I think the M.O. sometimes takes on some of the duties performed by home and mother for the boys back in the States. My new outfit is shaping up very well. In fact, G. [Major Gittler] would be green with envy if he could see our setup.

19 March 1943; North Africa

... This Africa is quite a place. I'd never have believed that it could rain so much if I hadn't just experienced it. I've moved my quarters on up ahead from the little Arab village, but am keeping some of my equipment back in the town under a dry roof. The mud is sure deep out in the sticks. I'm sleeping under 5 blankets every night, and Africa is a "tropical" country (oh boy).

Every time a tank goes by, or I hear of one being around, I run to see if it could be Jack. I certainly would like to run into that boy. I'd sure talk to him about his good-looking sister.

Our diet is very nourishing, but very monotonous. I'm now living in a tent with 3 of my men up in a muddy little cactus patch about 2 acres in area several miles from here. We were able to get hold of a gasoline camp stove, so we (or rather the boys) do our own cooking. Last night one of them found a can of whole grain golden bantam corn somewhere (I wish I knew) and we had that plus our hash. I've never tasted anything so good. The first I've had in 6 or 8 months. Once in awhile, we get a can of pears or plums or something and zip, it's gone. I've heard something about fresh tomatoes back in the U.S.A., but I don't believe such tall stories anymore. We finally managed to get in touch with a Veterinary officer to come and inspect a cow that the natives want to sell for slaughter. We have plenty of meat, but it's all canned of course, and we'd walk a long way for a good fresh steak. Hope he gets here soon.

Must close as I have much to do. I'm going to put some sails and a rudder on my jeep if the weather doesn't change pretty soon.

Ordeal at Fondouk Pass, North Africa: March 26–April 12, 1943

The 34th Infantry Division was tested in two battles for the key mountain pass at Fondouk in central Tunisia between March 25 and April 9, 1943. Col. Richard F. Wilkinson reported in *The Breakthrough Battalion*, "Fondouk Pass was a stronghold area for the German forces in early April 1943. It was vital to the Germans that the pass be held because if the Allies breached it, they would cut the supply line to German forces who were in the south battling the advance of the British 8th Army under General Montgomery" (23).

In his book, *An Army at Dawn*, Rick Atkinson notes that the first battle at Fondouk had been a somewhat half-hearted attempt in which the 34th Division made a lot of noise and captured nothing, at a cost of 527 casualties. There was poor coordination with the British IX Corps and French troops, a last-minute change of plans in the attack plan, and miscommunications.*

The second battle of Fondouk Pass had also been a costly failure. Not only had the Allies failed to catch the retreating enemy and end the fighting in Tunisia,

---

* *Army at Dawn*, 468–473.

but they had also paid a heavy price in men and equipment. The 34th Division had lost almost two thousand men, counting dead, wounded, and missing in action. It had also suffered a severe loss in self-esteem and in its reputation among the British officers. There was, however, a brighter side to the outcome of the battles at Fondouk Pass ... they can, in retrospect, be seen as a turning point in the war. The Americans had, in a few bloody days, learned a great deal about how to fight a war.*

The Narrative History of the 109th Medical Battalion's North African Campaign, 8 November 1942–15 May 1943, gives this status report from March 30–April 10, 1943:

> The aid station area was strafed by a German plane, hitting their station tent and destroying one ambulance. Fortunately, all men were in their foxholes at this time due to enemy bombings just ahead of the area. Miraculously, no casualties were suffered. This action was done in clear violation of the rules of land warfare (from)the Geneva Convention. The station tent was clearly marked with a red cross on a white 5 × 4 white background, and also a large red cross panel 12 × 18 feet was laid out in clear view. This action continued for another day—there was considerable enemy air activity.
>
> - April 3–5: Things rather quiet. April 6, preparing for heavy action; April 7, moved to new site; April 8, moved station four miles forward to speed up evacuation. Action and casualties very heavy.
> - April 9: Afternoon brought the much sought breakthrough and gave us the opportunity of clearing the field of the dead and wounded. April 10, moved our station forward near Fondouk Pass, mopping up and collecting of prisoners is being carried on.
> - April 10: second phase of the attack on Fondouk; after Fondouk battles, kind of in a vacuum—Germans had retreated Northward, hotly pursued by the British 8th Army. No longer at the front of the fighting; "Our surgeons had worked hours without rest, and litter bearers, ambulance drivers, and attendants went without sleep and toiled day after day without complaint." Our total casualties handled during the Fondouk action was 583 men.†

After the Fondouk fiasco, the Americans motored north, one hundred thousand strong, as the Allies maneuvered to attack the Tunisian bridgehead. Although the desert spring was bursting with flame-colored poppies, budded hawthorn, apple blossoms, and golden wheat fields at their peak, none of this mattered to the exhausted and bedraggled American troops. All they could see was the topography that lent itself to exposure from enemy fire, ambush sites, and groves of cacti that might hide a German 88. Embedded journalist Ernie Pyle, who was with them at the time, wrote: "They were dead weary.... They were young men, but the grime and whiskers and exhaustion made them look middle-aged."‡

---

* *Meeting the Fox,* 304–306.
† Patrick Skelly, Senior Historian and Archivist for the 34th Infantry Division Association from 2003 thru 2017, 34th Infantry Division Association: *"Division History."* Edited transcription. http://www.34ida.org/history/109_med.html.
‡ *Army at Dawn,* 480.

Letters: April 3–12, 1943

3 April 1943; North Africa, V-Mail

… It is now just about dusk and we are sitting around waiting for chow. An overcoat feels good, though. The weather has dried up considerably and now we have a few sand or dust storms. My bedroll has about a quart of sand in it all the time now. But it's clean sand so I'm getting used to it.

I wish I could tell you what is happening here right at this moment. Every time I sit down to write to you, or nearly every time, we get some excitement. I always knew you were an exciting woman, but *such* remote control!!!

Right now, we are receiving small bouquets of poppies from some people on the next ranch, or rather the people right across the road are receiving them and we could hear the postman knock. Ho hum, it's strange, and yet rather nice how quickly one can get used to one's environment. I slept through a whole celebration several nights ago, so it'll be all right for you to snap your chewing gum in bed if you want to.

… It's getting too dark to see, so must close. Be sure to let me know about Jack's address. I love you very much. Don't worry, I'm all O.K. with never a dull moment.

8 April 1943; North Africa

… I hope you are properly appreciative of this letter because it is written with the typewriter on a closed medical chest (locker) under a camouflage net in a cactus patch. The wind is swirling and sweeping over the landscape and carries a cloud of dust with it. If you get out your canteen cup to take a drink you have to move fast or the water will be a little gritty. Here I was complaining about the rainy weather some letters back. I guess I'm never satisfied. In addition to the dust and wind (which are really minor matters), this letter is being "penned" to the accompaniment of a symphony of sound. That is, if you're on our side it's a symphony because there are many "bundles for Berlin" being dispatched around here right now, of varying caliber. In other words, your fond husband is not very far from some very exciting and interesting goings on, but for this time our outfit can watch a little instead of doing.

One thing that I can promise you that will happen when I get home is the big smile that will constantly be on my face. I have to grin now to even think of it. After knocking around overseas for the length of time I've been here (17 mo.), such minor inconveniences as a leaky faucet, house on fire, train wreck, or squalling babies will merely bring convulsive snickers from yours truly. I wouldn't say that I'd gone silly or maybe "balmy," but it's very good training for persnickety and sensitive young Americans (husbands included) to be separated from good old America and those they love for awhile. You are going to be appreciated with NEON CAPITALS when I get home, babe, and I'll never let you forget it.

12 April 1943; North Africa

Well, I'd certainly like to see the headlines in the American newspapers of yesterday morning and this morning. I'll bet they're just turning handsprings about the super "colossal" over here in our neighborhood. Of course, it WAS a good show, but I wouldn't rate it more than three stars. Some of the scenes were a little stiff, but on the whole, it was a very credible performance, if we do say so ourselves. The important thing, I believe, is that we sure are learning fast and there is absolutely no teacher like the real thing. One day in battle is worth two weeks of maneuvers.

I wish I could find the words to describe the change that has come over this part of the country in the last couple of days. Two days ago, this valley and pass were reverberating to the syncopated rhythm of explosive reports associated with organized efforts of two groups of men to inoculate each other with an epidemic of acute lead poisoning. Right where I am sitting now would have been rated class "Z" (double minus on a plus four scale) as a health resort, two days ago, but now everything is peaceful and quiet. I know that you must think that some of my letters sound a little crazy, but it's against censorship rules to mention "enemy action, casualties, desertions, killed/missing in action, etc." until the news has been published in an American newspaper, so that's the reason I can't explain any further.

Uncle Hoiman suddenly decided he had to sit up with a sick friend elsewhere about two days ago and he "ain't benzene" since. We moved on in to a small valley and spent the day and night there. It was wonderful. The valley contained a couple of nice farmhouses, a real wheat field, an almond (I think) orchard, and a carpet of low wild desert flowers covering the uncultivated parts of the valley. The perfume from the flowers, especially at night in the moonlight, was almost unearthly—and the peaceful quiet was just like a "movie" scene. There were quite a few grouse in the valley. Wish Hefty had been here to get us a nice mess.

We moved back out of the valley yesterday and are now sitting awaiting further developments elsewhere. Once the pass was opened, a different type of troops belonging to our British cousins streamed through and kept up the negotiations with Hoiman's shirttails. After all, you know, he can move very fast when he wants to.

It's now 9:00 a.m. and my aid station is located in the inevitable patch of cactus. I have the typewriter perched on 2 metal lockers and I am sitting on a "petrol" can, under a camo net. The sky is blue and quiet, with just a few wisps of clouds in the air, the sun is already beginning to bear down so that I have on my sun glasses as I face the white paper, and have my collar turned up to keep the sun off the back of my neck, to the rear. It's odd how keyed up we all were. I had my first real good stretch this morning right after I got up for breakfast at dawn. I feel relaxed and very good.

Of course, one of the main reasons why I have such a pleased expression on my face is because yesterday I received 8 letters from you, four from Mother, and one

April 1943, North Africa: "Capt. A.L. Ludwick, M.C. Aid Station in a cactus patch, camouflaged." [Lud's caption in quotation marks.]

from Will Power [Waterloo friend, stationed in South Africa]. I'm inclosing the one from Will. Darn his picture, I feel like kicking him in the pants. I'm going to write him a letter and draw him a few pictures 'bout the facts of life ("Swami" Ludwick now on the air).—(Jean, if we ever go broke practicing medicine, we can still make a living running a column on advice to the lovelorn in some syndicated newspapers.)

... In your letter of Feb. 11th, you mentioned the medical officer and 15 EM [Enlisted Men] from Iowa that were prisoners of the Italians. That was Capt. Burdick, from Des Moines. In that same letter you suggested that I give your address to Leslie or someone like that so that if anything happened to me he could write to you about it. Of course, you understand that such an arrangement would be impossible because casualties, etc., cannot be mentioned in private correspondence until after the next of kin have been officially informed or it has been published. This is as it should be, because during battle there is much general excitement and the rumors fly thick and fast. Someone will be "positive" that someone else was "wiped out," and then the "wiped out" person will stroll in to camp in a couple of days wanting to know what all the excitement's about. That is the reason you should never believe rumors you may hear through unofficial sources. The War Dept. in Washington is very reliable and is conservative and has had much experience with this sort of thing. They check and recheck pretty carefully before they issue statements. As a medical officer, I can testify to the latter.

It's beginning to get right warm around here now, the weather, I mean. The nights are still somewhat cool and are grand for sleeping. I sleep like a log. The continuous noise and rumbling keep some of the "nervous souls" awake, but lull me to sleep like the bass drum in a dance band.

Must close and get to work. Have lots to do during this lull. How would you like to give half of Cedar Falls some shots tomorrow?....

13 April 1943; North Africa

... Our forefathers faced danger and deprivation, disappointment and loneliness with equanimity and fortitude, and in so doing purchased a freedom, both temporal and spiritual, that cannot be bought by self-indulgence. It is sort of interesting, in a somewhat morbid way, I guess, to watch "young America" be stripped of some of its "Hollywood-ish" ideas in combat on the battlefield. You know that making speeches is one of my weaknesses, but some of the "glamour" that has been dished up to us as essential during the last few years fades to superficiality when you are crouched in a foxhole with the earth vibrating to the crash of incoming artillery and shrapnel is buzzing over your head. Next lesson next time. More thrills in the next chapter.

Interviews: The Battle for Hill 609: April 27–May 1, 1943

PL: So, you're still in North Africa?

Dad: Yes—after Fondouk, we trained intensively for a couple of weeks but kept on pushing forward and were ordered to take Hill 609, a towering bastion in the desert. It was about 609 meters or almost 2,000 feet in elevation. Taking Hill 609 would clear the way for our advance to the east and eventually, Italy. Maj. Gen. Omar Nelson Bradley had taken over as commander of the II Corps on April 15 from General George Patton, who was preparing for the next phase of the war: the invasion of Sicily. Bradley's the one who decided the 34th Infantry Division could do the job and restore the confidence they had lost at Fondouk.

* * *

General Eisenhower had contributed a generous accolade for his West Point classmate, Omar Bradley, in this old yearbook entry: "True merit is like a river—the deeper it is, the less noise it makes."*

Historian Rick Atkinson notes that:

> It was Bradley who insisted on using the 34th, "Red Bull" Division to take Hill 609. To seize the hill, Bradley turned to troops whose self-esteem and reputation may have been the lowest in the US Army. Since the fiasco at Fondouk three weeks earlier, the 34th Division had spent every day in remedial training, practicing night attacks, tank-infantry tactics, etc. Now Bradley told the division commander, Charles Ryder, "Get me that hill and you'll break up the enemy's defenses clear across our front. Take it and no one will ever again doubt the toughness of your division."†

---

* *Ibid.*, 485.
† *Ibid.*, 506.

In its history of the 133rd Infantry Regiment, the 34th Infantry Division Association states: "After Kasserine Pass, the Allied objective was the capture of Bizerte and Tunis, crucial ports which the Germans used for bringing in reinforcements and supplies by way of Sicily. But Hill 609 [Kjebel Tahent], a rugged mass of rock in a mountainous region, barred Allied armies from these vital ports. This hill was also the last heavily fortified German position left in North Africa." These National Guardsmen, "Citizen Soldiers" from the Midwest, were being asked to carry out one of the most difficult assignments given to any unit in the entire war.

Veteran journalist and author Orr Kelley, in his book, *Meeting the Fox,* describes what the 34th Infantry was facing: "The Germans had turned this whole jumble of hills into an intricately connected defensive complex. Machine gun nests, carved out of the rock with explosives and jackhammers, covered each line of approach. Mines lay hidden, thick along all the roads and trails. Distant guns waited to fire airburst artillery at any troops trying to take the hills."

The directive to take Hill 609 was no small task. The toughest German combat units were now entrenched in Northern Tunisia to defend their last remaining toe-hold in North Africa. As noted in Lt. Col. Homer R. Ankrum's: *History of the Iowa National Guard:* "It was at Hill 609 that the 168th was finally provided with armored support by attachments from the 1st Armored Division recently equipped with the new, more effective Sherman tanks. The seizure of Hill 609 cracked the Axis lines and German resistance. Soon, all of the Allied Forces were advancing." pp. 2–12.

Dad (cont'd): And once again, the Germans pulled back to a 45-degree position and dug their machine guns into the rock. They always seemed to have the advantage of higher ground and defensive positions that were entrenched and fortified. But we finally pushed them back and took 609, and that was a big feather in our cap for the 34th Infantry Division. We, the 168th, had redeemed ourselves and had become a fine-tuned combat machine. Taking Hill 609 was our last big battle in North Africa and was essentially the end of the North African campaign.*

The Germans finally surrendered—and we had captured about 40,000 prisoners. The 168th was now beginning to regain its reputation that had been sullied by losing over a thousand men, about a quarter of the regiment, without being able to put up much of a fight … captured by the Germans at Kasserine Pass. However, we went on to fight with distinction at Hill 609 and throughout Italy's bitter battles.

* * *

---

* "Men of the 34th Division had more than the enemy to contend with at Hill 609. To avert malaria, orders were issued to administer dosages of Atabrine to American troops. The Atabrine 'backfired' in more ways than one because the prescribed dosages caused acute diarrhea. It was incredible how the 34th Division men, weakened by days of fighting and uncontrollable bowels, could summon up the energy to bring the battle to a successful conclusion." *History of IA Nat'l Guard.*

3. North Africa

After the siege of Hill 609, one soldier described the battle scene: "The summit of 609 resembled hell's half-acre, a fire-scoured wasteland covered with bodies, spent brass, bloody bandages, and, oddly, family photos, as if those about to die had pulled them from their wallets for a last farewell.... 'Those who went through it, wrote Ernie Pyle, 'would seriously doubt that war could be any worse than those two weeks of mountain fighting.'"*

Sgt. Milo L. Green, in his World War II frontlines "Brickbats" newsletter column, summed up the grueling routine of combat:

> ...the tiring, ceaseless grind of maneuvers ... the nerve-wracking strain of marching and driving miles in trying blackouts and of living day and night in fox-holes and dug-outs under the ceaseless tension of fire, on a diet of "C" rations ... the terror of Stuka dive bombers shrieking down on you, or the demoralizing suspense of listening to the whine of enemy artillery shells coming closer and closer—tramping through mined fields and cactus patches under enemy observation and artillery fire, carrying stretchers and blankets with which to pick up your dead buddies who have been closer than a brother ... for weeks and weeks, just to have a slight rest, then have to get up and do it all over again [141].

PL: How did you earn the Purple Heart? [near Eddekhila, Tunisia]

Dad: Doctors in combat do not carry arms. They wear a Red Cross armband instead. My driver was a sergeant from Texas, and he carried a Tommy gun underneath the seat of our jeep, even though we weren't supposed to do that, according to the Geneva Convention. The enemy is not supposed to fire at any Red Cross personnel, but they did—and my driver took very good care of me, I'll tell you that. Of course, it was in his best interest to do so. His name was Sergeant Hubert "Hub" Mott. He was a good driver and got us out of a lot of sticky situations. He was my right-hand man, one of the boys I brought over with me from the 133rd and one of the few boys who never showed any reluctance to go into and then out of some "jams" we found ourselves in during combat.

Our troops were making an approach march along one side of a shallow valley. In an approach march, the soldiers walk about twenty feet apart in single file, going toward the enemy to get into position. They're not bunched together so that if an artillery shell lands, fewer are wounded or killed. It takes a long time for an approach march to get the men there, but then, they get there, you see. And in fact, they won't get shot at very often because they aren't concentrated enough to shoot at. So I was there, with my driver and jeep, which had no top on it—and I had a stretcher across the hood and one across the back seat—that's how we got the wounded out. I was up front with the men, because I could never stand to stay back in the protected aid station the way a doctor should, I guess. Doctors are considered too valuable to be killed—but I was where I thought I needed to be.

Well, I came upon this guy who had gotten hit and was lying there with a bad wound to his armpit in his right axilla. He was bleeding badly. We had parked the

---

Army at Dawn, 509.

jeep on a small arroyo, and I went out to work on him. As I started to cut away his shirt and bandage him, some artillery shells began landing around me. The Germans were shooting French 75 cannons across the valley from about six/seven miles away. Of course, they couldn't see seven miles away, even with binoculars. I was moving all the time, and they couldn't see the Red Cross armband I wore. But they started shelling us, me and this wounded man. The shells were landing all around us—BAMM! about twenty yards over here, and twenty yards over there, and I was afraid he'd get hit and killed. There was a shallow wadi, a dry stream bed about three to four feet deep and about ten feet across, where my driver was crouching. I tried to get this wounded man into that small wadi to protect him from shrapnel and landing shells. But I couldn't move him, so I just threw myself on top of him. A few more shells were coming in, and one of them landed close enough that a little piece of shrapnel about the size of a kitchen match head, got into my back—I could feel it, but luckily it was a superficial wound and didn't penetrate very deeply. It wasn't much. But I was scared to death.

I gave the wounded soldier a shot of morphine, splinted his arm, and put a dressing on his armpit. My driver [Mott] was crouching back in the wadi, and he came up and we both got the soldier onto a stretcher on the hood of my jeep. I put an EMT tag on him (emergency medical tag) and I sent him back by my jeep to the nearest *real* ambulance. I think I went with them a little ways back. He was then taken back to the collecting station, which is usually two to three miles behind the front, and from there he was evacuated to a clearing station, about five miles behind the front, and then to our surgical hospital (which wasn't in place yet—it was too early.) I don't know what ever happened to him.

This was to be the 168th's final battle in North Africa—the Germans had finally surrendered and we had captured about 40,000 enemy prisoners.

When I got back to my aid station that evening, I mentioned to my assistant battalion surgeon that I had gotten a tiny little piece of shrapnel in my back. "Well," he said, "let me look at it." He looked at it and picked out the embedded metal with his fingernail or something, and said, "Well, I'm going to make an EMT on you." I said, "Oh, nawww—don't bother with that." But he insisted on it. So, I got the Purple Heart for that very minor wound.* After so much heavy fighting, we were allowed to sit out the Sicilian Campaign and prepare for the Italian Campaign.

* * *

---

* The 168th Infantry had been fighting in the Eddekhila, Tunisia area, May 5–9 1943. [See July 6, 1943, letter.] The Purple Heart Medal was first established in 1782 by George Washington, then the commander-in-chief of the Continental Army. It is awarded on behalf of the President of the United States for "Being wounded or killed in any action against an enemy of the United States or as a result of an act of any such enemy or opposing armed forces." In 1931, the medal was redesigned and revived, with the first medal awarded to General Douglas MacArthur. It is the oldest military award still given to U.S. military members. *Wikipedia.* https://en.wikipedia.org/wiki/Purple_Heart.

3. North Africa

My father was embarrassed to have been awarded the Purple Heart, having only received a superficial shrapnel wound which was easily flicked out of his back by his medical assistant. "Kind of like squeezing a pimple," he said. He felt this minor injury was nothing compared to what many soldiers in his unit had suffered. But in listening to his account of the incident, the intense danger he was in while treating one of his wounded men, and the courage he mustered to protect this fallen soldier, I believe his Purple Heart commendation was well earned. That day, amidst fields of red and yellow poppies covering the surrounding valleys and hills, my father, his driver, and a critically wounded soldier survived.

Dad (cont'd): We then went up to Bizerte in May of 1943, and were billeted in an orange grove. We set up our regiment there and staged the 1st Division, which was an elite fighting division of the regular army, and provided them a place to stay overnight before they boarded a ship at Tunis. We didn't know where the 1st Division was going. It turned out four or five days later, they were landing in Sicily. And that was a bloody battle. Patton fought in that—a lot of armor and artillery.

By then, we were all more experienced in combat. Americans learn fast. At Camp Claiborne, back in the U.S., and for the ten months we were in Northern Ireland, we weren't too well-trained, like the British said, because we weren't regimented the way the European troops were. The Germans, the English, and the French are all regimented—they'd do exactly what they were told. But Americans have more imagination and innovation, and in addition, learn quickly—at least I did. Yeah, I'd say we all did.

They didn't teach us many critical things in Louisiana like, for instance, looking for mines and being ever vigilant. That little spot ahead of you that's been disturbed in some way: take note and be wary. The enemy has tried to camouflage it, smooth it over so you won't see it. But if you inadvertently step on that trigger or land mine, it will blow your foot off, at the very least.

I can remember a terrible thing that happened in North Africa. It was dry farming there. It does rain a little bit there, about like it does in Wenatchee and eastern Washington, maybe ten inches a year, and the landscape was very similar, although they raised oranges, wheat, and olives. The French farmers had nice little one-story houses, kind of California bungalow-type in style. That's what we lived in. These houses were all empty—the people had fled, and the Germans would mine the driveways and the trails up the hills where the mess sergeants, who would have to deliver the evening meals, would regularly travel. They were scared to death they'd step on a mine. They'd drive as far as they could and then they'd have to take the Marmite cans, the big five-gallon thermos cans with hot food in them, to the troops and feed them in the mess line. They, the cooks, were kind of protected—they were back about three to four miles. We were all very aware of those things. When you'd walk into a house that we wanted to check, we were always looking at our feet, because you didn't want to step on anything that had been recently moved or changed in any way.

This was such a tragic story. The day after the Germans surrendered and all the fighting in North Africa was over, two American soldiers in a jeep with the top down, came upon this nice house. We weren't allowed to keep the tops up on our jeeps because of air raids. The Germans would fly along a road and shoot up all the American vehicles, and you had to be able to dive for the ditch. You couldn't have a lid on, even in the rain.

Don't know if these two soldiers wanted to just look or loot anything, or take a souvenir or something. Anyways, they ran up the driveway and they hit a mine—and it exploded, blew their jeep apart and killed both of them. Dumb guys—"careless" was my first reaction, although I felt badly for these two young soldiers. They thought the war was over and they were safe. I received a letter from the father of one of the boys about two weeks later. My aid station was still in a tent, a pyramidal tent that normally sleeps eight men. My desk and typewriter and everything were there, and he wanted to know how his son had died. I never could answer him. I couldn't tell that father that his son died because he did a very foolish and careless thing the day after the Germans surrendered and the war was over. He drove in this driveway of an unoccupied house and hit a mine, and it killed him. I just thought maybe it was better for him not to know, so I never answered that letter and I couldn't lie. I felt terrible about it, but I was also angry that those soldiers would be that careless—that's the way I looked at it—because I had learned the hard way. I had walked up many driveways and many trails looking at my feet all the time. This kid was most likely a replacement, probably hadn't been in combat over a couple of weeks. It was an adventure to him. He and his buddy were probably driving along and were naïve and curious, and here was this nice house.

1943 North Africa: "Deep study..." Note the Remington typewriter in this photograph. Ludwick carried a typewriter with him at all times during World War II, even on the frontlines. [Lud's caption in quotation marks.]

"Let's go in and look at it," they must have said *to one another*—such unnecessary tragedy and deaths. And one of the hardest lessons of war, was that for an invading army to win, young men must die.*

About six weeks later, in early August, we were sent back by motor convoy into Algiers again and wound up in Sidi Bel Abbes, a little town of about 5,000 and the national headquarters of the French Foreign Legion. They had more prostitutes there than you can imagine. We were there about a month or so, bivouacked in an evergreen woods-of-sorts, fairly close to the ocean. There were orange groves and evergreen trees twenty feet high.

We started training and building up our stamina because my commander, Colonel Frederic Butler, didn't think we were in top shape. Every day, we had two hours of calisthenics and we started running about two miles every day in our leather Army boots. We tried to make a mile in about twenty to twenty-five minutes. Forced marches were taken with full field pack, done in double-time, but I didn't carry a lot. I trained with the men voluntarily—the medical officers usually didn't, but in this case, almost everyone participated.

We also trained replacements, repaired uniforms, and conducted combined arms training with tanks and artillery in live-fire exercises, which we had never done in Northern Ireland. By fall, we felt well-prepared and ready for the Italian Campaign.†

Eventually, at the end of September, we went up to a little town west of Oran and stayed a week or so; then we boarded a ship and were delivered to a small town just south of Salerno, Italy.

Letters: May 10–September 13, 1943

10 May 1943; North Africa

> … Well, I suppose the headlines are pretty big these days back home. It's all over for us here now, although the British are still having a little party in another part of the "corner." It certainly is nice out tonight. The moon is bright and all the stars are out and all the men are encamped in a tented city. I can hear some of my men

---

* "The now tough, combat-hardened men of the 34th were justifiably proud of what they had accomplished, but they were acutely aware of the price they had paid: total battle casualties of the 34th in the Tunisian Campaign numbered 4,049, of which half were missing in action." *The Red Bull in World War II*, 34th 1941–1945, Infantry Division Resources, four-page pamphlet (October 23, 1944) [hereafter cited as *Red Bull*]. http://34thinfantry.com/history/history-133rd.html.

† From Lud's typed two page "Confidential" training schedule of the 168th's Medical Detachment, this eight-day intensive training included: Thomas Hip Splint, circulatory system, treatment of wounds, respiratory system, sterilization & aseptic technique, hemorrhage, dressings, nervous system, principles of splinting and padding, shock, unconsciousness, use of human plasma, fractures, water, movement under enemy observation & fire, military discipline, concealment, use of cover, waste disposal, dental first aid, anti-aircraft security, and improvised litters.

singing in one of our tents just down the line. We've been resting and cleaning up for the past three days, and believe me, it certainly is wonderful to know that the job is done. It was a "tough go" all right, tough in many ways that the press is not permitted to talk about; but I'll tell you about it when I get home. Don't go getting any ideas about an early return, just yet, anyway. We'll have to see what happens. We learned a lot in the last campaign and it is only now that we can be classified as seasoned fighters. The nice thing about it, though, is to know that the Germans CAN be beaten, and by American forces entirely by themselves. The next few months should be very interesting.

The "war of nerves" is just now beginning on our friends "Adolf" and "Musso." I'll bet they're all in a dither over where we'll strike next. All the Axis propaganda about Europe being a "fortress" doesn't impress us as much as it once did. There are plenty of draughty places in their house.

Must close and get to bed. Another big day tomorrow. I have plenty of responsibilities that make all my days full. I have the health and sanitation of a large number of men to look after as well as all the records of casualties, etc., during the "fracas."

11 May 1943; North Africa; V-Mail

... We are still encamped right where we stopped fighting. We are in a broad flat valley ringed with low rolling mountains. The mountains are a dark green color, covered with a low evergreen scrub. The flat valley land is either in pasturage or in wheat and both are beginning to turn brown under the ever-increasing heat of the sun. The valley is dotted with white stucco farmhouses with red tile roofs and a few trees surrounding them. I was walking with the Colonel [Butler] last night and he mentioned that the country reminded him very much of California.

I have been writing "V-Mail" letters almost exclusively for the past two or three weeks for a very definite reason, and that is that we have had it strongly emphasized over here that there is only a limited amount of space going to the states for air mail and that space is practically all reserved for official war department correspondence. They tell us that letters that we send airmail will probably be shipped by boat to the states, while "V-Mail" is now being photographed and flown across. Your airmail letters, however, seem to come just about as fast as "V-Mail" and take on an average of three to four weeks to get here.

16 May 1943; North Africa

[Near Bizerte. From a letter to his uncle, George L. Gallaher, published in the Harlingen, Texas, newspaper, "Facts From the Firing Line"]

Dear Uncle George,

As you no doubt know from the radio and headlines, all the fighting is over here in North Africa. Altogether, this outfit was on the front line most

June 1943, near Sidi Nsir, Tunisia: L-R: Ludwick, "Capt. Moses Cohen, my 2nd Bn. Surgeon. This picture was taken during the last big push around Sidi Nsir … at the 2nd Bn. Aid Station which I had dropped in on about something. The fancy duds (tie, etc.) were prescribed for all officers by 'Fancy Pants' Patton, during combat. That thing over my right shoulder is my neck cloth, which hangs from the back of my helmet to keep the 'tropical' sun off the back of my neck. Here, Capt. Cohen is 'at home,' hence no tie, etc."

of the time for the last two months. There were many exciting times and many experiences that one would like to forget, but which will remain forever in one's memory.

Right now the regiment is encamped in some low hills bearing olive groves, which are situated about three or four miles from the Mediterranean. We are close to one of the final objectives of the Tunisian campaign, but further than that, I cannot say, concerning our location.

We are all enjoying the rest a great deal, following combat. Right now, we are experiencing some let-down in tension as would naturally follow the sudden cessation of hostilities. I certainly do wish I knew what is in store for us in the future. It is too much and too illogical to hope that some of us would get back to the States, but one can't help thinking about such things. I've been over here a long, long time, well over a year, as you may remember.

Instead of being a little dissatisfied over being kept away from home so long, I should be very thankful for recent deliverances. Several times the hand of the Lord was on my shoulder to steer me along a safe path. As I look back on it now, I realize that only His mercy kept me from being where some of my less fortunate friends are now. I guess I'll not complain, although one's instinctive desires are not easily stifled.

There is a good deal of conjecture here as to where the next blow against the Axis will fall. We are just as much in the dark about it as anyone and the rumors fly from one group to another. The delusion about the invincibility of the German no longer exists, although it's true that he is well versed in his profession. The "War of Nerves" is just now beginning for Mr. Hitler and colleagues. I imagine that they'll be pretty frantic trying to plug the many drafty places that exist in their house.

Before closing I can't help but tell you how much I enjoy the letters that you write. Making war on a foreign soil is a curious mixture of almost hysterical excitement and mind-dulling boredom when there is inactivity. In either case, a letter to bring back the memories of normalcy and to remind one of the existence of more ordered ways, is much appreciated.

16 May 1943; North Africa

… Darling, I certainly have needed you during the past ten days. I guess it's the reaction after the tension we all were unconsciously under during combat, but I certainly have been depressed. None of us know what is in store for us or the outfit in the future, but it's pretty certain that there'll be no return to the States, at least for the vast majority of us who are capable and able bodied.

On the other hand, Jean, I know that I have a great deal to be thankful for (pardon the poor grammar). The only reason that I am writing to you today is because the Lord was there to protect me from harm. In a recent letter I hinted at a nick in the back that I got while I was working on a fellow, but it was just a scratch and I kept right on working. I'm in the best of physical health, I sleep like a log, my appetite is voracious, as usual, and when I think back on what has happened to some of my very good friends, I realize that there must have been a Higher Being directing things to let me escape, when they did not. I still don't worry about the future, either. Although I certainly don't deserve it, I believe completely that I'll come through whatever additional action we are in. Maybe it's yours, and Mother's, and Joan's, and your Dad's prayers that have done it all. I don't mean to imply that I've suddenly got "religion," or anything, but I can certainly assure you that there is no atheism in a foxhole, or when one is out on a bare hillside with large packages lighting up all around you.

21 May 1943; North Africa

… For supper this evening, we had "hash," canned spinach, canned green beans, boiled cabbage, lemonade, muscatel wine, bread, butter, peanut butter, rice and raisin pudding and one Atebrine tablet (malaria). That sure is better than special combat rations which consists of three types of canned food: vegetable stew, meat & vegetable hash, and meat and beans. They are all delicious when eaten singly, but when you have them for 72 meals a month, as we did once, it gets a little monotonous. I suppose the American soldier excels at "griping," however, as our German prisoners thought the combat ration was quite a delicacy and thought that we ate too much of it at once. One prisoner only ate half a portion, was surprised that he would get another can for the next meal—he thought it had to last all day.

Well, it's one and a half hours later, 8:00 p.m. to be exact. The sun is still shining over the hill to the west of our bivouac. We recently turned our clocks up one hour for "daylight" saving. I can hear the muffled cheers and yelling of two baseball games going on across our little valley from the medics' grove. The medics have their tents (Hdq. Section) pitched in a shady olive grove on the side of a gently sloping hill. Just below us is a field of barley that's about ready to be cut.

In looking back over this letter (which has taken about 2½ hours to write) I'm somewhat surprised at the undercurrent of "griping" and even cynicism that pervades this whole thing. Don't let it worry you, darling. I'm all O.K. and I'm sticking this thing out as long as it's my duty to do so. Mr. Hitler is the boy that needs the sympathy.

Please send:

Cadet bag
Insignia (maybe that's premature, but hope not)
100 Gillette Blue blades
½ doz. tooth brushes & one or two containers
Pr. swimming trunks
Box Candy bars

23 May 1943; North Africa

… Last night some of the boys had a bull session, mostly about U.S. War and Foreign policy and there were some pretty hot arguments. Some of the boys who are a little short sighted, get pretty much excited and feel pretty sorry for themselves. For instance, they blurt out: "How is it that there are 'eight million' soldiers sitting on their fannies back in the states while we're over here fighting the battles?" Of course, I always listen to them about such things and then try to show the boys the true situation, that they're not fighting the battles all by themselves, that it won't be long now before the big push, which will involve many of the soldiers that they are envious of. Well, anyway, I tried to cheer some of them up and referred one of my truck drivers to the article mentioned above (*Saturday Evening Post*, Feb 6, 1943—"As It Was in the Beginning," by Stephen Vincent Benét), but he couldn't wade through it. Ho Hum.

One point that I want to make in passing, Jean, is to explain to you that while some of my letters may have sounded a little depressed during the last few weeks, I never reflect that attitude before the men. I sort of have to have someone to sound off to once in awhile, and you being my wife, you're elected.

29 May 1943; Tunis, Tunisia

… Another sunshine-y day; that's about all we have around here now. It's peculiar about the sun, though, although the sky is always blue and clean, it is only during a few hours in the afternoon that the sun really beats down. In the mornings everything is balmy and fresh, just like a "May morning" back home. There is frequently a cool breeze that comes over the low hills between us and the sea, four miles away.

Day before yesterday, I visited the city of Tunis and the ancient ruins of Carthage, or rather, the Roman ruins that still exist at the site of Carthage. There weren't many ruins left and those present were not as well preserved as those I saw at Sbeitla or Haidra. You see, we can now mention some of our experiences over here, but censorship still prevents us naming any names or numbers of units, except division or higher.

Tunis is a nice place, all right, but I didn't like it as well as Oran, and the boys who have been in Algiers say that there is no comparison between the two cities. I've heard some say that Algiers is one of the most beautiful cities in the world. Of course, Tunis was jammed with soldiers, many of them British. The British are all wearing cotton shorts now and look right natty. I think we'll be getting cottons pretty soon, although I've not been real uncomfortable yet in the wool. There certainly was very little merchandise to be had in Tunis. Most of the stores were closed.

3 June 1943; North Africa

… One of the boys just finished tearing down, repairing and cleaning and re-oiling this typewriter. I see already that the paper holder bar is a little greasy and it has come off on this paper, but I don't want to waste the paper, so forgive the untidiness of this letter.

I must stop temporarily and go to chow. It's 5:30 p.m. and I don't want to miss the eats. We certainly had a whang of a meal several days ago. We had fresh frozen beef, cooked as roast beef. It wasn't this native stuff, either, but the very best grained American beef and it sure was delicious. It was quite a shock to all of us. First time in months since we've had American beef (uncanned). We also had canned whole grain corn and spinach, etc.

Yesterday we also had another "treat." Several days ago, I spotted some boats that had ice cream freezers on board. Yesterday afternoon, after some of my boys here in the headquarters, had "policed" (polite word for mooching) up a case or so of condensed milk, sugar, egg powder, vanilla, etc., we drove to the boat and I climbed on board to negotiate with the skipper for the use of his ice and freezer. The deal was readily consummated, so the boys froze five gallons of ice cream and it sure was good. We have about 20 mouths to feed in Hdq. Section of the medics, plus 10 specially invited guests, so the ice cream didn't last long. I sent the Col. a plateful. He was much mystified as to where I got it and was mildly curious about the whole deal today at mess. (Just a little advertising).

I've been swimming pretty regularly this week. The water is getting slowly warmer. The wind is sometimes very soft, when the day is hot, but often there is quite a breeze which is quite refreshing when one is dry, but a little chilly out of the water when wet. The mornings are always delightful.

I suppose you've thrown up your hands in despair about my sudden turn into a gold digger, but I have several more "items" you can send me, if you like: Wrist watch strap (for Westclox "Judge"), Pipe (light weight bowl, medium length straight stem, yellow bit), and a small French-English dictionary.

We've been lighting our office tent at night with kerosene lanterns, as usual, but a couple of days ago we found out that a neighboring company (anti-tank co.) had picked up an enemy electric generator powered by a gasoline motor. There was some "extra" juice available, so we ran a power line (I have electricians, carpenters, ball players, salesmen, ministers, farmers, typewriter mechanics, motor mechanics, and various other trades represented in my outfit), to our area and now we have electric lights and can play our radio. We get the BBC and some Italian stations mostly. The wops are sure getting jittery. They put out the most fantastic & ridiculous stuff you've ever heard.

One of these days we're going to have a big fried chicken supper. Do you remember my mentioning in a letter written from Oran last January about the soldier "Mott" who was my orderly and who gave us such good laundry service and incidentally always got a bottle of wine from the landlady? You remember that I said he was an older fellow (37) and that he ran a very successful cleaning and tailoring business in Texas? He was the best orderly I've ever had but was also very good in the aid station because he'd once worked for a doctor. Well, I asked Gittler for him (and five others) when I transferred and they followed me to the 168th [from the 133rd] about two weeks later. I've made most of them non-commissioned officers, made Mott a "T-5" which is a "Corporal Technician." Well, Mott is quite a promoter and he has been continually policing a flock of chickens of frying size. He now has about 20 in a wire pen near our aid station. He trades cigarettes for them to the Arabs who bring him a few every night and also a small bag of wheat, occasionally. A cat got about four of them on two nights, but we fixed the cat, so now the rest are getting bigger and bigger. I don't mean to bore you all the time with such mundane subjects as food and eating, but I'll let you know how the fried chicken comes out.

Must close and go to the band concert. The 133rd band [The Rhythm Majors] is coming over to our place tonight to give us a concert. Guess I'll see some old friends, especially the boys that played for the medic's parties we used to throw on Swamp Island.

12 June 1943; North Africa

… The news reports sound pretty good these days. The Isle of Pantelleria fell yesterday and today's radio said that the largest number of bombers ever to go over Germany was used yesterday. Things look better and better. We are all pretty sure that Germany will fold suddenly once she starts, just like she did here in Tunisia, but of course she won't be a push-over. There'll be some pretty vicious fighting on the continent, all right, but the outlook certainly is more cheerful than it was 18 months ago. I remember when we first "lit" on Swamp Island (Northern Ireland). There we were, a pitiful fraction of the larger unit (the newspapers flubbed the story, of course), all by ourselves, convinced that we'd be plastered by a German air raid at any minute. We scurried around through the blackout and I remember that I packed my "ditty" bag with an extra pair of socks, a suit of underwear, my toilet articles and a couple of cans of food and hung it right over my bunk so that I could grab my gas mask, helmet and the bag as I tore out of the farm house we were living in … you know … just before the bomb struck.

I have to laugh at the antics we went through. We thought we were right in the middle of the war, and that the old 133rd was going to have to take Berlin by herself. That's the way you feel when there's just a "handful" of men in a foreign country. After the other troops began to arrive later, we felt better. Ho hum, "Them were the days!" Now I sleep through the heaviest artillery barrages and we usually tell one of the light sleepers to wake us up if they start dropping them within 100 yds of us.

18 June 1943; North Africa

… Your brother, Jack, is leaning on the table that we have under our canvas fly where we write most of our letters, as I write this one. I made a trip to the big city with Ed Rohlf yesterday and when I returned, I found Jack here waiting for me. He sure does look good. He's very tan, has been stationed close to the seashore and said he'd been acting as lifeguard at the beach and so was able to get an "overnight" pass to come down here. He is stationed about 70 or 80 miles from us and said that he had just received my letter last week, the one I wrote on April 30. He stayed overnight with us last night and has made some of the rounds through the outfit here this morning. I sure was glad to see him and to know that he is all O.K. He is now connected with a "school" as a gunnery instructor, seems to think the job is fairly permanent, although we both know that things may change suddenly in the army. Jack says that his recommendation (appointment) for sergeant is now in the red tape mill at his headquarters (most units wait varying lengths of time for a bunch of promotions to accumulate before issuing an order announcing the whole lot), so I guess it won't be long before he is wearing stripes. He's filled the vacancy (where have I heard that one before?) ever since he left the States.

Since writing the last paragraph, we've eaten lunch and Jack says he must get over to the next town early this afternoon in order to make connections with a truck back to his outfit. I'm going to run him over. I'd sure like to have him stick around for a few weeks as neither of us know if we'll be able to see each other again over here, but here's hoping. Must close so we can make the "train."

"Jean—finally found Lud. Had nice visit. Will write when I get back to outfit." Jack [from Jack Hoyer, Jean's younger brother, handwritten at bottom of Lud's letter]

23 June 1943; North Africa

... We are still within three miles of the sea, but the beach here is not as good as the one at Gertie's Place (the "Villa"). Also, there's more wind here; in fact, there is always a cool breeze in the afternoon, which has discouraged us from swimming a little. The ground is very dry and crumbly, so we had a load of damp sand put in our tent as a floor. It worked fine as long as it was damp, but now it's completely dried out and has drifted all over the tent from the steady breeze.

We are on a special job in this new location. There is absolutely nothing for you to worry about because it's of a peaceful nature, for us. However, it gives me a chance to function in a much larger scope than I ever have formerly and in this way, will teach me a great deal from an administrative standpoint. For a few weeks I'll have a bigger job than Col. Fourt has now.

About fifteen minutes ago there were six Arabs in the aid station tent. Two of them were patients: one man had a lymphangitis ("blood poison") in his left hand, and a little boy about 5 yrs old had a bald spot about the size of half a dollar due to fungus (ring worm) of the scalp. The first Sgt. of the anti-tank company (whose area is right next to ours) is of Syrian extraction. Both of his parents were born in Syria, which is the modern center of Arab culture (something I never knew until recently). He speaks Syrian fluently, and of course is understood perfectly by the Arabs. Arabic and Syrian are practically identical languages. I've made some arrangements for him to teach me some Arabic, so look for a change pretty soon—you know my luck about arranging for language lessons. I'm afraid that the smattering of languages I'm picking up is going to be hard on you. You'll probably go wild trying to interpret the jargon that I'll mutter in my sleep.

25 June 1943; North Africa

... Major Beaumont (Council Bluffs) who was the 168th Regt'l Surg I replaced when he was captured by the Germans, wrote that he was now chief cook in the officers' mess in the prison camp and also that he had just "finagled" or was trying to get a French horn to play in the band. It sounds a little less depressing than it might be, but I sure do feel sorry for them, especially the "docs," who must follow along where the line officers lead them. When I stop to think of the tremendous task Tom [Corcoran] and others will have, after the war, of re-adjusting themselves to normal civilization, I'm certainly not envious. It will be difficult enough for us that have just been living in tents away from civilization, but of course will not be in any way insurmountable. I imagine that the most difficult thing for a prisoner to do would be to keep the galling hate and cynicism from creeping into his heart at his enforced "twiddling."*

The officers of the regiment are having their first party tonight. It's to be held in a little casino-like restaurant that is built out over the beach at a little seaside village a few miles from us. It's to be a stag affair, strange to say (the Col. thought it up), and we are going to eat more water buffalo steaks and have some extras on the side. In fact, we may even have some fresh vegetable salad, which will be quite a treat. The truck gardens over here are frequently fertilized with human manure, etc., and so many of the natives have intestinal parasites, amoebas, etc. Thus, we have never permitted any fresh vegetables to be served in the men's (or officers') mess. That, of course, is one of my jobs, to keep a check on the kitchens to see that they behave themselves along this line. However, for this party, I relented enough to allow them to use fresh tomatoes, cucumbers, and cantaloupes providing they scalded the outside by dipping them for 20 seconds in boiling water. That will kill the eggs of the helminths and the amoebic cysts that might be present but, of course, is impractical for use regularly in a large mess.

27 June 1943; North Africa

... The temperature was 101 today at 1:00 p.m. in our aid station tent. The old sun is really beginning to bear down, so much so that we had to go swimming in the Gulf this afternoon. The beach isn't quite as nice as the one at Gertie's Place, but the swim was much enjoyed by all. The Mediterranean is a "swell" place to swim.

I have another Arab rug for you. This one is a colored Kairouan rug. These rugs are made in Kairouan, which, next to Mecca, is the most holy city in Islam. It is said that seven trips to Kairouan equals one trip to Mecca. The rug is hand-made and has maroon, orange, and brown colors in it. It is not as soft and luxurious as a Persian rug because the "knot count" per square inch is much lower than that of a Persian rug; but, nevertheless, it is a good example of a Kairouan rug and has a much nicer pattern than the average I've seen. The average of such rugs have rather garish designs, although this one is certainly colorful.

I also have a couple of other souvenirs to send home. Several of the ambulance drivers assigned to us have taken some captured empty brass German shell cases and have cut out some letter openers from them. They've pounded the brass into shape and then soldered some Tunisian coins on the handle. I have two of them, and am waiting to get one more if I can before sending them.

Our practice amongst the Arabs has never been heavier. We are all always

---

* Capt. Thomas E. Corcoran, commander of Company C of the 109th Medical Battalion attached to the 168th Regiment combat team, was tragically captured by the German army in retreat from the Kasserine/Faid Pass debacle and became a POW.

very friendly to them and frequently slip them a few cigarettes or something. There is one little boy about 5 years old that comes every day to get his eye treated. He has an ulcer on his cornea. He brings three of his friends with him and it's quite a sight to see them. They are all about the same size and shade of light brown skin. They all wear the little red caps that the Arabs wear here, and they all stand or sit on the floor of our tent, very close to the patient while he is being treated and they all look very solemn and take everything in.

1943 North Africa: "This is the boy I wanted to bring home in my barracks bag. He is irrigating a small field by directing the flow of water using a hoe on the ditches."

1 July 1943; North Africa

... It is now 8:45 a.m. and is still in the cool of the morning. My sick call is over and I'm stealing a little of the "company time" to write to you. Since we've taken over our temporary "big job," I've sent Capt. Horowitz out to one of the battalions to replace an absent officer there, so have to run headquarters sick call myself, which I enjoy doing. As soon as I finish this letter I'll have to start making my rounds to see that the war is being "fit" properly. Right now, my job is that which would normally be filled by a Lt. Col., but it's not a regular or permanent job, so I have no further delusions of grandeur.

5 July 1943; North Africa

... Capt. Leslie dropped in on us this morning, just to pay a friendly visit. He is the regimental surgeon now at the 133rd, since Gittler has gone to division. He invited me to an officers' dance the 133rd is giving next Saturday evening. He said he'd arrange for a nurse for me. I hope I can make the party, but don't know yet. Don't worry about the nurse, dearest. She'll probably give up in disgust after I've talked about you for a half an hour, just as a starter.

... We had an officers' stag party at the beach casino night before last. It was held in honor of Lt. Col. Moore (the major you asked about once) who has been ordered back to Washington. He left the outfit this morning. What a lucky guy, but he looked pretty sad as he was pulling out.

6 July 1943; North Africa
[Purple Heart details]

... Whooee! This day is sure a scorcher. At 10:30 this morning it was 104 degrees F in the aid station tent, and now at 1:00 p.m. it is 110. Our tent is made of green duck (dark) and it really absorbs the heat. You can hardly hold your hand against the canvas. We have all the sides rolled up, of course, and we get a little gust of breeze every minute or so, but the breeze feels just like someone had opened the doors of a blast furnace. I'm sitting at the desk with just my underwear and shoes on. I wish we could get a little extra canvas with which to make a tent fly, but none is available.

Last night some of the boys wrangled a few gallons of beer from the brewery. Beer is hard to get here because the one brewery has been sewed up by the British and they only allow us so much per capita per week. By taking down a little present of a can of corned beef to the yardmaster of the brewery, the boys were able to circumvent (ahem) the obstructions and brought home a couple of water cans full. Someone else got about 50 lbs. of ice and last night I had a pint of ice-cold beer. Boy, oh boy, did it taste good. I could stand some right now.

... I don't see how Glen knew that I had been scratched [injured]. He has always been located three or four hundred miles behind us. I wasn't going to mention anything about it, it was so little. In fact, there was much too much fuss made over the whole thing. I was working on a boy on an exposed hillside who had been badly hit by fragments of an artillery shell that had landed about 15 ft. away from him. He had compound fractures of the right arm and a severe penetrating wound of the right axilla so that the axillary vessels were damaged ... his hand was blanched. He also had a big shrapnel wound in the muscles of the front of the right thigh as well as other wounds in the back. About the time I got a splint on his arm and had given him morphine and dressed his wounds, the enemy artillery opened up again and started laying 105 mm shells practically right at us. I had to drop to the ground to continue working. I had just crawled over him to carry him out with his arm around my neck when a shell lit about 40 ft. away. I got a tiny piece of shell fragment, about the size of a bb shot, in my back, between my shoulder blade and my spine. It just barely penetrated the skin and I didn't do anything about it until evening when Capt. Horowitz grabbed it with a hemostat and pulled it out at the aid station. I could hardly feel the wound the next morning, so I never quit work. I WISH, Jean, that you wouldn't tell this to a soul. It's just between you and me. There are so many others who have done much more than that, that I just don't want to talk about it. Incidentally, after I was hit, I tried to pull him along on the ground (I could stand, but didn't want to make a better target), but his morphine had begun to work a little by then (we give them ½ grain) and the splint caught on the rocks and ground, so I saw we weren't getting anywhere. I knew I couldn't get him out under that fire, so I beat it back about 150 yards where there was about a 3 ft. deep ditch with a little trickle of water in it. There I crouched with my feet in the water, catching my breath (I did that 150 yd. in about 15 seconds) and scared as hell for about 5 minutes. At the end of this time, I flagged a peep slowly crossing the ditch (he didn't know about the shelling ahead) and together we drove up the hill to where the boy lay.*

The shelling suddenly ceased about this time, so we were able to lift the boy into the front seat of the peep and the driver took him on back to the aid station. I walked on back to the ditch and sat down. The boy had not been hit during the five minutes I was away from him. Maybe I shouldn't have run out on him, but when I saw that I couldn't get him out by myself, I figured there was nothing to be gained by my getting hit there with him again ... and maybe I could get help to get him out, which I did. I'll never forget my sensations when that shell hit. It's hard to describe. I was dazed just for a moment by the concussion. I'll tell you about it later. Now you see, you'll be worried sick the next time I'm in action ... that's the reason why you should never ask me to tell you any details about such things again. I don't know whether I'll mail this letter or not. If I do mail it, don't worry about me. You learn the knack of taking care of yourself, a little, and besides, I have great faith that God will keep me "lucky." I really believe this, Jean.

I've drunk a quart and a half of water while I've been writing this; it sure is blistering hot. We get salt tablets, however, so everyone gets along O.K. Most of my boys have gone down to the beach for a swim. I didn't want to get out in the sun, it's so hot, so stayed home and took my clothes off. I'm tan enough, anyway.

Guess I'll close and start arguing with myself about whether to send this letter or not. Danged if I know whether a husband ought to confide such things to his wife or not. I guess the heroes don't, but I'm not a hero—I was just a scared kid for a few minutes....

10 July 1943; North Africa

... The officers' party (dance) given by the 133rd is being held tonight. It looks like I'll be able to make it all O.K. It'll be nice to see all of the old gang again. I suppose the nurse that I'll have for a dancing partner will have a face that will stop a clock, but I'll look over her shoulder and think of you, and that way maybe I can pretend that you are there. Gosh, kid, I'd sure give a million to have you here....

... What have you done with the car? Do you still have it—is Sally still running or wheezing along? How is our bank account coming along, or do

---

* According to the "Victory Division News," a 5th Armored Division newsletter, referring to a jeep as a "peep" was common to armored division soldiers. In fact, this was a point of pride and distinguished them from their infantry comrades. Wikipedia notes that a "peep" or "baby jeep, quad, or bantam," was a quarter-ton/smaller jeep vs. the half-ton or three-quarter-ton Dodge Command Reconnaissance vehicle.

we have one? It's going to take me a few months to get back on my feet (self-supporting, for two) when I get home, so you'd better lay away a little kale so that we can live in more than one room—you know, TWO bedrooms so we can change from one to the other.

... You are my life, my very breath. I think of you night and day; in fact, it sometimes interferes with my efficiency in my job, but on the other hand, it keeps me at it so the brass hats shouldn't kick. Just remember that throughout all the world's history, no woman, lady, wench, girl, or babe has ever had a man that loved her more than I love you ... that's a very big statement, but you know that it's true.

12 July 1943; North Africa

... The 133rd party was a moderate success. There were a few nurses there and more French girls. It's the funniest thing about the French girls. They always bring little brother, mama, sometimes papa, and usually one or two male cousins or boyfriends. If 100 American soldiers would want to give a dinner-dance for their 100 French girls, they'd have to lay covers for about 400 people. As it is, we always run out of food and drink feeding the rest of the family. One bunch of soldiers, who got a little teed up at another party, got so mad because all the girls came heavily escorted, that they broke up some of the furniture, threw some of the food out, and stomped out of the place. I can see their point, but they certainly should have had enough good manners to stick it out when they saw they were "stung."

13 July 1943; North Africa

... This noon we had the biggest and best meal since we landed in North Africa a long time ago. We had lots of fried chicken, mashed potatoes (not the dehydrated kind), chicken gravy, fresh tomatoes, deviled eggs, fresh cucumbers, pickles, canned corn, canned peas, dumplings, iced tea, and cherry pie. I just read off this list to some of the boys to see if I'd left out anything and several said they'd never write such things home 'cuz the folks would think we were living off the fat of the land. Sometimes our rations are a little on the thin side, especially the nauseating corned beef, but now and then we have a real feed and this was the best. We had to chip in a dollar (50 francs) a piece for the chicken and some of the extras, but it was sure worth it.

... I am getting to be quite a walker again, although not necessarily by choice. I wonder how high in rank you have to get in the infantry before you can quit walking—I guess, never. This morning, while it was still cool, I walked 4.6 miles in 55 minutes, and sister, that is traveling. The first few times I did it my back felt like it had been run over by a truck, but it doesn't bother me any now—guess I'm used to it.

The other day I wrote you that the thermometer had climbed to 110; that was early in the afternoon. It finally went up to 119 in the shade, but that is the only extremely hot day that we've had. It is very pleasant here now as I write this letter at 11:00 A.M. out under the canvas fly that we use for a supply tent.

3. North Africa 117

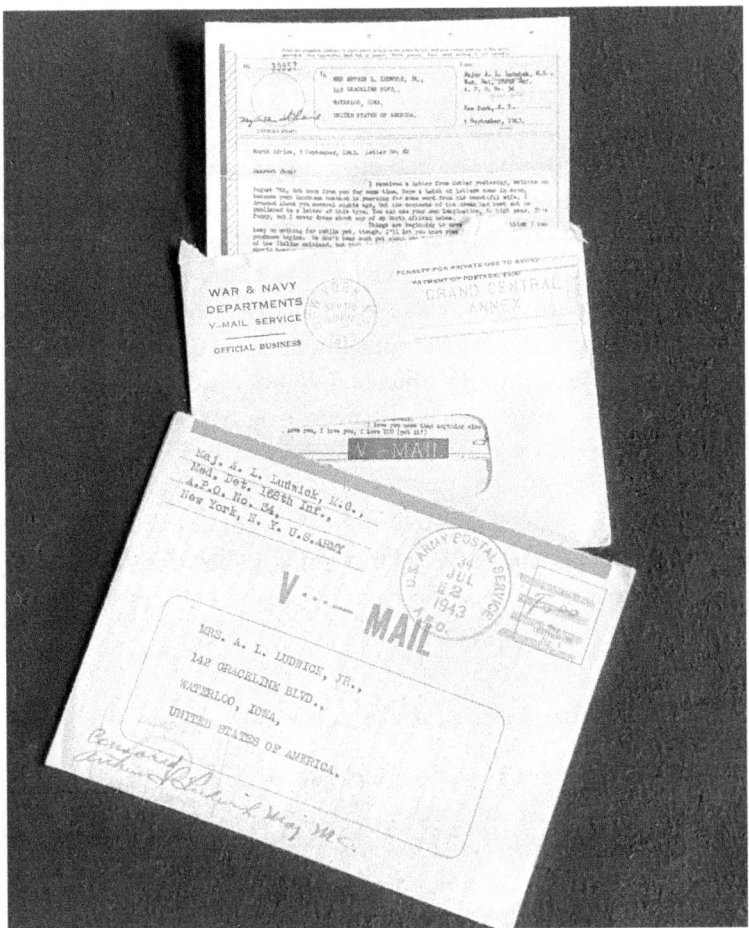

Examples of 2 types of V-Mails: some were folded to make their own envelope, others had a separate envelope with address window. V-Mails were used during the war to save space in plane cargo compartments.

19 July 1943; North Africa V-Mail*

This is going to be another scorcher of a day. It's now 1:20 P.M. and the thermometer in the aid station tent read 105 F in the shade. It'll probably go up to 116 or 118 by mid-afternoon.

I went to division today and while there dropped in on Major Gittler for a

---

 * According to the National WWII Museum [hereafter referred to as *WWII Museum*], V-mail (Victory Mail) was a special postal system put into place during the war to drastically reduce the space needed to transport mail, thus freeing up airplane space for other valuable supplies. Although the V-mail system was only used between June 1942 and November 1945, over one billion letters were processed through these means. It provided quick mail service to and from soldiers overseas. A special form was used which permitted the letter to be photographed in microfilm, then reproduced and delivered. Https://www.nationalww2museum.org/war/articles/mail-call-v-mail.

chat. I learned that several medical officers are going home on rotation service. This "service" is designed to permit deserving officers to get promotions that they can't get over here due to lack of vacancies. I thought there must be a catch to my majority—G [Gittler] says that of course officers who have been promoted in the past six months would not be considered. He is sore about the whole deal, as he thinks something ought to be done about it, especially since his application for rotation was turned down (too valuable a man). He hits the ceiling every time I talk to him about it, and I'll admit it's sort of a funny deal. I'm certainly not giving up hopes of getting home this Fall or Winter, though. I still have other irons to heat. I did not apply for the rotation because the C.O. here discouraged any such action on the part of his officers. I wonder if the powers that be at home realize how long some of the men and officers over here have been overseas? They probably think the overseas service started with the African landings last November.

In a few days, I won't be able to write to you for about a week or so, but there's nothing to worry about. We're just going to do what we've been doing plenty of since who knows when. Some of my airmail letters should be arriving during that time to fill in the gap.

2 August 1943; North Africa "V-Mail" #1

This is the first letter I've had a chance to write you since July 23. We've been pretty busy during the past week or so. We've moved again, and are about 800 miles from where I last wrote you.

... We are now located in a wonderful place, that is, for an open-air camp. We are situated in a real pine forest in one of the most fertile valleys I have seen in North Africa. The good roads skim through acres of green and well-tilled rows of grape vines that are now loaded with purple grapes, while in between the vineyards are yellow fields of recently cut wheat stubble. The farms all look prosperous; the towns are neat and progressive, for Africa. It rained a little this afternoon, just enough to settle the dust and cool things off. About 23 miles away is a very nice town of about 10,000 population. It has three French "movies" and one American. The shops display the first real selection of leather shoes that I've seen—they look like they might be American made.

On the trip I stopped to see Jack. I knew that we would pass by his camp the first day out, so I left my part of the convoy (the Col. put me in charge of one march group) that morning and drove on ahead. It took me about an hour to find Jack after I arrived at his camp because he had recently transferred over to the truck battalion which was several hundred yards down the road. Jack looks fine and likes his new job, although he said he had a lot to learn about it yet. He's in charge of about eight trucks that go out on freight runs pretty regularly. He said he was learning quite a bit about the job of a mechanic because he has to check over his trucks and frequently helps the driver in making minor repairs. We had dinner together after several hours' visit, and by that time, my part of the outfit was passing by, so I fell in line and went on. Jack had just begun to receive his mail. I read one of your letters to him that he'd received just a few days before. His camp is located about two miles from one of the nicest beaches that I've ever seen. The country is hilly and where he is, there are quite a few trees, which is a little unusual for that part of the country. It gets pretty hot and dusty there, the roads get a layer of dust on them about three inches deep off the pavement, but altogether, he has a pretty nice setup. The shade is fine and they feed well. I hope he can stay there for a long while.

My paper is running out, so I'll have to start another....

2 August 1943; North Africa V-Mail #3

This is the third section of letter No. 66 that I'm writing tonight. I must be bats about the girl. What makes me do these things, anyway? I love you, hon.

... We are working pretty hard in our new location; don't have the time off in the afternoon that we had at the other end. I'm in top physical condition—my legs are as hard as rocks. I'll walk the legs off of you when I get home. I'm sure glad that you've quit smoking, if only for a while. I wish you could sleep better at night. I know you must get enough exercise with your job, swimming, and all. Do you still ride your bicycle? By job, I meant your working at the Pres. while the tech. was on vacation. Don't you think you get along better when you're working? I never really wanted my wife to have to work for a living, but under the circumstances that we face together, I think you do better when your time is regularly occupied—only I sure don't want you to be tied down by long hours. I've begun smoking again—about a month ago. I couldn't be bothered with it in combat, but during the easy life I had at the other end and after the excitement was over, I started again—hadn't smoked over a dozen cigarettes or so since we landed in Africa.

6 August 1943; North Africa "V-Mail"

... As you know from my last letter, Jack was still in Africa on July 26 when I saw him at his camp during our recent move. I don't think he will move any time soon but, of course, one can't say for sure.

... We are very busy all day long now, just like we were back on Swamp Island. Every day is full, but we are in a nice bivouac with plenty of shade and the food is really swell for a change.

... The radio news today has been the best we've heard in a long time. The Russians have taken both Orel and Byelgorod, which were the main bastions of the two-pronged pincher movement of the summer German offensive. The reports, which you'll know by the time you get this, say that the losses in equipment on the part of the Germans, have been large. The Allies have taken Catania and it looks like the beginning of the end for the Axis in Sicily.

10 August 1943; North Africa

... About the letter of July 6 regarding my "hit." [shrapnel wound in back at Eddekhila] I expect that my outlook that day was considerably influenced by the fact that several days before my little episode on the hillside, Lt. Robinson was killed (lived 20 minutes) by a shell fragment in the back—a much larger one, of course. It was just a shot in the dark, an unlucky hit. Robbie went through the La. Maneuvers with me and he always asked me a great deal about you and used to admire your picture that I carried. I felt pretty bad about him—he was in the 133rd. I guess that's what got me a little excited, but when I stop to think of it, the women of this world (thank God for them) have been undergoing just about or as great a danger every day in the routine job of bearing the next generation....

... While in the big city, I went into the Officers' Sales store and bought a hum dinger of a trench coat. It cost $31.00 and is the neatest I think I've ever seen. It is waterproof and has a heavy removable lining of blanket, with a half lining of sateen, has a hood that buttons on the collar which you can pull up over your head. The coat is wind proof, warm, but light in weight. You'll probably think I was crazy to buy one in the heat of the summer over here, but I was afraid that I'd not get another chance. Besides, the wind is always chilly at sea whatever the season. I almost bought one several times on Swamp Island, but never did....

17 August 1943; North Africa

[location near Oran]

Dearest Jean,

We've moved again. We are now located about a half mile from the sea on a bald and dusty hill that overlooks the Mediterranean. There's no shade, but we are only about a half hour's drive from the city, jammed with American soldiers, sailors, nurses, Red Cross girls, etc.

We are up here for a certain type of work [training] which comes under the general category of the type that we did all the time we were in camp back at home. It's a rough bivouac area all right; no shade, no grass, and dust from a half inch to three inches in depth. It's impossible to keep yourself or your bed clean. Ten minutes after a bath your ankles are black again, unless you keep standing in the bucket. Oh, for the life of a soldier.

This is our first day at the new camp, and is devoted to getting the place cleaned up. There were other troops here previously and as I think I've told you, the gentle Arabs ALWAYS dig up every hole in which the old cans and garbage have been buried. What they ever find in them is beyond me, but we always have to rebury everything as soon as we move into such an area.

Beginning tomorrow, we'll have a pretty stiff schedule every day, and I wouldn't be surprised if I got wet occasionally. I went swimming last night after supper. It's surprising how cold the water is compared to the warmth up near Carthage and at Gertie's place. The latitude is about the same.

... Today was payday for the boys, and although it's only 2:45 P.M., the crap game is already going strong in the aid station tent. I imagine that the lucky ones will want to go in to town this evening for a last fling before the schedule begins. I suppose I'd better go along to see that they don't turn the town over—just my patriotic duty, of course. The town (city) is the same one we lived in last January. It now looks different in many ways. There is much more merchandise in the stores, and much of it looks American, but am not sure that it is from that source. I've seen several windows full of men's leather shoes, modern styling, etc. In Jan. I didn't see one leather shoe (men's) and only two or three women's shoes in the whole place....

18 August 1943; North Africa

[Villa location—in/near Oran?]

... Don't be surprised if you get a money order for $100.00 from McKinney, Texas, one of these days. My right hand man, Hubert Mott (Corporal), one of the boys that I brought over with me from the 133rd, and who has been one of the few boys who never showed any reluctance to go into some "jams" that we got into in combat. He's already sent about $1,500 home to his wife in Texas, but last month he lost heavily in one of his gambling games and had to borrow $100.00 from me to pay up.... He is writing his wife to pay you a money order—be sure to let me know when it comes through.

19 August 1943; North Africa

Dearest Jean:

Besides your V-Mails, I received a "V-Mail" from the wife of a former member of the detachment asking about "how come no allotment," etc. You'd be surprised at the amount of correspondence I get from the families at home. Some of them get pretty excited when they don't hear from their boys for three or four months while they (the boys) are held incommunicado awaiting shipment from the states and while they are rattling around over here from one replacement depot to another before they finally land in a permanent assignment.

One of the fellows in the outfit has a "fiancé," at least she says she is, in the states. She must be a dizzy female because she's written me twice saying she has heard rumors that her boy was missing. I wrote a nice letter to her the first time, explained that rumors get pretty wild in war time, both over here and over there, and that she shouldn't pay any attention to them, to wait for official word from the War Dept. The boy in question is all O.K., just doesn't seem as enthusiastic about the girl friend as she thinks he is.

... Everything seems to be going all O.K. here. The Col. [Col. Frederic B. Butler] is right on my tail all the time. He's a hard-boiled guy all right, but I admire him very much, especially for his inflexible integrity of purpose. He never volunteers much encouragement to me, but everyone else in the division that I talk to says that he praises my work pretty high when he talks about me. I think he was especially pleased by the way we handled the so-called "shell-shock" cases back in the campaign. We really got on the job on that deal and cut the incidence of that trouble to almost nil. The American public certainly needs to be educated as to the real nature of shell shock. Some of the boys that get the screaming jitters and beat it, leaving their buddies flat, actually get to be "heroes" back home.

As I've told you before, I've had the *sh*** scared out of me five times a day in combat, and so has everyone else, but the great majority of the boys manage to keep their head. The trouble with these "birds" that get the jitters is that they don't realize that the rest of us also get a few qualms once in awhile. They think that because the boys successfully conceal it, that they aren't bothered at all and are really enjoying some of it. In their own mind, the comparison of how they feel with what they think Johnny Jones feels, or doesn't feel, makes them feel pretty sorry for themselves. Fortunately, though, there aren't very many of those fellows and they are gradually disappearing. You have to handle the situation adroitly, though, whenever it pops up, because the disease is very "epidemic" if it gets started.

Well, anyway, the Col. [Butler] seems to think I'm doing all O.K. so I feel pretty good, although I'm going to let him see that there is another officer in the outfit that is capable of taking over my job in case I get a chance to leave. I don't want him to think I'm indispensable, which of course, I'm not.

The boys just turned on the radio here in the aid station, and there's sweet swing and hot jazz coming over the ether waves. It's 8:45 p.m. and the sun is now a red ball as it sinks into the haze of the horizon into the Mediterranean. There's a show going on down at the "amphitheater," but think I'll turn in early. Last night we had another French Vaudeville show. It was better than average and following that, we had Marlene Dietrich, Randolph Scott, and John Wayne in "Pittsburgh." It was pretty good, all right, although Marlene is losing her grip a little. Baby Snooks is now on the radio, so I'd better close and give ear to the Brat and her Pa.

21 August 1943; North Africa

... Yesterday afternoon I decided "to heck with the war" and took off with my driver, Hub Mott. We went down to the officers' beach club at Wagner's hospital, had a swim and a shower, changed clothes and then went on in to town. I bought a new pair of oxfords at the officers' store, left the old ones to be repaired and then roamed around town a little. There are always big crowds of people in town, but there's not much to do. I went up to the swanky (?) officers' club in town—costs two whole dollars to become a member, had a couple of steak sandwiches and a couple of drinks and watched the crowd go by for awhile. Saw Wagner there with escort, but didn't talk to her as she was well occupied. I also saw a nurse that I knew I'd seen before somewhere. Finally, on her way out, I talked to her—found out she worked on the Contagion Ward at Ancker [Ancker Hospital in St. Paul, Minnesota] when I interned there. She's with an evacuation hospital near here—a hospital that we may see more of in the future.

About 9:00 P.M., I left the club and went down to the Red Cross Officers'

Club where they were having their regular Friday night dance. The dance is held in a big room which was jammed full. There was a Negro orchestra and all the girls were French. The second lieutenants, many of them newly commissioned, were cutting the rug in great shape....

... As I mentioned, there isn't much to do in this burg. There are a lot of people roaming around trying to have a good time.... I'm sure lonesome for you, darling. Lately, I sometimes find myself not giving a hoot about the war, world, or life in general. I wish the army would realize what the score is in regard to long separations. Someone ought to instruct them on the psycho-physiological functioning of the male sex. I often wonder how much longer this is going to go on, although I know down deep inside that I'll stand it O.K., I guess, but not without a great deal of bleak lonesomeness. I know you feel the same way.

The boys in the detachment are working on a party that they are going to give this next week, if it can be arranged. We have $850.00 in the company fund (canteen dividends) and I don't want to carry that much cash around (it's in the bank) indefinitely. I told the boys we ought to spend it for the mutual benefit of the men, or at least part of it. The party won't be an $850.00 blowout, but at least it will give the boys a good time and whittle down some of the pile that I'm responsible for. Must close and get ready for sick call.

27 August 1943; North Africa

... This is sort of a sad day in this outfit. Yesterday, while one of the sections was out in the field with their battalion, one of the medics picked up an old "dud" shell and threw it against the trunk of a tree, under which some other medics were sitting playing cards. The boy that threw the shell was killed outright in the resultant explosion and one of the card players died on the way to the hospital. Two others, including the section sergeant, are seriously wounded; both are under oxygen tents at the Station Hospital—all this in spite of the fact that the men have been frequently warned not to touch any duds or anything that might be a booby trap. The longer I'm in the army, the more I realize that whenever one is dealing with groups of people, one has to treat them as children, at times. You have to explain and explain, repeat and repeat, so that the idea finally gets around to everyone—and then convincing them of the truth, is another matter. We are leaving for the funeral at 1 p.m. I'm waiting for the trucks to show up.

29 August 1943; North Africa

... I've thought a great deal about you and your new job the last day or so. How do you like it by now, and do you think it will be too hard on you? I suppose with the scarcity of doctors at home, that no doctor can very well turn business away from his door....

... I've wondered quite a bit recently where all my medical equipment is. I suppose they are still using my microscope, etc., in the office? Are my medical books still there? How about my diplomas and my state licenses? I can't remember whether I packed my diplomas away or not when I left for the army. If they've taken the licenses down off the wall, as I imagined they have, be sure that they are stored in a safe place. I expect the girls have already attended to everything, but I'd like to know where the stuff is.

It was very nice of the Blackhawk Medical Society [Waterloo, Iowa] to send that check; quite a surprise. We'll need a little backing when I get home because I'll have to spend some months or maybe a year in some hospital in order to get back in the swing of things. I've always thought I learned the basics of medicine pretty well, but the newer techniques will be pretty new to me at first and I'll have to give them a going over before I again inflict myself on the unsuspecting public. I'll be darned if I know where I'll go to brush up, but I'm going to try to get the army to foot the bill if at all possible ... we'll have many other things to do for ourselves, and that will take a little dough. Do you think you can support a war-wrecked husband when he comes home to pick up the threads of civilized living again? Don't worry about it, because I certainly don't.

I'm going to be up most of the night tonight: Business, so guess I'll knock off a little and take a short nap. I sure will be glad when we move out of this dust. The hair at the back of my neck gets gray with dust after driving a few minutes along one of the trails around here, and shirt collars are brown in the inside a few hours after you put them on.

The news still sounds pretty good; hope the Russians are good for a long race this time. Remember that I love only you and am counting the days until we are together again.

1 September 1943; North Africa

I have a mountain of paper work to do today; monthly reports to write out and reports on investigations made, etc. It seems that the Colonel must think I'm a good "finder outer," because I've had quite a few to make recently....

... Don't work too hard in your new job; and you'd better eat more than a sandwich for lunch. I want something to put my arm around when I get home this winter (I'm straining to make it true), as well as something to look at. That was one of the minor differences in the way of doing things between Hefty and me. If he had an office full of people at meal time, he'd work right through without eating. But not your Uncle Dudley. I always thought I did a better job if I knocked off and had a square meal at the right time in spite of the daily crises. Maybe it's better for me that way 'cuz I sometimes get a little owlish when I'm real hungry....

5 September 1943; North Africa

... Things are beginning to move over here. I think I can keep on writing for awhile, though. I'll let you know when the break in the correspondence begins.

We don't hear much about the British-Canadian landing on the toe of the Italian mainland, but that is the way the Sicilian campaign started out, so we should hear more about it in a day or two.

I'm going to another regimental headquarters officers' party tonight. A large shipment of nurses arrived fresh from the states a few days ago, so we are doing our best to help them get acquainted with Africa. I have quite a little fun at the parties, but my mind is never free from the longing to be with you....

7 September 1943; North Africa

[Villa]

... Your account of the discussion on the yacht about things people are deprived of was very interesting to me. It's funny, and yet it's not, how a person's individual experience influences his/her ideas. Those people have never experienced very much in the way of hardship. The fact that they're unable to get whole hams is, no doubt, quite a catastrophe. Fortunately, we're going to win this war so they won't have to learn some of the things they would shudder at with Nazi domination. All in all, I'm sure that one eventually experiences a deeper and richer life for having gone through some of the experiences we've gone through, but it's painful during the "going through" process.

Last night I went to another party; that's about five or six I've been to in the last two weeks. This time it was given at the General's Villa and was for the division medical officers. The Villa is the palatial seaside place of some wealthy French family that the General is using. There are terraced gardens going down the rather steep hill to the beach. On one of the terraces, under a sort of arbor of low, twisted and gnarled trees, they've built a nice dance floor. Some of the trees are over 600 years old. There were drinks, sandwiches, potato salad, pickles, and cake. All very nice and I had a fair time. Saw Wagner there, talked to her for a few minutes, but when I looked for her to dance with later in the evening, she had apparently already gone home with her boyfriend. I think I'm "partied out." I sure will be glad to get out of this place. It gets pretty boring at times.

The American radio station over here just finished Fred Allen's program and now they are playing dance music. Sounds good, makes me homesick. Short pause while the lights go out and we all watched the search lights pick up a plane about 7 or 8 miles away. Guess it was friendly as there was no tracer climbing up, and the lights went back on in a few minutes.

We changed over into wool uniforms today. It's still hot here, but orders are orders; can explain why later.

... I'm getting sleepy and hungry. Fix me up a sandwich and a glass of milk and let's go to bed. This burning the candle at both ends is getting me down. Sweet dreams....

13 September 1943; North Africa

> This is a very short one because I am so very very busy ... all the last minute work is "referred" to me. My duties as medical officer are just a sideline now. I'm lawyer, shipper, and otherwise make myself generally useful. This may be the last letter I'll be able to write for some time, but will try to get another one in.
>
> ... Our mail isn't coming through very well now, but I know it's on the way....

4

Italy

Battle Hardened,
September 21, 1943–May 5, 1944

"It's a cold day and I'm set up in the basement of a large farmhouse. The only source of light is a window that must be left open and my fingers are getting a little stiff from the cold. It's beautiful outside today. As I stood on a terrace behind the house, beside a green orange tree, I could see for miles across the valley in the sunshine. The mountains in the distance are all snowcapped—very beautiful in their quiet majesty, but hell to fight in."

—14 February 1944

Interviews: September 25–November 29, 1943

PL: When did you finally get to Italy?

Dad: About the second or third week of September 1943, we sailed from Oran in a relatively small convoy and were delivered to a little town just south of Salerno [at Foce del Sele, near Paestum], Italy. Our ship pulled in to the Gulf of Salerno and then we boarded amphibious "ducks"—those are trucks with wheels, but they also have a propeller in the back and a prow in the front. (It's built like a boat, but is also a floating true ETE)—and we were run up to the beach in those and then we went in.

The initial invasion of Italy had been made about two weeks previously, and had pushed the Germans back ten miles or so into a semi-circle. That was a bloody battle with major losses on both sides. So we, the 168th, did not actually land under fire; but the Germans were about ten miles away—we could hear their artillery fire, and they could have shelled us if they had wanted to. We didn't see any action for a while, in person.

Incidentally, when we were in North Africa and moved from Sidi Bel Abbes up the coast to that little town just west of Oran, I think that's where I got Hepatitis A, the infectious virus that is spread through contaminated drinking water—from drinking out of untreated well water. After we arrived in Italy, and our first engagement with the enemy after crossing the turbulent Volturno River, north of Salerno, I began to lose my appetite and not feel very well—had aches and pains, a low-grade fever, and jaundice. We called it "Catarrhal Jaundice" back then, not Hepatitis A. There was no bottled water then. Local water was "purified" with chemical tablets, and tea was added to kill the awful taste.

September 1943–May 1944: Map of Italy and major locations where Lud and his 168th Infantry camped and/or engaged with the enemy. Not to scale. (Invisible Ink Corporation)

We were just getting ready to tackle the enemy—engage in our first major battle in Italy. So, I kidded my friends, "Well, I guess I finally turned yellow." About two hundred men in the regiment also got jaundiced. Again, the Colonel wanted me not to evacuate them, because if we evacuated them, they'd be gone two months before they were finally rehabilitated, you see—and they'd probably be sent to another regiment. In the meantime, we had received fresh, raw recruits from the U.S. and he wanted me to save our own trained regimental men—or really, he just didn't know what to do, and I didn't either.

So, I set up a little "jaundice camp" with pup tents, like I had done with the combat fatigue soldiers, and kept them there. But we had to move at night—and it rained, and they didn't have any tops on the trucks. And here were these sick men, in about five or six trucks—and they were miserable—wet, sick, jaundiced. And I was also jaundiced—I've never been so tired in my life. I'd walk just two blocks to the officers' mess, and I'd have to sit down and rest. Finally, after a day or two of that, I said to the Colonel, "I can't do this anymore, Colonel, I've got to evacuate these men to a hospital." And he said, "Okay, whatever you say." So, I did. I evacuated a whole bunch of them—about a hundred; but, I didn't evacuate myself. I kept going, and pretty soon, after about two weeks, I felt better, and my jaundice, which was fairly mild, subsided and I got over it. Well, that impressed the Colonel, I think, my ability and determination to carry on, no matter what.

* * *

To the 34th "Red Bull" Infantry Division, Italy's terrain of frigid fast-moving rivers and wet, snowy mountains proved daunting. Their three dangerous crossings of the Volturno River were interspersed with a series of three vicious battles. One soldier's first-hand account underscores the challenges: "Swimming in a swift current with clothes on in icy cold water while holding a rifle aloft, takes mental toughness and physical stamina beyond imagination. When reaching the other side, invariably the banks and any flatland would be mined."

—Breakthrough Bn, 75

My father is mentioned several times in *Mud, Mountains, and Medicine: The World War II Diary of E.W. Paulus, M.D.*, Commanding Officer of the 109th Medical Battalion:

October 13, 1943: The Volturno River crossing ends at 2 a.m. Both the 135th and the 168th cross easily and with moderate casualties. But the bridge is not completed during the entire day and no vehicles can cross. The 135th uses a raft to float wounded back but the 168th cannot use one and has a number of casualties on the far side.... Connell and Ludwick try to evacuate the 168th Regiment casualties [158].

These valiant troops were wet, miserable, but relentless in pushing back the enemy defenders. Their ranks were critically thinned by the minefields, machine guns, mortars, multi-barreled rockets, and enemy artillery fire. They kept expecting to see a fresh unit coming forward to relieve them and give them an opportunity to dry out or change their wet clothing, but that never happened. As described in the *History of the Iowa National Guard*:

> After all regiments of the division had made their final crossing and achieved their objectives, fighting through many small Italian towns high up in the snowy mountains, they began their drive to the Rapido River and Cassino, where hundreds and hundreds of them (the Red Bull men) would become wounded or lose their lives. The Red Bull men literally bartered their arms, legs, and blood for each objective in Italy [8–10].

Letters: October 3–December 8, 1943

3 October 1943; Italy

[hepatitis camp]

Dearest Jean,

    I suppose by now you are tearing your hair out over wondering what has happened to your wandering husband—and rightly so, because I haven't written very much during the last few weeks, for several reasons. One reason was that we didn't have any carrier sea gulls around, and so forth. We are still not allowed to tell our whereabouts, which seems sort of silly as it seems that everyone at home has guessed it already. One of these days, some brass hat will tell us, "Oh yes, of course you can say where you are, didn't you know?," where upon there will be one less hat drifting around.

    … Hub Mott (I promoted him to Sgt Technician recently) told me today that he'd received a letter from his wife in Texas stating that she'd received his letter requesting her to send you a $100.00 money order to pay for a personal loan that I made to him over here. He is one of my best non-coms, but is an inveterate gambler and was caught a little short one month, though still is way ahead of the game. Let me know when you get the M.O. from her so that he'll quit stewing about it.

    … We are in a very peculiar setup here right at present. We're "right near" all the excitement, but haven't really contacted any as yet, and we thought we'd be right in the middle of things as soon as we arrived. Guess it's part of the grand strategy and no doubt we'll know the answer soon. Don't worry about me; I'll come out all right, with a little help from Providence. The Lord has been very good to me in many, many ways in my life, and when I think of what might have happened in some of the situations I've been in, I get pretty disgusted with myself for ever griping about anything.…

    P.S. Wash your hands after reading this letter and after throwing it in the wastebasket. It might have some of the virus of catarrhal jaundice on it, but probably doesn't. Pass a hot iron over the pictures.

9 October 1943; Italy

    … Last night I received your airmail letter written on Sept. 12 as well as a letter from Mother written the same date. I certainly was glad to get them as, once again, mail from home is about the only break we get from a time-consuming job.

I still can't tell you where we are, although as I've mentioned before, you have probably guessed it correctly. As usual, the weather is not just exactly the way the Chamber of Commerce advertises it. We have sunshine every day in between several showers. The soil is more of a loam than in other places we've been recently so that the ground is very muddy and travel is slow.

The natives are very friendly to us. It's surprising how many of our soldiers turn up as being able to speak their language. Many, or I should say, a few, of the people have visited the United States previously, or at least they tell us they have.

I won't be able to write as often as I'd like for some little time, probably several weeks.

… I'm glad that you received the box of "junk" O.K. It really was "junk," but thought it might be a little interesting to you. I wish that we would stay in one place long enough for me to find and buy really nice things, but we are a combat outfit and when we move through a place, the native merchants have all hidden their fine things from the shelling or bombings, etc., and sometimes it is several months before these wares begin to reappear on the markets. Another thing is the money. They won't bring out their luxury goods until the money situation is stable and, of course, they don't have a lot of luxury stuff in many cases. To really get nice things you had to get well acquainted with a native merchant and pass the time of day with him several times before he would bring out his better wares. You can't hurry these people. They just won't do "over the counter" business.

18 October 1943; Somewhere in Italy

[Pompeii, near Salerno and south of Naples]

… I'm snatching a moment to write to you to tell you that I'm all O.K. I'm standing in the muddy courtyard of a house in a small town in (censored). The typewriter is setting on the hood of my jeep and artillery shells are whistling both ways overhead.

We've been very busy the last few days. Very frequently one goes 36 hours without sleep, or only a few moments, and by the time you get yourself cleaned up occasionally, it's time to move again. It's rough going—the terrain, I mean mostly, although it's rough in other ways, too. Several nights back I climbed into an upland mountain valley, or ravine, where there were some wounded awaiting evacuation and it took about an hour to go a mile. Altogether, though, everything is working together much better than on the last continent. The soldiers are more experienced and, in many cases, are darned good, so that for the present, we are making good headway considering the terrain. Jerry certainly must be putting up his best fight, since this is the best place for him to do so, but it isn't quite good enough to stop us.

October 1943, Pompeii, Italy: Lud wearing trench coat amidst Pompeii ruins. See August 10, 1943, letter re: purchase of trench coat in North Africa a few months earlier.

Several letters back I mentioned the fact that you should wash your hands after reading the letter. The reason for that was that I had a slight attack of catarrhal jaundice (Infectious Type A Hepatitis) soon after arriving here. I have recovered quickly so there's nothing to worry about. I managed to keep on duty because I knew what was coming up and knew that we needed every man. Felt a little rocky for a few days, but am all O.K. now. Fortunately, we were just sitting in a field for a few days prior to moving up.

I received an airmail letter from you last week. The letter is under my pillow in my bedroll. It sure was a morale raiser because I received the letter in the evening after I was dogged tired from wading a cold river and climbing mountains most of the day.

21 October 1943; Italy

Dearest Jean:

The order came through yesterday that we could state where we are in our personal correspondence, so "surprise!"; we are somewhere in Italy as you've probably known all along.

There is a great deal to write about this country and about the action we've been in; don't know whether I'll get it all recorded or not, but if I don't, we'll have all the more to talk about on long rainy evenings after I get home. And speaking of home, I see by a fairly recent "Stars & Stripes" that just arrived this far forward, that the committee of five U.S. Senators which visited North Africa a couple of months ago recommended, among other things, that there be a definite period or term of overseas service established. It looks like someone's brain is beginning to cough out a few revolutions on the crankshaft over there, but I suppose it'll be some time before the motor is really racing.

All the Italy that we've seen consists of rough mountain ranges with flat valleys containing good farmland in between. The soil is much better than in Africa; in fact, it looks much like the good old brown Iowa variety. It is of fine texture, a loam that has apparently been washed down the rivers by erosion for centuries (alluvial soil).

There is much more food visible to the eye here in Italy than there was in Africa. In the back-country, away from the towns, one sees apple orchards loaded with fruit, small piles of corn ready to be ground, baskets of potatoes, etc. One never saw food standing around like that in Africa. The poor Arabs either ate it up right away or hid it. There are also some fairly nice-looking cattle here; and quite a few oxen, which are used to pull carts, etc.

I haven't been in any large city yet; hope to in a few days. The "back country" is really primitive. We've been in many isolated little mountain villages that look like something out of the middle-ages. The buildings are a ramshackle stone variety with tile roofs, all piled on one another with narrow archways, dark alleys, and smoky windows. Most of the men wear shoes, but most of the women and children go barefooted. In most houses the pigs and chickens roam right through the living quarters and in some cases the "master's" bed is right beside the manger. Things are pretty dirty and smoky and depressing looking. The narrow streets twist and turn and are cobblestone. One expects to see some character like Robin Hood or Sir Lancelot come clattering down the street between the arches at any time.

One thing that is immediately noticed by the stranger is the manner in which the women are used practically as beasts of burden. The women here carry large weights of various things on their heads. On the way forward I saw a woman carrying a hogshead (large wine barrel) on her head and have seen them carry large bundles of straw and hay, furniture, large casks and jars, etc. Every once in awhile, one sees a man courteously helping the woman to get the load balanced properly on her head. Boy, am I learning how to handle women!!! I think I'll use a combination of the Arab and Italian methods when I get home. Say, do you think you'll be able to support me in the style to which I'm accustomed—without, of course, interfering too much with my own affairs?

We did not go into action right away after we landed, but stayed around the beach for a week or so, which was fortunate for me at the time. We soon moved up, though, and began our combat in this campaign with a river crossing. All the bridges were blown, of course, so the assault battalions had to wade the river at 2:00 a.m. under fire, etc. I went with one battalion and believe me, the water was plenty cold and very wet. The fire wasn't as heavy nor did it last as long as we expected (Jerry pulled out rather quickly) so it wasn't really very bad and our casualties were light for the crossing. The engineers, however, couldn't get their pontoon bridge in that day due to artillery fire, so we had to evacuate our wounded on rubber boats by pulling the boats along a rope stretched across the river. The current was very swift. I waded the creek three times and almost got swept downstream in water waist deep. The bridge went in O.K. the next day, but by that time most of our outfit was several miles down the road.*

Right now, we are resting after having secured our objective. The regiment certainly has improved over the early days of Africa. It's hard to explain, but in every way, this outfit behaves like a crack combat unit. There are very few cases of jitters (so-called "shell-shock") and the boys know how to work the country—to work past Jerry's machine gun nests and then clean them out. We've taken a moderate number of prisoners. The rough country makes it slow going. You can't whiz through the mountain gulches (no road) with tanks the way you could cover some of the territory in Africa. You have to crawl slowly forward, punching it out from one ravine to the next.

We (the Hdq. Sect. of the Medics) are now housed in a small mill at one end of a town of about 2,000 population. It's the first roof we've had over our heads

---

* "Near Limatola, the medical detachment of the 168th Regiment braved the swiftly flowing water of the Volturno River and swam ropes across to the opposite bank. The going was tough with heavy enemy resistance, but the advance continued and a bridgehead was established." *History of Iowa National Guard*, 7. [Hereafter cited as *History of IA Nat'l Guard*].

for some time and the boys enjoy sleeping dry. The living quarters of the family that runs the mill are in the adjoining buildings. When we arrived, everything was empty, as the civilians move out when we fight through a village. Yesterday, when it was safe to do so, the family returned. One of my boys speaks Italian, so he made it right with the miller and we are still occupying his mill. There is no electricity in town so that he can't run his grinders anyway.

We have quite a business at the aid station from Italian civilians. Quite a few of them have been hurt by shelling, etc., and, of course, the little kids are frequently picking up things that they shouldn't and getting killed or maimed. The Italians, at least out in the country, are a simple people, much like the Arabs in many ways.

The Italians really hate the Germans. Several days ago, two men came to the aid station at separate times, asking for help in locating their daughters. The first man said his 24 yr. old daughter had been missing three days; the second man burst into tears and told us that his 15 & 18 yr. old daughters had been gone 10 days or so. The Germans blow up the bridges to delay us, and frequently dynamite the houses on both sides of a narrow street to block it for a few hours. I've heard many other stories, but most of them are probably rumors. The Italians are a very emotional and excitable race and I imagine rumors spread very fast ... but one thing is certain, they hate the Germans.

24 October 1943; Italy

... Things are still rather quiet for us, so I thought I'd better get another letter off to you while I have the chance. I don't think that we will be "quiet" much longer—will probably be at it hot and heavy again shortly, maybe tomorrow.

I am sitting in the back of our small truck writing this letter and every few minutes the truck and my eardrums are shaken by the blast (air concussion) from some large artillery pieces of ours that are firing just in back of us. They are pretty big guns, aimed 6 or 8 miles down the road and when they go off, the whole earth around here shakes and your hair stands on end for a second. Last night the air compression (concussion) made the flame in our lantern in our tent leap up twice as high as normal every time the wave of sound hit it—somewhat like the old experiment in physics lab....

30 October 1943; Italy

[valley above Pratola; Ariola?]

... I don't know whether this letter will be a success or not, but here goes. I am writing it in the 9 × 9 wall tent that the three of us officers sleep in whenever we are situated where we can put it up. It is a dark green tent so that we can use a lantern in it at night without advertising our presence to Jerry over there on the next range of hills. The lantern light is just "fair," however. I think I'll try to work the supply officer for one of those Coleman gasoline lanterns whenever I get time to go back to his bailiwick and put up a hard luck story.

It is very quiet outside the tent right now. When I started this letter, the artillery behind us was steadily pumping out its evening serenade and Jerry was sending a few back. The incoming shells have a peculiar peee-er-er-er-er followed by a "thwhamp" that shakes the ground when they light. We are situated about halfway up a hill that is about 1,000 ft. high. The hill is part of a range of small mountains that runs around a flat and green valley. We are at one end of the valley and Jerry is at the other, but our forward elements (the battalions) have possession of about ⅓ of the floor of the valley. Jerry has been shelling the road that we use down the center of the valley almost all day.

We have a beautiful view from our place, when we are here to watch it. None of the incoming shells have come within 500 yds. of us, so there's nothing to worry about. BANG! One of our howitzers just let go right behind us, but actually, in the next ravine behind us, probably 300 or 400 yds. away.

Near us are several of the quaint little Apennine mountain villages that I've told you about. [likely Sant'Angelo d'Alife] In every village there are one or several churches (as well as many wayside shrines, etc.). Most of the churches have small church bells that chime or ring out on the hours. It's very touching to look out over a moon-drenched valley (when it isn't raining!) and hear the church bells ringing and echoing through the hills—also in your tent at night, or as you creep along some country lane in a blacked-out column of vehicles. You can frequently hear the clear, high notes of the bells, pealing in the shadows. Its pastoral beauty is hardly appropriate as a setting for war. The cheerful bells and the sound of cannon just don't go together.

Your story about how you're going out on calls, etc., for Hefty is very interesting. I grinned a mile wide when I read it. Jean, there are very few women that could do that the way you can. You'd make a fine doctor. I wonder and have wondered if you'd ever want to study medicine yourself in case we ever set up a practice in a university town, but suppose it would interfere with other things you'd want to do. I'd never particularly wanted you to go in for the practice of medicine seriously, but would just be interested in such a thing if you would be. I'd also be interested if you took up architecture or apple pie making, or procreation.

As a whole, this division is rapidly coming of age as far as combat is concerned. It is many times better than it was in the early part of the African deal. In fact, they are beginning to handle themselves like seasoned veterans. Most of the "jitterbugs" (so-called "shell-shock" cases that run and hide, etc.) have been weeded out (just another medical problem, maybe you think I didn't have a headache the first month in combat?); and the business of smacking Jerry where it hurts the most is becoming ordinary daily routine. The boys from Iowa (and elsewhere) are turning out to be darn fine combat troops. You remember that I hinted some criticism of ourselves in my letters in March and April, long before I ever read any magazine or newspaper articles on the subjects (they didn't arrive over here until several months after being published). Well, now I'm prophesying just the opposite—you're going to hear us referred to as "crack troops" one of these days, although I always hope that we'll remember that "pride go-eth before a fall" and keep our ears and eyes alert for possible slip-ups.

9 November 1943; Italy; hand written

... We've been the busiest that we've ever been during the last week. Jerry had tightened up considerably and it has been pretty tough going for the boys—but we've made it.

... Our dept. has been busy day and night—we've done a good job, as has the whole outfit. In fact, I cannot praise the behavior of the outfit high enough. They have accomplished an almost impossible task, at high cost, and have succeeded.

I am not supposed to mention casualties until they are announced by the War Dept., but we in the 168th Med. Det. have been very lucky. I feel pretty bad, though, about some of my boys back in the old outfit [133rd].

This is the first real relaxation I've had in a week. I'm writing this by candle light in a room of a house that is jammed against the foot of a cliff (Jerry is over the second hill forward). The boys have a good fire in the fireplace—how strange it feels to absorb external heat for a change. It's 7:00 p.m. and there's moonlight outside. If we didn't have to watch our blackout, we could let a little moonshine in. It's cold out tonight in the foxholes.

... The "1%" per month rotation home has been started (and yet *not* started) over here. For Oct and for November we have been asked to submit the names of 1% of our commissioned for rotation home—as the basis of length of overseas service—and we have submitted the names, but no action has been taken on the recommendations—something has stopped it up above somewhere—although we hear that rotation is going ahead in other units. I guess I ought to slow down some so the Col. will think I'm worn out and rotate me home. As it is now they tend to want to keep the ones that are difficult to replace. It has astounded me to find how pale is the blood of many of our American physicians who shudder at the thought of going out into the field—and under shell fire, too!!!

13 November 1943; Italy

... The mail has been coming in well of late. Many Christmas pkgs are beginning to show up and the boys certainly do appreciate them. They are invariably opened within two minutes after they are received and the edibles are promptly devoured by all within hailing distance. Of course, it is impossible to get men who live a little dangerously at times to wait for a specific date as none of them know just what sort of climate they may be in on that date.

Our food has been really wonderful since this last little lull began. We've had roast beef two days in succession now, and the other morning we had pancakes and real Karo syrup for breakfast. Usually we have to make our own syrup by melting down our hard candy ration (try peppermint syrup sometime on your pancakes) and diluting it considerably with water, but somehow someone crashed through with some maple syrup and boy was it good. We had French toast and oatmeal & coffee with cream this morning. The boys deserve the good food, because they certainly did "put out" during the last little deal—a night river crossing through mine fields. The Jerries are devilish in their use of mines, but they didn't stop most of us. This outfit certainly has "what it takes" now. I'm very proud of the way they behaved, although the piper was somewhat expensive.

... For the last three days we've had it very cozy. We moved the Hdq. aid station into part of a deserted house, one room. There is a fireplace in the room and we are really enjoying the heat. The house is said to have belonged to an Italian engineer. Of course, it was deserted when we appeared on the scene. The neighbors say that the engineer was carried off by the retreating Germans, but we've found quite a lot of official receipts and fascist literature in the house so I imagine that he went off with them voluntarily. Anyway, we are enjoying his room and fireplace. It's nice for the men to stand before the fire to be examined, instead of shivering in the breeze when I listen to their chest.

... I saw Major Gittler and Leslie at a meeting this morning at G's place. They both looked well and G. yelled at everyone as usual. He's a great old boy. He's one of the most conscientious men I've ever known, and he's a square shooter. Sometimes I think it's better to yell and raise hell like he does than to try to be smooth. Anyway, they think a lot of him up at Div.

16 November 1943; Somewhere in Italy

Dearest Jean:

This morning your letter written on October 17 arrived, and believe me I certainly was glad to get it. Several soldiers standing nearby looked at me in a startled manner. This in turn sort of surprised me because I thought all the guys around here knew I was a little odd at times, especially when reading letters from my wife—(they say he gets that faraway look in his eyes).

... Things are rather quiet around here for a change and very, very wet. We of the headquarters section have it pretty soft, but the boys out on the line have nothing to do but sit in the cold rain all day long, and it is no pipe. In some places they can't even put up a tent or tarp for shelter because jerry is looking right at us, and of course a fire for heat would attract immediately the kind of attention they don't want. All these things are taken into consideration, however, although the boys still get cold and wet for a certain length of time.

We are still located in our lucky find: the farmhouse with the fireplace in it. The boys of the hdq. section sleep in a tunnel which was part of an old quarry of some sort, so we are able to keep fairly dry and the fireplace dries out our clothes when we come back from backing up our boys in front of us. The reason you are getting this typewritten letter is because we possess the luxuries of a dry roof and a table and chair right at the present moment.

... I wrote to your father a day or so ago. In the letter, I did something of which you may not approve. I asked him for some advice on financial matters and asked him to advise you in that regard. I explained to him that I was certain that you had saved some money, and that I was perfectly satisfied as to your capabilities of both saving & handling the money, but I wanted him to advise you concerning the possibility of inflation after the war and to suggest a possible "hedge" against it.

I know you well enough to surmise that you have a definite program of savings already started and probably want to surprise me with the amount when I get home. You may not like my sudden inquisitiveness concerning it, but it has occurred to me that maybe (IF we have enough money to do so) that we might buy some sort of tangible property which might hedge us against inflation. I've lost contact with the business world in the states, and asked your father what he thought of such an action.

We can get along all O.K. even if we are broke when I get out of the army. I don't know of any woman I'd rather share poverty with than you. I was just day dreaming some and planning for the future. That's about all we have to do over here. It's a form of recreation.

... Things look better and better from an International point of view. The Russians are still rolling (God bless them!) and it was reported to me that a "second Front" was mentioned as probably soon by the radio recently. We surely ought to get a break one of these days.

It's surprising how few of the original shipload are left in the larger outfit. Many have gone home or transferred, etc. There is no one in the div that has been over any longer than I have, but I suspect that when they start going over the list they'll say "H—l, there's nothing the matter with that guy, he's always raising cain, etc., and pass on to the more decrepit." I think I'd better cultivate a limp or a funny look.

Must close—some business has turned up. I can't sign off without mentioning again how much your letters mean to me. They aren't like ordinary "wives" letters, I know, because none of the other fellows act like I do when they read theirs.

21 November 1943; somewhere in Italy

I'm beginning to wonder what's holding up the mail. I haven't had a letter from you since the one you wrote on 17 October, which arrived here 16 November. I guess I'm a little impatient, but I can't get too many letters from the one and only—so that's you, honey chile.

I happened to pick up the Sept. 7th issue of "Look" Magazine this afternoon for a few minutes and saw an article about how the Yanks took Hill "473." The battalion described in the article is one of ours. I "hepped" in that battle; in fact, Mott and I did our first crawling through the wheat fields that day. Some dope let us out on the wrong side of a hill and Jerry cut loose while we were strolling casually across it with a litter on the way to pick up a reported casualty. That was some fun.... I'll tell you a couple of funny stories about that day when I get home.

... I haven't received any Christmas packages yet, and am glad I haven't. About a week ago one of my trucks, with some mail in it, started to ford a swollen river and got stalled in it over night while the water kept on rising. My two boys got out all o.k. when the top they were sitting on collapsed in the current, but the contents of the truck got pretty wet. I was afraid my shirts were in the mailbag, but they were not. When I went down to the river bank the next day to check on the vehicle and to get it out, I almost died laughing at the antics of various inexperienced soldiers trying to get stuff cross the river. We are old hands at river crossings now—it's a little stunt to handle and engineer boats in a swift current, with a cross rope, etc., and I couldn't help laughing at these Joes who had not learned a few of the principles yet. What a day. I came home muddy and wet, but couldn't keep from giggling. No one was hurt, just scared.

Today (this afternoon) I went up to inspect one of our aid stations in the hills, and noticed that one of the higher mountains in the distance was covered with snow. On the way up the winding mountain road to that place yesterday we came through the hardest rain storms I've been through in a long time, and there was quite a little hail present. The mountain gullies were full of cascading brown columns of water within a few minutes. Due to the rough and inaccessible terrain, about the only way you can get to this aid station is to run in from the flank on the outpost line, right out in front of Jerry and everyone. When we started home this afternoon we had to wait while Jerry shelled a little mountain village that we had to pass through. The mud is still with us in quantity.

I suppose you've heard the terrible story about the kid who persisted in saying that his name was Adolf Hitler Brown to the teacher at school. Finally, his teacher called up his mother, saying: "Mrs. Brown, I cannot understand why your small son persists in saying his name is Adolf Hitler Brown." The mother replied: "That's his name alright, and I am MISS Brown, if you please."

... Must close. We are still in the house with the fireplace. It will be a tough time when we finally have to give it up and move out into the mud, but we really don't mind since every day is so busy we don't have much time to think about it....

28 November 1943; Italy

[one day before battle of Monte Pantano]

I'd better write you a note now, for I may be pretty busy for a few days. I can't say that I've been sitting around any during the past week or so, but my work will revert to "outdoor" type very shortly. During the past ten days I've had a chance to catch up a little on "paper" work and administrative detail, which seems to mount ever higher over here. I think I'll probably practice a little law on the side when I get home and maybe get interested in a couple of insurance companies, if the practice of medicine begins to get dull.

We had a very nice Thanksgiving. The day was a little moist inasmuch as it rained almost all day, but we were snug in our farmhouse with the fireplace. We had a large turkey dinner (at headquarters—you must remember that part of the outfit that was on the line had only "C" rations a la foxhole) with all the turkey we could eat, riced potatoes, escalloped corn, noodles, gravy, dressing, nuts and apples, and cake with apricot sauce. Someone also found a bottle or two of "John Jamison" for the officers' mess.

I arrived a little late for the feast, it had already started when I sat down beside the Colonel. He immediately wanted to know how much I wanted to drink. In a sort of absent-minded manner (I'd just come from working on reports in the office) I replied, "About a tablespoonful," so amidst the whoops and laughter of all concerned, Colonel Butler picked up a tablespoon, poured out exactly the desired amount and then insisted on holding the spoon while I "took" the drink. They didn't urge me further, 'cuz several others kept a vigilant eye on the bottle. They are a swell bunch of fellows. It's surprising how much fun we have at times. Altogether, it was quite a blowout.

I received a letter from Jack yesterday, the first I've received in Italy. His letter was written November 4 and was from the vicinity of the location where I saw him in July. He said he was all O.K., was sleeping in pyramidal tents and off the ground, so guess he is in a fairly permanent setup. I hope he can stay there for the duration of his stay overseas. It's very nice around there, close to a fine beach on the blue Mediterranean. From the fact that he has been in the one spot so long, I believe he'll probably stay there.

The Christmas packages are really coming in, and the boys are doing right well. Today the headquarters section of the medics (19 men) got a sack of packages, mostly fruit cakes and candy. The edibles don't last long because they are all promptly passed around.

... I love you very much, Jean,
Merry Christmas, Babe! Lud

Monte Pantano, Italy: November 29–December 4, 1943

A Crucial Battle and the Silver Star

"Dearest Jean:
Your 'V-Mail' letter written November 18th arrived here on December 6th, and there never was a more welcome letter. It came just at a time when I needed a great big pickup and it was just that. Your letters are knocking the stuffing out of Hitler, because as far as this little boy is concerned, they are the most important thing in keeping up his morale...."

—8 December 1943, Italy

The Germans had established a series of military fortifications in southwestern Italy called the "Winter Line," a string of three heavily entrenched and well-equipped lines designed to defend that section of Italy and slow down the advancement of Allied forces. The primary "Gustav Line" was centered around the town of Cassino, through which ran the important Highway 6 leading directly to Rome. Winter in the mountains contributed greatly to the German's tactics in delaying the Allied advance. The wretched wet and cold weather not only made the soldiers of the 34th constantly miserable—it also more than doubled their disease total.

Why was it so slow going in Italy? The terrain. As described by *Yank* magazine staff correspondent, Sgt. Joe McCarthy:

> Miles on the map here don't mean anything. They may tell you to advance to a point three miles away. But by the time you get there, up and down ridges and around chasms, zigzagging up the sides of mountains, you will cover 8 or 9 miles. The squad on your right may be within talking distance. But there is a canyon dropping down between you and them. If you want to get to them, you have to walk a half mile to the rear and then a ½ mile forward again on their side of the canyon [5].

But before Cassino, the 168th had to first capture Monte Pantano, the anchor in the German Winter Defense Line. The high command in Berlin had ordered the Winter Line held at all costs. This seemingly impossible objective assigned to the Iowa boys of the 168th Regiment, was to become its defining test of courage and will.

The 34th Infantry Division gazed up at the snow-capped mountain peaks of Monte Pantano and Monte Marrone. Towards the end of the North African campaign and since their landing at Salerno, Italy, this division of soldiers had become battle hardened. They had developed into a well-honed fighting machine despite the miserable conditions and thinning ranks.

On November 29, 1943, Col. Frederic Butler's 168th Infantry Regiment set out to take Monte Pantano on the left flank, and on the right flank, the 133rd, moved out to attack Monte Marrone. Monte Pantano was a short-lived, but intense and brutal battle. The *Stars and Stripes Weekly* staff writer Sgt. Milton Lehman, wrote: "During the attack on Pantano, the weather was clear to begin with, but quickly changed to fog, drenching rain and snow, which made the trails and mountain top a slimy mire."

At first, as the 168th cleared out the bunkers in the foothills, success seemed imminent. But the Germans had entrenched themselves in a saddle near the crest and, as was their custom, viciously counterattacked.*

Retired Lt. Col. Homer R. Ankrum adds further details to the drama that unfolded:

"Running low on ammunition, some of the 168th Infantry men threw C-ration cans at the charging enemy who, in the darkness, mistook them for grenades, thus

---

* "There was hand-to-hand combat. Bayonets were affixed to rifles and were used. The Krauts were driven back only to regroup and attack again and again. For seven days and nights the battle waged for control of Monte Pantano. This was the first heavyweight slugging match of the Italian Campaign." Howard D. Ashcraft, *As You Were*, 61–62.

buying enough time for those with a few rounds to reload and fire. Grimly, the 168th Infantry held on, advancing inch by inch, refusing to give up ground gained."*

Interviews: November 29–December 4, 1943: Monte Pantano, Italy

PL: How did you earn the Silver Star for "Gallantry-in-Action?"

Dad: It was about 15 miles south of Cassino, Italy, along the Volturno Valley, and the regiment was given the assignment to go up a very steep hill, about like Saddle Rock [a popular hiking destination in Wenatchee, Washington]. There were just rocks up there, no field to speak of. And the Germans were on an adjoining little mound, and they were dug in with machine guns and mortar shells. They had fortified their position with concrete and steel bunkers. Once again, the enemy had the advantage of occupying the high ground, looking down our throats.

There was a curtain of mortar fire in intervals. Our guys were up there with the battalion commander, the Lieutenant Colonel I knew from Iowa—he was one of the better ones. They had casualties lying on the ground everywhere. I didn't know what had happened to their two aid men who are usually with each company. There were a couple of companies up there, so Colonel Butler said, "Doc, they have heavy casualties that need to be evacuated. We have to get some litter bearers up there."

Apparently, there weren't any medical aid men up there—they were afraid to go or something. I felt I couldn't just say to someone else, "YOU go," you know, because they might get killed. I would never have asked someone to do something that I wouldn't do myself. I was a Major by then—and so I said, "Okay, I'll get 'em. Come on, let's go." I rounded up four litter bearers and a litter and said, "C'mon, follow me," and we started up.

I had my trench coat on because it had been raining and I didn't know what I was getting into. So, I took a litter squad up there, through this curtain of mortar fire. We were just lucky, I guess, and got through to the top where I immediately came upon a guy with a compound fracture of his skull—and his brain was showing. I knew his chances of survival were slight, so I left him there. I had to decide whether to try to evacuate him or not. He was unconscious, not suffering, and the chances of him living were—well, with modern brain surgery, he might've made it, but not in these circumstances. That bothers me to this day. But essentially, I had to triage and quickly choose.

I picked up another guy who had a fractured femur and put him on the litter. We had one with wheels on it—two bicycle wheels in the middle. We found the trail that we'd gone up and we got him back down and evacuated. I had only my lightweight canvas musette bag with me that had a few dressings, a tourniquet, some iodine, morphine, syringes, and my surgical tools kit.†

---

* *History of IA Nat'l Guard.*

† The M1928 Musette Bag was a khaki-colored, heavy canvas backpack and was the standard issue to Army infantrymen and Rangers until 1944. It was used to carry only the essentials for soldiers in combat and on the move.

Lud's canvas Musette Bag ("rucksack") and contents that he carried onto the battlefield to treat the wounded.

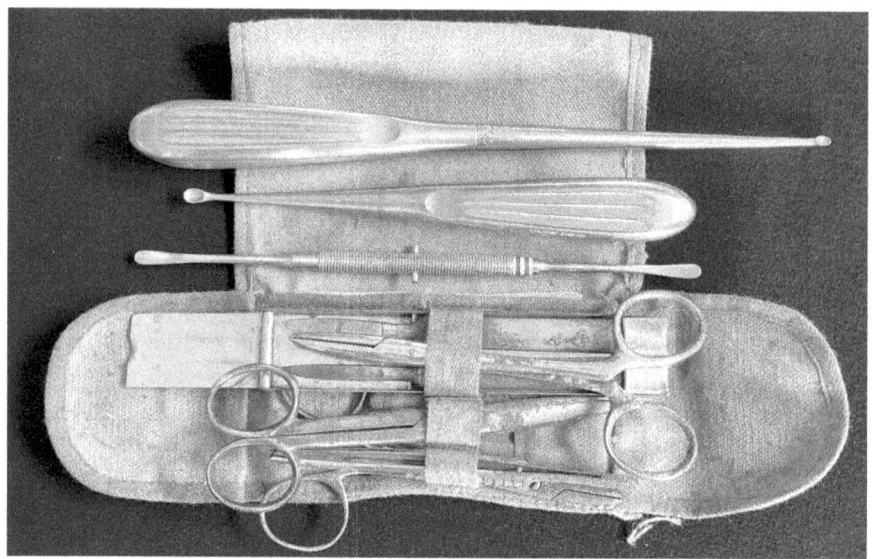

Lud's emergency surgical tools kit in canvas pouch that he carried with him in his Musette Bag.

There were some other wounded up there that were "walking wounded" and kind of dazed. We were able to guide them down the trail behind the litter squad.

I'm not sure how many times we went back up—I wasn't counting. But we got a few of them out of there. Eventually, we kicked the Germans off the mountain, but then they counter-attacked. They always did that—the Germans always counter-attacked. They were tough and experienced fighters. But we eventually got them, and we prevailed on Monte Pantano.

About a month later, I was notified that I'd been recommended for the Silver Star by Colonel Frederic Butler, and it would be presented to me in Benevento, Italy, which is way south.

* * *

Gordon Gammack, embedded *Des Moines Register* staff journalist with the 34th Infantry, wrote in his March 8, 1944, column:

> Access to Pantano was limited to one major trail up the steep eastern slope, with minor paths on the flanks, so rough and twisted, they were virtually unusable. With the severe weather conditions of drenching rain, snow, sleet, and bitter cold, the trails became slippery, muddy quagmires. The men were soaked to the skin and their wet clothing froze. Overcoats became stiff as boards. The soldiers shivered in foxholes with six inches of water, as they had not been issued winter clothing. But they would not come down off that mountain, because they knew any gap in their lines would be disastrous. They elected to die rather than quit the fight. Military men with wide experience have said that the physical discomforts of Washington's army at Valley Forge could not compare to those suffered by these men.
>
> With such adverse weather and logistical conditions, hard choices had to be made: the dead were left in place and no rations or water were brought in. Within 24 hours, Col. Butler had lost the three battalion commanders who had served with him since Tunisia.

The Germans pounded both Pantano and Marrone viciously with mortar and artillery fire, then strafed the area with fighter planes. Over the course of seven days and nights, battle casualties for the 168th Regimental Combat Team on the approximately 3,600-foot Monte Pantano amounted to 35 officers and 429 enlisted men. Non-battle casualties were extensive because of the harsh elements and because the Fifth Army troops had not been issued winter uniforms at that stage. Many suffered from frostbite, trench foot, pneumonia, and the flu. Litter bearers operated in relays, carrying casualties down the hillside for long distances, while others had to be lowered by ropes down steep cliffs. Some, who were still able to walk, slid down the icy mountainside.

Coming down out of the snow-covered mountains and blood-spattered hills came the brave Red Bull men, many with trench foot so severe, they could hardly walk. The feet of hundreds had to be amputated.*

"As it turned out," journalist Gordon Gammack went on to write, "the battle of

---

* Trench Foot, or Immersion Foot, is an injury of the feet from prolonged exposure to wet and cold conditions. Injury occurs because wet feet lose heat 25 times faster than dry feet. Therefore, to prevent heat loss, the body constricts blood vessels to shut down circulation in the feet. Skin tissue begins to die because of lack of oxygen and nutrients and due to the buildup of toxic products. Affected feet may become numb and turn red or blue as a result of the poor vascular supply, and may begin to have a decaying odor due to the possibility of the early stages of necrosis setting in. As the condition worsens, feet may also begin to swell. Advanced trench foot often involves blisters and open sores, which lead to infections, gangrene, and eventual amputation. Walking on the affected feet may cause permanent tissue damage. If trench foot is treated properly, complete recovery is normal, though it is marked by severe short-term pain when feeling returns. As with other cold-related injuries, trench foot leaves sufferers more susceptible to it in the future. U.S. Occupational Safety and Health Administration. https://www.osha.gov/sites/default/files/2018-11/fy12_sh-23584-12_TrenchFoot.pdf.

Monte Pantano, fought high above the clouds in December 1943, was one of the fiercest battles of the bitter Italian campaign. The gallantry of the veteran Iowa and Minnesota soldiers and the many men from the other states who fought with them, was extraordinary."

In its drive that started in the fall of 1943 with the capture of Benevento and culminating in the incredible battle of Monte Pantano, the 34th Division had been in combat for 79 consecutive days. Relief came December 14 when the 168th Regiment was finally pulled out of the frontline for rest, training, and replacements. This respite was brief, however, for on Christmas Eve, the order came through to return to combat. The Germans were far from being finished—true also, of the mighty "Red Bulls."

Interviews: December 8–31, 1943

PL: What happened after the bloody battle of Monte Pantano?

Dad: After Monte Pantano and being in heavy combat for over two and a half months, we were finally pulled off the frontline to get some rest and rehabilitation. However, the medical detachment continued its training after learning valuable lessons in heavy combat the previous few months.* Then, soon after Christmas, we were ordered back on line for another major engagement. It turned out to be the battle for Cassino.

PL: Tell me about this framed print that has always hung downstairs in your home office? It looks rather gruesome.

Dad: This is an etching by the artist Baron Rudolph von Ripper. He was Austrian by birth, and was an artist embedded in our unit. He was also a member of the Reconnaissance and earned two Silver Stars. He hated the Nazis. I've often wondered about him. This art piece is overly stylized, but it shows a couple of litter bearers carrying a wounded man, and also the dazed "walking wounded." [Baron Rudolph von Ripper was considered one of the greatest combat artists in the world, and one of his prints, "Hitler Plays the Hymn of Hate," appeared on the January 1939 cover of *Time* magazine. See Appendix C.]

In the battered town of San Pietro, Italy [the Battle of San Pietro, Dec. 8–17, 1943, just south of Monte Cassino and halfway between Naples and Rome, was a major engagement], the medics had set up a first aid station. All the inhabitants of the towns that we fought through had already fled, back behind the Germans. The

---

* According to Lud's original typed schedule, the 168th Medical Detachment's two-week training during this time period included: pitching of wall and pyramidal tents, map reading, location and function of Aid Stations, medical tactics in combat, Articles of War, manual transport of sick and wounded, concealment and use of cover, sterilization and aseptic technique including use of morphine syrette, improvised litters, elementary bandaging, hemorrhage and shock, treatment of unconsciousness, spinal fracture, loaded and obstacle litter drills, ambulance loading, purification of water, contents of aid pouches, lice control, dressings and bandages, venereal prophylaxis, use of plasma, as well as daily vigorous calisthenics and fitness training.

Germans would occupy them, but we were pushing them back through these towns. The Italian inhabitants didn't want to get out into "no man's land," in-between, and so all these towns were deserted. And some of them were badly damaged by artillery fire. This print is sort of a depressing picture, but it shows that everybody was depressed and scared to death. I mean, the fact that we were there doing our job didn't mean that we weren't frightened, or that we weren't worried. We saw a lot of tragedies, and I thought this piece of art captured all of that.

As I said, in Italy, all the little villages we occupied were up in the Apennines and were deserted, because the Italians had been allies of the Germans, and the Germans had occupied Italy as a friendly ally. The Germans didn't think much of the Italian soldiers, because they weren't nearly as well-trained or as competent as their own. The Italian civilians also became allies of the Germans, and so when the Germans pulled back, the Italian civilians went with them. I don't know what the Germans said to them—they probably told them that if you cross no man's land tonight, or try to resist and step on a mine or something, the Americans will think you're attacking, and will shoot you—they're your enemy.

So, the Italians all retreated back with the Germans, leaving their homes empty. I slept in many Italians' vacated houses. I had my own folding wooden cot, and a bedroll. I had a roof over my head, but was also surrounded by these people's furniture, rugs, and cooking utensils. I didn't use any of them or take anything—but it felt strange and intrusive—that I had invaded someone's private life in this way.

A lot of these villages didn't have running water, just wells, and I was afraid to drink out of them—which, I think, is how I got Infectious Hepatitis back in North Africa—from untreated well water.

It was a week or two before we finally got to Cassino. We never did take Cassino, but were very close. We pushed on, but just couldn't get much past Cassino, so they finally ordered us to go around by ship to a cemetery there for U.S. soldiers. We had kind of leap-frogged the Germans a little bit and had come around on their flank. We later learned that it had taken nearly five divisions of Allied troops over the course of three months to finish what we had almost accomplished.

In the reading I've done since about the war, I think Cassino became the gold standard for measuring the fierceness of battles. The enemy *always* seemed to have the military advantage of the "higher ground": Kasserine and Foudouk Passes and Hill 609 in North Africa, the Salerno landings, Monte Pantano, and then, Monte Cassino.

Letters: December 8–30, 1943

8 December 1943; Italy

[post Mt. Pantano]

Dearest Jean:

Your "V-Mail" letter written November 18 arrived here on December 6, and there never was a more welcome letter. It came just at a time when I needed a great big pickup and it was just that. Your letters are knocking the stuffing out of

Hitler, because as far as this little boy is concerned, they are the most important thing in keeping up his morale.

We just finished a very busy time again—"outdoor life"! ! ! [combat] It was the roughest we've had, but now it's all over for this time and we'll be able to catch up on our loafing again for a little while.

One of the Christmas packages that you sent arrived with the letter. It was the package containing the "duffle bag" with the toiletries in it, plus the extra soap, shoe polish, dental floss, nose drops, etc., as well as the canned nuts. Thanks very much, dearest. The package pleased me very much. It was just like walking into an American drug store again. Many of the articles are unobtainable over here, of course.

... The papers are playing up the big conference between FDR, Churchill, and Stalin in Iran. It certainly sounds good and from my "private wire," I hear that there is good news ahead. I can't say that I like any part of Italy that I've seen yet—it is so blasted wet and muddy all the time, but maybe it's just as well that I'm here, at least for the present. I'm still waiting for that ticket home to you, though. What a day that will be.

... I think I wrote you that I received a letter from Jack several weeks ago. The letter was written on November 4 and he was still located near where I saw him in July. He did have a different outfit address, however. I don't know whether that presages movement or not, but doubt it if weather in this part of the world has anything to do with it. An outfit of that type wouldn't get around very well over here most of the time. I'll keep my eye open for him, however.

Must close and get to bed, have a little trip to make tomorrow. I love you very, very much, dearest. Remember the guy that loves you the most when you get lonesome around any "4-F'ers"! ! ! This mess can't last forever, and we'll have a lifetime together. I can hardly wait.

I love you, Lud

... P.S. I hate to be mundane, but have you written me about our bank account? I'm mildly interested—to know how soon we can get off the government when I get home.

12 December 1943; Italy

[after Mt. Pantano; in the small village of
Sant'Angelo d'Alife, a farm village.]

... We have moved since the hurried note that I wrote you last. We are now licking the wounds of a fairly hot deal and everyone is duly appreciative of the lull. We are located in a quaint little mountain village. I am living with Capt. Armstrong ("Buck," the dental officer) and Lt. Spoo (my Med. Administrative Corps Officer) in one of the larger houses in town, the home of one of the leading families.

The house is quite a place, quite large, with many balconies, gardens, balustrades, stairways and passageways, tiled floors and old-fashioned furniture. I spotted the place when we first looked over the town and made arrangements for a room since it was located near where our headquarters was to be. After we arrived, the whole regimental officers mess moved in with me, so the rambling structure is full of American officers ... and also the band.

It's strange how well the people take the whole thing. They are very polite and really don't seem to mind our occupancy and do many things for us spontaneously. I have watched for some evidence of their dislike for us, moving in on them this way, but have never seen any. Tonight I was called in consultation to see one of the family who has been ailing. Her husband is a dry wiry little fellow who dances around muchly trying to be nice to us all. It's all very interesting in a desolate sort of way because I certainly am homesick to see YOU, and incidentally, the good old U.S.A.

14 December 1943; Italy

Dearest Jean:

This afternoon your airmail letter written on 7 Nov. arrived here. I feel a thousand percent better than I did this morning. That's how your letters affect me.... In carefully reading your letter I see reflected therein the depression and the lonesomeness that I frequently include in my letters to you. I wish it were not so. If I were the good husband that I ought to be I'd never confide my depressions and lonesome or uncomfortable times to you, because—just remember that your Uncle Dudley is a pretty tough character as long as the Lord is nearby, and inasmuch as He gets around in an unrestricted manner, you won't need to worry about my welfare. I've always had every confidence and faith that I'd return home unscathed and so far, my faith has been justified, as I have been in many hair-raising predicaments as witness the fact that I'm getting more bald all the time. My hair isn't going through the grey state that some go through in times of stress. It has stood on end so many times that it is just getting thinner ... don't worry, though, there are still a few wisps left.

In regard to the shirts—do what you think best, but send them on if you want to. Right now, we are in a quiet time again, back a few miles from the main excitement, getting acquainted with the new fellows and working them in. During these times, some of us get to go to the big city once in awhile. They've established a large "rest camp" in one of the large cities near us [Naples], with hot showers, clean clothes, real cots to sleep on, movies, sightseeing trips, etc., all for the front-line soldiers. All of my medical officers and most of my men have been to the camp for from four to nine days, as well as the men from the rest of the regiment. They certainly did like it—it is a wonderful thing and just what they need, short of a trip home.

I haven't been to the rest camp yet, probably won't have time to go, but I may get a chance for an overnight trip into town, or something. The boys tell some pretty wild stories about the big city [Naples] and from my one trip there, which I wrote you about in October, I believe many of the stories are true. Apparently in many parts of the city an American soldier has to push his way through crowds and swarms of boys and young men of all ages who are assisting their womenfolk in the practice of a very old profession. I thought Picadilly Circus was pretty rough along that line, but it is certainly exceeded in the "big town" near here. War is a terrible thing in more ways than one. I feel very sorry for the people on both sides that must suffer for the selfishness of a small class of selfish and power-mad people that started the whole thing. The situation I described above is also a headache from the medical officer's point of view, in his "eternal" war to keep soldiers fighting fit, but it is really a secondary headache compared to the pity that I feel for the people who are reduced to such suffering. Somehow, I feel that there are countries that would resist such a state, even in defeat, but it takes the help of a strong moral code to accomplish it.

... The weeks and months are steadily clicking by. Pretty soon I'll be the senior officer in the regiment in point of overseas service. In fact, there are three of us left in this outfit that all came over on that first boat with the "old outfit" [the 133rd Regiment; he's now in the 168th].

Must close and hurry down to the officers' mess for evening chow. I'm late now, but waited to finish this letter. The weather has eased up on the rain for the last few days, although it's still cloudy much of the time. It hasn't frozen yet down in the valley where we are, but sometimes the nights are pretty chilly. Today the sun shone some and we were comfortable all day with just field jackets on. The roads are getting a little dry for a change, but I imagine that the rains will start again soon. What do you think about living in Phoenix, Arizona, when I get home? That is the "Sunshine Capital" of America (A h e m).

19 December 1943

[at Sant'Angelo d'Alife ~37 mi north of Naples, 22 mi north
of Caserta; in Province of Caserta]

Dearest Jean (You WONDERFUL Woman!):

Two days ago your second Christmas package arrived—what a package! ! ! It's the best one I've ever received, bar none, and I was tickled to death to get it. With all the variety of things that were in it I don't see how you hit on so many things that I wanted.

The underwear was fine, especially the "T" shirt, which I have wanted for a long time. It's little things like that which you see in the magazine ads that you know you'd like to have, but in the hurry and hustle of a busy job you forget that you'd like to have one. The slippers are fine, too, because I can slip them into my musette bag and carry them right with me and not have to put my feet in my shoes to get something from the other side of the room or tent. The shrimp and jam were big surprises. I'm saving them for a real blow out when I can sit and think about the wonderful wife I have at home. The little box of Dad's old insignia really bowled me over. You must have dug those out of the old trunk. I've been wanting some miniature leaves for a long time to wear on my shirt collars, but once again thought it was too small a thing to ask for, and besides, I guess they are pretty scarce now in the States. The Gillette razor blades were tops, cuz I haven't been able to get Gillette blades for about four or five months and what we do get frequently are just the better grade "saws." The pipe I'd forgotten all about—and immediately lighted it up, thanks. It's practically impossible to get pipe cleaners here, so that package comes in very handy. I've been short of tooth brushes for some time, in fact mentioned it in one letter to Mother recently since I happened to think of it when I was writing to her—and there they were in your package. One thing, though—they are Fuller Brushes. What I want to know is, what kind of guys are Fuller Brush men nowadays? I'd sort "of" like a report on this guy, the Fuller Brush man. I've seen a lot of cartoons about him in Esquire and they say he is sometimes a pretty fast worker—how about it? The sewing kit was perfect and the all-day sucker was much enjoyed. The dress socks will also come in handy if I get to go to the recreation camp at the [censored—cut out] but right now I'll have to put them away as the weather demands the thicker type of socks over here in the field. We've had a little trouble with some of the men's feet after being in cold water for several days at a time.

... I can't imagine anyone worrying about his job in the good old U.S.A., but I guess it's all in what you are used to. Believe me, it'll take a world-shaking catastrophe to even make me turn my head when I get home. I can think of no civilian problem that won't be duck soup after a couple of night river crossings, for instance.

In my last letter I enclosed a clipping (picture) showing two medics working on a "patient." The one man, Mott, is one of my boys here in hdq. section. It was his wife that sent you the $100 money order from Texas. He's my right-hand man and we had some pretty exciting times together in Africa. He's 38 years old, though, and I have had to have a reliable man in my aid station, so during the Italian campaign he has spent most of the time back in the aid station.

Recently I've thought a great deal about the picturesque country that we are in. I wish you were here once in awhile to see everything that is interesting, but I'll try to describe some of it to you.

We are living in a little village perched about one quarter the way up the side of a mountain, at the side of a broad valley down which we pushed the Germans a month ago. The place is torn up quite a little from shelling and bombing so that there are many houses with gaping holes in their walls and in some cases, there is just a pile of broken stone and plaster jutting out part of the way into the street. Many of the houses are still intact, however, and right now, the medical officers at hdq. are living in a regular mansion that belongs to the mayor. I've described some of it to you in my last letter. The room we sleep in looks out back into the garden. There is one tall French door that opens (in) onto a small balcony. There is an orange tree growing right against the house so that one branch with several oranges on it lies on the floor of the balcony. The fruit isn't quite ripe yet, but the oranges are a pale yellow against the dark shiny green leaves. The grass and many shrubs in the garden are quite green and in the next garden, over the wall, there are some roses blooming. It seems strange that these plants are so green because it's rather chilly most of the time and most of the time it's cloudy and overcast. You can always see your breath (indoors or out) and the atmosphere is usually damp, although for several days lately, the rain has ceased and we've had sunshine.

Beyond the garden wall, the hill starts to rise rather rapidly and goes up about 600 yards to a smooth rounded point which is barren of vegetation, and on which is situated the ruins of an old stone castle. It's bleak, yet somehow beautiful, like the illustrations in an old fairy tale.

I'll have to quit pretty soon, because the lights have now gone out for good this evening and I am writing by the light of two candles perched right beside the typewriter. Another time I'll tell you about some of the quaint shops that are still open in town. One of them is very interesting to me—it's a cabinet-maker's shop. He does everything by hand. All of his boards are rough-hewn and crooked and he planes them off and smoothes them entirely by hand before he even starts to make a box or a bookcase, etc. His boxes are beautiful works of art, with the corners all neatly dovetailed together. One day I saw a pair of French doors that he had mortised and made by hand. Look at the door of your bedroom and think what skill it would take to make one with just hand tools, out of a slab of rough wood. The work is slow, but it's expert, the way they've done it over here for hundreds of years. Several of his hammers are American made.

Then there's the olive press that I watched in operation yesterday, but that'll have to wait until next time.

27 December 1943; Italy

[officers' "rest camp" at Hotel Minerva in Sorrento, Italy, overlooking the Mediterranean]

Dearest Jean:

What a Christmas! It was hard to believe in a way, yet very little things loom very large at times over here. Last night I returned to the outfit after a four-day trip to the officers' "rest camp" or "leave camp," located in a famous resort town across the bay from a very large metropolis in Italy. I certainly did have a good time.

A month or so ago the Army took over one of the large old resort hotels in this coast village and retaining the civilian staff that has worked there for years, made it into a "rest camp" for the old broken-down army officers, like me. The rooms and appointments were of the best: real beds with clean sheets and mattresses, hot and cold running water in the room, and a semi-private bathroom with an honest-to-goodness "john" in it. What a place. I used everything all I could (ahem!!).

The service was excellent. The moment you approached the front door a doorman opened it and a porter took your luggage away from you and there were also nice chairs in the lobby where you could pass out comfortably from the shock. The dining room served excellent food (best G.I. ration, with an

Italian twist on the culinary interpretation) and a nice little string ensemble that wafted soft music between bites. The ensemble also had a very pretty and petite Italian girl with Hollywood dimensions who had a golden coloratura with which she had the boys all groggy in short order. Downstairs there was a billiard and ping-pong table as well as a post exchange, and the bar opened about 11:00 a.m. and closed after midnight. There was a spacious glass roofed winter garden with potted palms and wicker chairs and from the veranda, as well as from the balcony of my room, one could look out across the water at night toward the lights on the shore across the bay, or at the dull red glow of a volcano [Vesuvius] in action.

The town itself was rather quiet; that is, as quiet as a hundred officers and their drivers would let it be. There were many fine shops where "objects des arts" were sold. The main attraction as far as souvenirs were concerned, were the inlaid wood boxes made there and the fine hand worked (embroidered, I guess) linen and laces available. I was pretty much entranced by the whole place, so I squandered a wad on some boxes and linen which you will receive one of these days. I don't know whether you'll want to use them or not, but I wanted some souvenirs of the place. I'll always kick myself for not buying a little linen on Swamp Island back in the days of our destitution.

… Christmas night we had quite a dance at the hotel ("albergo," in Italian). An American orchestra played sweet and hot and the gentry from the town turned out. It was quite a cosmopolitan crowd. There was "Kiki," an American gal of perhaps 40 years of age who had married a wealthy Italian some years ago, a countess (pretty smooth) of something or other and some princess of somewhere. The latter two were young and not bad. Of course, there were lesser lights there, including one or two "ahems" you can always count on some affectionate but enthusiastic officer bringing to any party. I certainly did get a kick out of watching both groups, the officers and the guests, as well as participating in the party. There were a few American nurses and a couple of Red Cross gals also present. It sounds as though I added their names as an afterthought, but they really stole the show, as always, since no European female can hold a candle to the American girl in any way.

The amusing thing about the whole deal was the action of the Italian men. Of course, all the native girls (sounds South Seas, doesn't it?) brought their husbands, etc. Boy, they looked the part. Most of the time they moped around the wall while the American (and a few British) officers did the monopolizing, including yours truly, to a limited extent, of course. For a brief instant I couldn't help imagining how a bunch of us wild Americans would react to such a setup of wolves. Somehow, I couldn't see a bunch of American men "renting" out their women for a dance, but the moment passed off quickly as the party waxed gay. They know where the bread is buttered, though. About one such party per year is about all I could stand, however. There is something about that class of Europeans that makes me want to clip one on the chin just to see him fall apart, although I suppose there were many there of genuine integrity. One cannot help wondering how long ago they were dancing and wining with the Germans, although, again, it's probable that some were genuinely anti-fascist—in a discreet way.

Well, the show is over and the memory isn't lingering very long. I'm back at the outfit now, but my "rest" from my "rest" will be rather short. The officer that I left in charge during my absence was a little new at the job and we are soon going back to work…. I won't be able to write much for a few days beginning tomorrow. The place where we are going is just back of a hot spot in the cold and wet mud, and I mean wet ! ! !

The first issue of "Newsweek" arrived yesterday. Your father sent it to me for Christmas. It's the thin and small "Airmail" edition and I like it very much. Be sure to thank him for me since it'll probably be some little time before I have a chance to write to him.

30 December 1943; Italy V-Mail

… This is a peach of a day, the first real sunshine that we've had in some time. We certainly appreciate this change to let the tents dry out a little. The cold is not so noticeable when things are dried. I can't say dry, because that stage hasn't been reached yet. Whoever said "Sunny Italy" ought to make his fortune in California because he certainly started from "scratch" over here.

I'm beginning to seriously question the advisability of keeping some officers so long overseas, from several standpoints, none of which I can discuss here. I'm sure that the higher-ups know "something" of the problem, but doubt that they can fully understand it even if they themselves had been overseas this long, which very few, if any, have been.

Serving overseas in the comparative comfort of a quiet headquarters town at a base or far behind the lines is different from being constantly on the go amidst the conditions of the front. I expect I may sound self-centered, but when I wrote the last few lines, I was thinking of the "dough-foot." The first percussion of the problem as I outlined it, usually is felt by the medical officer in his dealings with the men. Fortunately, only a small percentage of the various outfits have been gone that long. I expect that officers who deal in large masses of men must consider the average of the mass and can't give much consideration to the individual.

At any rate, I've always felt, and expressed myself, that a definite policy of overseas service should be established and, incorporated in that policy, a more or less definite "term" of overseas service that would be considered reasonable by those "that are in the know." I've always doubted that all the boys would be "shipped home" immediately after the war is over—it wouldn't be practical or logical, and I think that such service should be organized with a long-term scale in view. The "brass" will be brought to it some time or another, possibly in a painful manner, but I'm confident that the problem is already being worked on. I hope so, anyway!

4. Italy

Approach to Cassino: January 1–15, 1944

[San Vittore, Mount Chiaia, Cervaro]

During the first two weeks in January 1944, after the bloody battle at Pantano in early December, the 168th Regiment continued to engage with the Germans above the timberline across Italy's mountaintops. They lived night and day in freezing weather with inadequate and wet clothing. They had little food and melted snow for water. Their mission was to protect the advance of the rest of the 34th Infantry Division, from San Vittore to Cassino.

Progress was slow and German counterattacks were fierce. Casualties were heavy on both sides. The 34th's numbers had been greatly reduced and there were no reinforcements. In John Hougan's book *ATTACK, ATTACK, ATTACK: History of the Famous 34th Infantry Division,* he noted: "Never were fresh troops more greatly needed ... none came ... indeed, thus far in the Italian campaign, reserves were an almost unknown quantity ... men wondered then and wonder now, how planners of the campaign failed to have sufficient reserves on hand...."

These brutal engagements under such adverse conditions were what distinguished the 168th's record and performance in the annals of military history.

The Regimental Surgeon's job was especially challenging during this time. Evacuating, let alone treating the wounded, became an almost impossible task. On the approach to Cassino, there were no roads fit for a vehicle such as an ambulance or wide enough trails for even a jeep. In desperation, horses and mules were employed, but with little success. Ultimately, the only way to evacuate the seriously wounded soldiers was by hand carry. Litter Squads ordinarily consisted of four bearers per litter, but because the trails were so treacherous, six men were needed for this work to safely navigate the icy, rocky paths.

Some of these evacuation routes (up to twelve miles) set records for longest carries in U.S. Army history. At one time, it required about 12 hours to hand carry a wounded man by litter back to where he could be placed in an ambulance. This became intolerable because so many of the wounded men would die during the hours-long evacuation. In these extreme circumstances, a plan was eventually established to have litter bearer *relay stations* so that at intervals, a fresh team could take over and not overwork any one group of men. At various times, not only were Italian soldiers used as litter bearers, but also the unit's men from the rear echelon including cooks, bandsmen, truck drivers, and clerks—essentially, any able-bodied and available man not in combat. Many of these men who served forward as litter bearers earned Purple Hearts, facing as much danger as anybody else. It was the Regimental Surgeon and his assistants who organized these relays and kept them functioning.

My father's good friend and former Medical Assistant, Lt./Maj. Morris J. "Les" Leslie, eventually became the 133rd's medical detachment Commanding Officer after Lud was transferred to the 168th Infantry as its Regimental Surgeon almost a year earlier in North Africa. In the snowy, treacherous mountains above Venafro, Italy, "Les" was instrumental in masterminding and coordinating the longest litter trail for the evacuation of the wounded in the history of the U.S. Army.

Embedded war correspondents, such as the *Des Moines Register*'s Gordon Gammack, and the more widely known Ernie Pyle and Bill Mauldin, lived with the men on the frontline. They did not write from some safe haven twenty miles behind the front. They did not share the comforts of heated tents, three hot meals per day, or special services and accommodations that high-level officers could command.

In his March 13, 1944, column, Gammack reported on the extreme challenges to evacuate the wounded. He tells how the Iowa men suffered the first two weeks of January in snowdrifts often four feet deep to forge a path through mountains 5,000 feet high to Cassino, and how 150 wounded were carried down treacherous, icy mountain trails where mules and human pack trains were the only transportation*:

> Engineers tried to build a jeep trail, but it wasn't possible. All rations, ammunition and water had to be hauled by mule. It became apparent that the wounded would have to be evacuated by litter. The regiment didn't have nearly enough litter bearers, so additional ones were drafted from units not in combat.
>
> The plan for removing the wounded was devised by Maj. Morris J. Leslie of Brooklyn, N.Y., regimental medical officer, and his administrative assistant, Second Lieutenant Roy L. Bates of Fairfield, Md.
>
> As the 168th regiment moved across the mountains of Italy, relay stations were established. Finally, there were twelve of them, each a mile apart. At each, a non-commissioned officer and 36 men were stationed. Each litter team consisted of six men. At every other station blood plasma, morphine and supplies for changing dressings were made available. The men lived at the stations in pup tents, and the temperature often was just a little above zero.
>
> It took from 12 to 20 hours to take a man the length of the trail. Most of the work had to be done at night when the Germans could not spot men moving on the trail and shell them.
>
> The battle casualty chart alone shows clearly that the most severe battles in Tunisia—Fondouk and Hill 609—were trivial affairs compared to the slaughter from San Vittore to Cassino.
>
> Iowa and Minnesota should be more proud than ever of their famed 34th, but THE PRIDE SHOULD BE REVERENT because many have died, many have been maimed, many have shrieked with pain, thousands have suffered from the biting cold of the Italian mountains.

Ironically, the extreme cold and wet weather conditions, combined with lack of sleep during weeks of continual fighting, contributed greatly to the

---

* "From footholds in the Sammucro heights they would have to cross several miles of mountain upland, over a maze of ridges held by the enemy. Supplies for this operation were carried by pack trains; by 11 January they were using nearly seven hundred mules." *Winter Line*, 97.

disease and poor health of the men. Sleep became a golden commodity no soldier could afford. Jaundice, fevers, pneumonia, trench foot, and weakened immune systems removed far more from combat units than did actual enemy action.*

Letters: January 3–14, 1944: Approach to Cassino

3 January 1944; Italy

[hills around San Vittore]

I can very well remember a year ago today. We had just arrived at the place where we were to spend the rest of the Winter, Spring, Summer, etc. [North Africa] We arrived in port about midnight on January 2 after having been rammed by another ship while still four hours out. The ship we were on was listing about 25 degrees, but limped in as fast as it could, to be close to land if she started to sink. Along about 3 a.m., she suddenly shifted from one side to the other. I can remember hitting the floor of my stateroom on the run, to try to make the deck before she turned over, but she didn't and we were towed into the inner harbor the next morning to disembark. It was amazing that not a single man was seriously hurt during the whole thing.

I can also remember, even more clearly, New Year's Eve two years ago. You know why. I can also always picture the events of the night before, when we received the telephone call from Camp. I certainly would have done things a little differently now, in view of my experience in the movements of troops in wartime, but I expect that I was as excited as the rest. I never will forget sitting in the Olds those last few moments with you, while the rain drizzled outside. I remember that I said, "I guess I can stand it" (being away from you), but it was a glib phrase on my lips. I guess I HAVE been able to stand it in some ways, but I little knew what the experience meant. I know that I loved you even more than I thought I could on that night and that your image will be engraved forever on my brain. You are Life to me; all of the hopes, longings, happy memories, and anticipations experienced by this lonesome man are tied up with you. You'd better take good care of yourself, because this guy is expecting to catch up on Life when he returns to you, and you'll just have to be around, that's all.

Yesterday I received your letter written on 12 December. That's pretty good mail service considering how far we are up in the mountains now. I liked the gifts that you picked out for all the family very much. It gives me a sort of warm feeling

---

* "At the front line, attention to basic hygiene is left undone; the main focus there is survival. A bar of soap, a comb, or toothbrush and toothpaste is excess baggage. Daily existence is reduced to the priorities of retaining only those essentials of a gun and ammo." (Ret.) Lt. Col. Homer R. Ankrum. *Dogfaces Who Smiled Through Tears: An Outstanding Chronicle of Heartbreaks, Hardships, Heroics, and Humor of the North African and Italian Campaigns* (Lake Mills, Iowa: Graphic Publishing Co., 1987), 87. [Hereafter cited as *Dogfaces*].

inside to think about them and to imagine that I were there to look them over when you showed them to me.

... I'm afraid that I might be a little exasperating to you by my inattentiveness at times, though, because I know that I would be looking from robe to brown hair, from scarf to a few freckles, from a sweater to very blue eyes. I know that in my awkward way that when I helped you wrap them up you'd have some tinsel in your hair and some fancy ribbons where they weren't meant to be. You are the only Christmas package I've ever wanted.

We had quite a little excitement here today, in fact this letter was interrupted near the bottom of page 1 and it's been three hours since I began first to write. We are all packed into this little valley in pretty close quarters and Jerry knows that, so he came over a few hours ago and gave us a few souvenirs. Remind me to tell you about it when I get home. Everything is settled down here now.

Before I forget, the Col. [Frederic B. Butler] is no longer with us—he's been transferred to Div. where he will soon become a Brigadier General. We have a new Col. who looks pretty good, but it'll be a long time before we ever see as good a commander as "Freddy" was. We also called him "Beebee Eyes" and other pet names. (TGWF—The Great White Father). He was a hard-boiled baby, a tough disciplinarian, but a square shooter and not afraid of anything. He'd do anything he could for his men as a group, but personal favors were out. It takes just such a man to hold together the thousands of personalities that make up a unit, especially after a long time overseas when nearly every man is feeling sorry for himself and occasionally loses his enthusiasm about going out and getting shot at time after time. Of course, the "Old Man" as we called him, will be around supervising our new Col. [Col. Mark Boatner] who was his classmate at West Point, so we'll still be in good hands.

Must close and get to bed. We are going to be very busy for a little while now.... I'm pretty sure I won't be able to write for a week or a little longer, so don't worry about a short pause in correspondence. Thinking of you, always.

14 January 1944; Italy

... We are right in the middle of a big deal over here; have been going at it hot and heavy now for about nine days with the end not yet in sight.* We are making good progress, however, so the headlines ought to begin to tell the story pretty soon. It takes this outfit to crack the "nuts" over here. The whole gang certainly knows their business and they go at it like veterans. There's never a dull moment

---

* Approach to Cassino, Jan. 6–15, 1944: "The 168th Regiment occupied hills north of Mount Chiaia and opened the way for the attack on the village of Cervaro, a typical assembly of stone houses set on the slope of steep hills. The 168th resumed the attack on Jan. 10 and eliminated the enemy from a number of hills just east of the town after close quarter grenade and bayonet fighting. For two days and nights, hand-to-hand fighting of the most fierce kind raged from street to street and house to house." *Breakthrough Bn*, 202–203.

as our business runs day and night. We've had the toughest deal on evacuation this time that we've ever encountered, with very long carries by stretcher to get the wounded out of the mountains and canyons. If there're any questions on mountain fighting that Headquarters would like to know about, just refer them to the 168th Infantry staff and they'll get an accurate and comprehensive answer in short order. One cannot help but smile a little when one remembers the big ballyhoo about "specialized mountain troops" that were or are being trained in the U.S. There is no teacher like the actual experience. I'd like to meet some of those "specialists."

    I received your Christmas boxes all O.K., and liked them very much, as I've already written you, but the shirts have not arrived as yet. It's just as well as I'm wearing the roughest outdoor clothes now and wouldn't put on a really good shirt. I haven't had a bath since I left the "rest camp" right after Christmas and I'm getting pretty rugged (ahem, I can tell). Last night, while we were coming back to the Hdq. from a trip up forward, we were crawling along a muddy trail in the dark in the jeep and approached one of the stone terraced walls that are numerous over here in the foothills. The road turned at this point, down a steep grade that had been knocked out of the terrace wall by the engineers, and the trail was a little too narrow, so our peep did a "barrel roll." No one was hurt. Three of us crawled out from under the overturned vehicle and with help rolled the buggy on over so that the fourth man could get out. We then started up the motor and continued on home. After I got home, I tripped over a branch on the ground and bruised my knee a little. I guess yesterday was the "13th" all right, but lucky for me. I expect I'm a cad for telling you these things, because you'll just worry your head off about it, but it's almost forgotten already over here, although I kid my driver a little about having propensities for a flying circus. My clothes and field belt, etc., were covered with about a quarter inch of thick brown mud when I finally got "home" last night, so you can see that "good clothes" are not appropriate at this time. I'll sure use those shirts some time, though, so I'm waiting for them. I asked for them because there are many "quiet times" in this life when baths and shined shoes are possible. We'll be getting a break again one of these days.

    The rotation quota for div. hdqs. allowed one major to be rotated home and he (although at that time the oldest and the senior major, both in point of rank and in overseas service) didn't make it: too indispensable. Today I learned via rumor that Major Karns of the 135th has been relieved, apparently not going home, just transferred back to the base section. He was regimental surgeon over there and a darned good man. It came as quite a surprise. That leaves me the senior reg't'l surgeon in the div. and also, as all along, the youngest. As I said, it's all rumor, and may not be entirely true. I can't imagine why he was transferred, but no doubt will learn one of these days.

    We ought to get a break sometime soon, because we've certainly done our share and more. Keep the home fires burning for me, because I love only you....

The Battle for Cassino: January 22–29, 1944

In September 1943, when the U.S. and Allies invaded southern Italy at Salerno, the Germans did not retreat north of the Alps as the Allies had expected. Instead, the Germans and Italians had constructed a series of military fortifications known as the Winter Line, comprised of a series of three heavily secured lines designed to defend the western section of Italy around Highway 6, the pathway to Rome. The town of Cassino sat at the foot of a cliff-like mountain, Monte Cassino, which overlooked Highway 6, and was a critical objective at this stage of the war. It was the final mountain barrier, guarding the entrance to the Liri Valley and the road to Rome. Whomever controlled the hills above Cassino, automatically controlled the town and valley.

The American Fifth Army's advance was very slow—less than a mile per day. The abysmal weather, rugged terrain, and entrenched German troops, all slowed down the 34th Infantry Division's progress.

And then, an almost impossible order came through, notes Sergeant Milo L. Green in his book, *Brickbats*:

> ... it was decided that the 34th [Infantry Division] would cross the Rapido River north of Cassino, attacking the hills overlooking the city and break through to Highway 6, isolating the city and the Abbey.
>
> They were already exhausted and understrength from the series of advances they had slowly been through. The Division attack began on January 24–25. The Germans had diverted the Rapido in front of Cassino, flooding the low land in front of the city, making use of American vehicles and tanks impossible [220–221].

Former infantryman, Fred Majdalany, recalls in his book *The Battle of Cassino:* "First the approach across the flooded valley, then the wading of the icy river, then the

Winter 1943/January–April 1944, Italy. Typical scene of the muddy conditions in Italy slowing down the progress of the 34th Infantry Division (2008.321.066, from the collection of the National World War II Museum).

pillboxes, dugouts, caves, and fortified houses along the lower slopes, and then—if they lived that long—they must fight their way up the mountains themselves and, wheeling left, bear down on Monte Cassino from the higher peaks around it: this was the task of the 34th Division" (92).

The months-long battle for Cassino and the monastery on the mountaintop (January–May 1944) was one of the largest and most intense battles fought during World War II. Neither side would yield.

It took a five-day drive for the 34th Infantry to reach the Rapido River's edge. On the other side was the city of Cassino that, in ordinary times, had a population of about twenty thousand. Behind the city was Monastery Hill, and on top of the mountain directly behind, was the Abbey. The rock-strewn mountain had steep slopes with little to no vegetation and was generally inaccessible. The monastery, sitting at the very top, was a huge fortress of stone with four-foot-thick exterior walls and about four city blocks square in size. It had been occupied by Benedictine monks for hundreds of years and would have been a perfect stronghold from which to observe the valley below and surrounding territory for many miles. There was also an underground network of tunnels and catacombs. Most of the Allied soldiers and those in command believed that Germans occupied the monastery.

American troops were unable to dig foxholes into the pure rock and granite of the 1,700-foot mountainside of Monte Cassino, leading up to the Abbey, so they piled rocks around themselves for protection. But when mortar and artillery fire landed, the rocky mountainside shattered, sending sharp fragments of metal and flint-hard rock in all directions and creating horrific shrapnel wounds, especially to the head and face. Many soldiers were blinded and disfigured. As a result, Field Surgical Units had to be supplemented by a specialized Forward Head Injury Unit, moving as far forward as possible, to deal solely with head and eye cases.

The war had bogged down on the banks of the Rapido River. The fortifications at Cassino were seemingly impenetrable. In his book, *Dogfaces Who Smiled Through Tears,* Howard R. Ankrum writes: "We are still at Cassino—the battle still rages. The 168th Regiment has had numerous casualties and must be withdrawn from the line to be reinforced with replacements. The 168th must be regrouped and rested—San Angelo [Sant'Angelo d'Alife], here we come!"

The troops had reached the limits of human endurance and on February 14, the 168th was finally relieved by elements of the British 4th Indian Division. Ankrum goes on to say:

> The spirit of the troops improved immensely as we loaded the vehicles and got on board for the trip to the rear echelon. No one shoots at you twenty miles behind the line. Seems you can sleep easier, breath normally, walk casually, stand up in full daylight and not have to be ready to duck. There is that element of fear at the front which causes a man to be keenly alert; coiled like a spring, ready to jump, fall or run. Fear of death or injury is a very healthy attribute—fear keeps you on your toes. One cannot be overcome with fear. Experienced infantrymen say that control comes when first your total attention is directed to the current circumstance. Next, you freeze in place long enough to assess the next logical step to take. Then, and only then, does action take over—control holds the upper hand [86].

The eventual, almost total destruction of the Abbey by Allied bombers on February 15, 1944, is still an open wound. There was much controversy and speculation about whether or not the Germans had occupied the Abbey and were using it as an observation point. Since then, exhaustive studies and analyses have revealed that the destruction of the Abbey was not necessary—that the Germans were not using the Abbey as an observation site; there was enough high ground surrounding the Abbey for this purpose. Germany's General Albert Kesselring held a high regard for the historical monument and did not want to jeopardize its ruin.

The bombing was finally conducted because many reports from the British commanders of the Indian troops on the ground suggested that Germans were occupying the monastery, and it was considered a key observational post by all those who were fighting in the field. However, during the bombing, no Germans were present in the Abbey. Subsequent investigations found that the only people killed in the monastery by the bombing were 230 Italian civilians seeking refuge there. Ironically, once the monastery was destroyed, it *was* occupied by the Germans who found excellent cover amongst the rubble for their heavy artillery and troops, more so than an intact structure would have offered.

The Battle of Monte Cassino, January–May 1944, was a costly series of four assaults by the Allies. There didn't seem to be an actual plan for the Allies in Italy other than to "Get Rome!" The Allies' 5th Army Rainbow Coalition of multicultural chains of command and forces from several countries (Britain, India, New Zealand) was not well coordinated—leadership and communications were poor, resulting in a stalemate, of sorts, with thousands of lives lost. In the mud, snow, and bitter cold, the killing went on. Some historians note that General Mark Clark's attempt to breach the Gustav Line was a bloodbath and suicide mission, with no strategic gain.

Letters: January 19–February 14, 1944

19 January 1944; Italy

[Approach to Cassino]

> ... We've had a comparatively quiet time for the last few days. We are still located right where we stopped [Cervaro?] which was considerably further than the brass hats at higher headquarters thought we would get during the allotted time. In fact, we beat the timetable by several days and against some pretty stiff opposition. They threw in some crack troops against us in an effort to stop the tide, but we brushed them aside and went on. Of course, the actual distances are small due to the rough terrain, but taking all into consideration, this outfit did itself proud in the last "go." It sure is a hell of a good fighting outfit. Some of the faint praise that we received during the early days in Afrique (and which was probably merited, as I wrote you) will be very much out of place now. These guys are tough, smart, and ambitious to go places. Things are looking up in Italy.
>
> I took my first bath today since 24 Dec. I decided to heck with the war, I was going to fix it so that I wouldn't have to use that clothespin on my nose at

night, so we got into the weapons carrier we have and drove about 5 or 6 miles back to where the showers are located. It was a shower unit belonging to an ordnance outfit. There were about 8 heads connected with a portable boiler so that the water was warm and "just right." They had put up a canvas fly around the showers and there was a duckboard to stand on under each showerhead. The tent for undressing was about 50 feet away. This made it a little inconvenient to walk through the mud barefooted back to the tent, but they had canvas buckets at the shower that you filled with water and took back into the tent with you to wash your feet. Boy, do I feel like a new man.

As I said, things are rather quiet here for us, but the boys over on our left are really having a time for themselves tonight. The hills are constantly flashing from their artillery, which has been pounding steadily for about two hours. The ripostes of the firing come so often that they merge into a continuous roar that rumbles back and forth between the mountains and across the valley. Guess they must be trying to catch up with us.

I passed Leslie on the road today. We were both in a line of vehicles on a fairly narrow road, so could not stop, but I yelled my congratulations to him. His majority came through finally last week. I know that pleased him very much. He's certainly earned it. I have to laugh when I think of all the antics we pulled back on Swamp Island together. He was the funniest roommate I've ever had, and I certainly enjoyed living with him. I can remember the time in the early Fall of '42, before I got my captaincy. I'd been filling the vacancy of a Capt. for 18 months and the future didn't look any too bright for him, [Leslie] either, because he was my assistant, so we decided we'd get out of the division. We armed ourselves with a portable typewriter and piled in the truck with plenty of paper and carbon paper and started out to work our way up through the various headquarters, getting approval as we went, on our requests for transfer.

We had quite a bout with Gittler, who was our first hurdle, and then went on to division where we really ran into a hornet's nest. They refused to approve our transfers so there was quite a to-do. The 5th Gen. Hosp. had said that they would accept me if I could get out of the division. That was the time when I cabled the Surgeon General in Washington and wrote a letter outside of channels to the Surgeon of the European Theater. I also sent it through channels, and division had just got wind of the deal. "Them" were the days!! I never could understand how I got my present job as I've been thrown out of more offices than anyone else I know of. I haven't had so much fun in a long time—maybe I could have some more if I'd just look around a little. As it is now, I keep G. [Gittler] in hot water quite a bit of the time. He is very patient with me, however. I certainly could give the boys in Washington an earful about the scrap over here and some of its medical aspects because I've learned that it's useless to be "subtle" or diplomatic when discussing a topic as realistic as war. War requires straight talking about the facts, without any cover-up and the sooner the public and their servants realize it, the better. In the long run, it will save lives.

It's now 10:20 p.m. and about my bedtime. The cannonading is still going strong and I just heard a machine-gun bark down in the valley. From the characteristic sound, I'm not at all certain that a Yank had pulled the trigger. We are parked behind a mountain on the right side of the valley, and noises travel for quite a distance. We are living in our pyramidal tent and are very comfortable without the pot-bellied stove set up. The weather has been much better this month than the two preceding it. It hasn't rained more than once or twice and the sun has been shining much of the time. This is a great blessing to the "G-I" who frequently must lie down in his foxhole to sleep and at best, has only his pup tent for shelter in quiet times.

22 January 1944; Italy

Things are still rather quiet for us since our little "push," that was so successful, it stopped a few days ago. The landing of Allied forces on the west coast of Italy, behind the German lines, was announced today. That was a smart piece of business, in my opinion and should help us a great deal here in Italy, although the boys up there won't have easy going for some time.

I haven't heard from Jack lately. Is he still in the same place? I certainly hope so.

I sure am lonesome for you, Jean. This war has dragged on interminably for me even though our days have frequently been very hectic. War is a terrible business, and in order to pursue it to a victorious finish, anyone with any responsibility must become a little calloused, a little thick skinned, a little hardboiled and possibly a little cynical. You'll have a big job on your hands, but I'm happy in the knowledge that you are the perfect one to lead me back into the paths of normalcy again.

I say that I may have grown a little calloused, thick-skinned, etc., and yet, I feel the same anguish when I see a wounded man that I felt when I saw the first one. It's just that one learns to go on with the job without batting an eye. I'm not complaining. Others have suffered and sacrificed far more than I have. I'm also very happy in my thoughts about the future—ours together.

I know that a great many men who are now overseas will be strangers when they return, and their secret need for understanding and companionship will go unheeded. No rough, tough fighting American is going to admit that need, but it'll be there just the same, and its frustration will come to the surface in a variety of action, reaction, and behavior. I'm going to need you very much when I get home.

4 February 1944; Italy

[168th in reserve/rest for a couple of days]

... This is the first letter written since the one dated 22 January, but it isn't because I haven't wanted to. We've been very, very busy for about 10 days now, busier than we've ever been before.* We are still busy, but tonight, I am back at the rear headquarters about two miles from the front and at least have a chance to get a letter off to you. For the past two days the regiment has been so split up that I have to stay back a little now for awhile in order to keep behind all three battalions.†

The last letter I read from you, I was standing in a partially ruined stone house serving as the second bn. aid station. There was quite a lot of artillery falling all around so I read your letter with an ear cocked to the "percussion" sound effects going on outside. I had gone to the aid station to see how things were going, from the forward C.P (command post) and met Lt. Spoo there who had come up from the rear C.P. (where I am tonight) bringing medical supplies and the mail.

I'm ashamed to admit that Christmas didn't mean as much to me over here as it should. Our days are so full that one day is about as bad or as good at the next. With so much misery and unhappiness visible on every side, one hardly realized it was Christmas, although, as I wrote you, I was in a sort of tinseled environment down at the leave camp on that day. In spite of the *comparative* gaiety, it certainly didn't seem like the way Christmas should seem. You'll have to watch me when I get home because I'll want to give everyone a full stocking, I'll be so thankful.

Am "sort of" surprised that neither Dirk or Smitty are home. I suppose I sound cynical, but it frequently seems to us up on the front that the boys back at the desk jobs in the bases get the breaks more often than we do. I do know that outfits, like ack-ack units, who live close to some big city and maybe get a slight workout once a week for a few hours at night, still send the same quota of officers home on rotation in fact, as also do the supply bases. I understand that some of them can hardly stand the strain of overseas service and "… why they've been overseas for a <u>whole year</u>," etc.—but don't let it throw you as it doesn't bother me. I'll keep on doing my job and be thankful for the Lord's protection. I think maybe I've learned not to envy the lot of others—I hope so, anyway, because it contributes somewhat to the serenity with which one faces life and the world.

In your last letter you quoted a rumor that had been going around about "not enough blood at Salerno," etc. It's all bosh, just misinterpretation of the facts, as many rumors are. This is the score: We have plenty of plasma, all we want, and

---

* "After a ferocious river crossing attempt on Jan. 27, 1944, tanks bogged down but the infantry forged ahead through minefields. Without tank support, the 168th men had to move back … In the higher elevations, the 168th made attempt after attempt, but was never able to drive the enemy from the hills." *History of IA Nat'l Guard,* 11.

† "… the line companies were weary. This time stretch had covered four weeks of intense fighting that had now become hand-to-hand combat in fighting over one building at a time. The buildings in Cassino were no longer buildings as such; they were piles of rubble four or five feet high. No territory was given up freely. Today we may hold a building and tomorrow the Germans may control it." *Breakthrough Battalion,* 81.

it's the best thing we could have for treating shock and hemorrhage in the field. They have large stores of it, thanks to the patriotism of the American people. However, it isn't quite as good as real fresh blood itself, of course. You understand, I know, that "plasma" when reconstituted by adding water, has no RBCs [red blood cells] in it—it's a pale clear amber color.

The beauty about plasma is that it can be stored and transported easily. It comes well packed in a strong carton containing a bottle of distilled water and another bottle of the dried plasma powder which are mixed together just before it is given. You can pack large amounts of the plasma in a truck or ship and handle it easily by hoist or ship hand, etc. Fresh blood, on the other hand, has to be refrigerated, etc., if it is stored, and then can only be stored for a couple of weeks. When a man is first wounded, let us say, in the abdomen, with perforation of the intestine, he comes into the aid station at the front in deep shock plus more or less hemorrhage. We give him two to eight units of plasma, as well as morphine, etc., to snap him out of the shock so that he can start the long

June 1944: American medics administering blood plasma in the field to a wounded soldier. (U.S. National Archives; U.S. Army Signal Corps Photo SC189916 [UNCLASSIFIED] photo #SC189916.)

rough ambulance ride back to a hospital. The plasma works well and has saved many lives.*

All along the way back to the hospital, at the collecting station and at the clearing station, they take a look at him and give him more if he needs it (one unit plasma is 250 cc). Now supposing after they have operated on him, probably the next day, and put in a Wangensteen [duodenal suction tube/pump], etc., he continues to do as well as any case of peritonitis may be expected to do.

After 10 days or two weeks he may still have the Wangensteen† down and unable to retain nourishment. His shock has been properly overcome in the early and critical stages of his illness by the plasma, but it didn't cure his anemia. He will get well faster if given a real blood transfusion at this point—so, some fast-thinking medical officer at some hospital got the idea of establishing donor lists amongst the soldiers near the hospital. With characteristic army thoroughness, the "call" for donors was sent to all units. I advised the Col. NOT to let any of our boys give blood because we are a combat outfit and it's silly to bleed a doughboy one day and maybe have to give him a transfusion if he is wounded the next.

However, it's different for the quartermaster, air force, and other personnel back at the bases whose lives are not in danger and who rarely get wounded. It is a good thing for them to give their blood for such cases as described above. I suppose some GI in this or some other outfit read the notice and breathlessly wrote home that they were so short of blood that the soldiers had to give it. The soldiers are given $10.00 a pint for their blood and it's entirely on a voluntary basis. None of our boys gave blood, although I know they would if called on in an emergency, but of course I put my foot down.

Several days ago, I received a "swell" Christmas package from your father. It contained a lot of different items: cigarettes, candy (butterscotch, oh boy), mints, cough drops, camphor ice, and among other things, a can of Pabst Blue Ribbon

---

* "Our main job continued to be to fight shock, which meant that we had to give plasma and control hemorrhage. Having done that, we improved the dressings that the aid men had put on when they first picked up the wounded. If an aid man and his patient were under heavy fire, the most important thing was to get the wounded man to a sheltered area. The aid men would place a dressing and try to control hemorrhage, but because they were anxious to get the wounded out of danger, their control of bleeding and their splinting were often inadequate. It was difficult to keep wounds clean. At the [aid] station, we would give morphine if it had not already been given. A red "M" on the soldier's forehead meant that he had been given morphine. If heavy fire prevented an aid man from writing this message, he would just stick the empty morphine syrette to the soldier's clothing." John A. Kerner, M.D. *Combat Medic: World War II* (New York: J. Boylston & Company, 2002), 81.

† Wangensteen Suction is an elegantly simple siphon used to relieve gastric and intestinal distention caused by the retention of fluid. This device maintains constant negative pressure without the use of electricity. It was first created by Owen Harding Wangensteen (1898–1981), the Chief of Surgery at the University of Minnesota. His novel approach to the most significant cause of death during gastrointestinal surgery was a breakthrough discovery in the 1930s that reduced operative mortality from 44% to less than 20%. Its use has since been credited with saving millions of lives, especially in the treatment of wounded soldiers in the field. *Wikipedia*: https://en.wikipedia.org/wiki/Wangensteen_suction

beer! I'm the envy of the whole outfit in regard to the beer. I'm still looking at the can every once in a while, and on some special occasion we'll open it and have a party. We haven't had beer since the early days of Swamp Island, and it'll sure be good. I could auction it off for $100 in war bonds, I'm sure, but I think I'll be a little unpatriotic and quaff it when I'm thirsty. Of course, about 10 other guys will have to have a taste also, but I don't mind.

This war can't last forever. Surely we're "over the hump" now. Maybe there'll be some way for me to get home before it's over.

I have plenty of vitamin capsules, etc. Mead Johnson sent me a bunch of samples. What I really need is some "Vitamin X," and I can tell that you need some too.

10 February 1944; Italy

[Cassino]

Hey! Over there, remember me? How about some letters? The mail has been trickling in fairly steadily during the last week or so, but there have been no letters from you—wondering if you are down with the flu or something worse. I keep telling myself that "tomorrow" I'll get a batch of letters from you, but they haven't showed up. Altogether, I received only five letters from you in January and, of course, none yet in February. I sure do hope nothing is wrong.

I received a nice letter from Jack on 7 Feb. It was written in Italy on the 30th of January. I suppose you know by now that he is in Italy. Of course, he couldn't tell me the location of his unit, but just as soon as this deal is over, I'll get on the road to find him. He said he was well and in good spirits, had received a Christmas package from your father, containing a can of beer (as did mine) which he enjoyed very much.

… This little deal that we're on now has been the roughest, toughest and longest one we've been in yet, and it's still not finished.* The boys are pretty tired; in fact, that's putting it mildly, and tonight there is a cold rain in the mountains. I am set up in the dry basement of a small mansion and have a wood stove constructed out of old oil drums, so that compared to the "dough-foot," I'm living in a palace. Believe me, it's no fun to crouch in a wet foxhole up on the hill tonight.

The outfit has done a whale of a fine job this time. In fact, much of what you are reading about the fighting on the southern Fifth Army front concerns us. Of course, I can't explain much, but we did something that the Jerries and quite a few of our brass hats didn't think we could do. In fact, when you look at all the engineering installations, including cast steel machine gun pill boxes that we

---

* "The months long battle for Cassino and the monastery on the mountaintop has been described as the fiercest military conflict in all of recorded history. On the night of February 7 and the morning of the eighth, a blizzard struck, depositing six inches of new snow atop the landscape. The entire Fifth Army is bogged down. The allied high command continues to order frontal assaults and our casualties mount daily." *Breakthrough Bn*, 82.

"galloped" over, one can scarcely believe that we got through as quickly as we did. Of course, the Russians have been doing this sort of thing for some time, but it's a little new to us yet and I imagine that when the press is allowed to open up, that the old 34th will get quite a spread. In one way, that works against our coming home, which is the thing that burns us up. We do a "better" job, and as a result, a lot of our pleas about being "stale," "homesick," and "washed up" are looked at with a smile by the higher-ups.

The job isn't completed yet, just part of it. The Jerry always has things fixed in depth and with lateral protection so that if one part of his line leaks, the next section can still hold fast. We did so well on our section that we are now working on another one—some system!!!

I am very homesick. I've wondered if maybe you are beginning to think that I like it over here and that I might be content just to let things ride. Don't ever let that thought get into your head, because each day for the past two years has been a lonesome and unhappy one for me. I certainly HATE war, in all its ramifications, and I'm here on the ground—I know. The only thing that keeps me from griping more than I do is the fact that there are thousands in the same situation that I'm in. While it's true that a few (much less than the schedule originally called for) men have been rotated home, the actual percentage is very low, about one percent in all, whereas the original idea was to send one percent every so often. Somewhere along the line the idea has been choked off by the higher ups and there isn't anything we can do about it except gripe.

Of course, the original plan made good newspaper copy. It's the same old system, like my promotion. Their intentions are good, but the consummation is ridiculous. All I hope and pray is that I can return home safe and sound to you, as soon as possible, and that I'll find you waiting for me. I've seen some of the others develop "psychoneuroses" or other more organic ailments and get home, but somehow, I can't bring myself to even consider such a thing, because if any moderate percentage of the guys over here did that, we might as well quit right now. Secretly, I know, down deep inside, that I should be and *am* very thankful that I haven't had to make the sacrifices that so many have already made. When you walk along a trail and see the sightless eyes of a dough-foot staring at the sky you realize that you're darned lucky to be alive and unhurt, and that you really haven't given so much after all, as hard as it has seemed just to be away from the ones that mean the most in life to you.

I don't know when I'll get on the list for rotation. Law's name was put on the list in Sept. and my name isn't even on the list yet. It gets pretty discouraging at times. You see, every "so often" they tell us that we can submit the name of an officer of certain rank and the names of so many enlisted men of certain rating. So far, they've never asked for an officer of my rank, the higher the rank the fewer the officers rotated. There aren't very many officers of my rank in the regiment right now (censorship prevents my mentioning how many), but the other Majors are all older than I am, and I think all of them have children, at least some of them do, so they'll probably look at my name and say, well he's young and energetic and besides we need him where he is, etc., although I've been overseas a few months longer than either of the others.

We've noticed that they don't like to rotate men who are difficult to replace, and of course that makes medical officers head the list. I've been very careful to groom my assistant to take over my job, and have taken pains to let the old C.O. see that Capt. Drye is a very competent man who could ably fill my shoes; but now we have a new C.O., so I'll have to begin my subtle campaign all over again. The catch, of course, for the medical officers, is that it would be difficult to replace Drye in his job. That burns us a little, too. I guess the American medical profession is just as patriotic as anyone else, but there is certainly a paucity of doctors who are clamoring for field service. See if you can't get some volunteers over there to come over to take my place up front in the mud.

14 February 1944; Italy

... Of all the reporters writing for the public about war, Ernie Pyle is the most accurate and has the most courage and skill in portraying the true state of affairs. I'm glad that you read his column.

Must close. It's a cold day and I'm set up in the basement of a large farmhouse. The only source of light is a window that must be left open and my fingers are getting a little stiff from the cold. It's beautiful outside today. As I stood on a terrace behind the house, beside a green orange tree, I could see for miles across the valley in the sunshine. The mountains in the distance are all snowcapped—very beautiful in their quiet majesty, but hell to fight in.

* * *

On Feb 15, 1944, the 168th Infantry Regiment was finally pulled off the frontlines of Cassino where their progress had been stalled and their objectives unmet. They were exhausted, badly battered, and essentially, unfit to fight. They retreated back to the desolate, small Italian mountain village of Sant'Angelo d'Alife, where they had been in December 1943 and January 1944. Lud's medical detachment returned to and occupied the same farmhouse, owned by the two elderly sisters, who warmly welcomed them back. This ten to twelve days of much needed rest and respite, allowed the soldiers to resume a rigorous training schedule to prepare for their next call to action.

Letters: February 17–March 16, 1944

17 February 1944; Italy

[Sant'Angelo d'Alife]

... We are now located back in the little foothill town where we lived when I wrote you letters 99 to 102 inclusive. We are living and using the same buildings that we had then and the Italian people seem overjoyed to see us back. Of course, the Italians are a demonstrative race, but when we left the little building where I had my office about 6 weeks ago, the two little old women who lived upstairs and in the back room downstairs and who had become fast friends with the boys, cried a little because we were going off to war. Their niece, the rather buxom young girl of 16 or so, who became shyly attracted to one of my clerks, wrote several letters to him after we had gone and invited us all back, day or night. We took advantage of the situation in that we arrived back in town about 2:00 a.m. on a clear, cold, moonlit night, and the boys moved right in and didn't have to sit out in the trucks until morning. Our ride to this place was about 34 miles and rather breezy. I got a little frostbite (trench foot?) on both feet which gave me some trouble last night, but they are much better this morning so I guess I can't go to the hospital (ahem).

It is quiet and peaceful back here in this little village. We use our headlights when driving at night—it certainly seems strange after weeks of creeping along rocky trails in the pitch dark. Our food is good again and we are having movies almost every night, and yesterday a vaudeville show, none of which I've attended as yet. We certainly need and deserve the rest, and things are rather "wonderful" here, with a roof over one's head, and yet, I don't believe I've ever been as depressed and homesick as I am right now.

We all frequently get a little depressed over here when we start thinking about the future, because the future, except for the very few lucky ones, is always the same ... an occasional rest and respite, and then intensive reorganization, replacement, and training of replacements to go back and do the same thing all over again. I've always managed to keep myself among the most cheerful of the outfit, but this time even I am pretty low, because of the restricted outlook that faces all of us. I've had many men tell me that there were only three things to look forward to in this outfit, and one of them, the happiest, was the end of the war, the other two alternatives being the two unpleasant eventualities of which my office compiles the statistics.

The above paragraph is certainly not inspiring, and is childishly plaintive in its note. I don't want to worry you, or to add to your lonesomeness or depression. I'll survive, all right, and I guess the dreary memories will fade soon after we return home, but I can't help but let you know occasionally how terribly lonesome and homesick we get, although we know that we have a job to do and will do it in spite of our feelings in the matter. It does sometimes seem strange, though, that after over two years of war, such a small number of Americans are still carrying the ball for Uncle Sam, and by that, I mean frontline combat service and not sitting back at the port at a desk job or working in a warehouse as thousands are doing.

If I were the drinking type, I'm afraid I'd throw a week-long bender right at this time, but even that still seems pretty futile to me. I'd be all O.K. in about 30 seconds if I could just get to see you. I'm going to talk to the Colonel about a 30 day leave to come home, but of course they aren't granting any leaves at all and it will take quite a lot of explosion to attract much attention and that will all be unfavorable. However, I'm even beyond the stage that I was in on Swamp Island, with lonesomeness and no promotion, so I think maybe the fireworks will start pretty soon. We can expect to be in a quiet period now for a few weeks or so—and, of course, one cannot pull histrionics while in battle.

I haven't had a chance to see Jack yet. My jeep is in the shop for a few days for needed repairs. However, I think I'll accompany two officers I am evacuating to the hospital tomorrow, take them in their jeep and use it to come home in and maybe run around a little. I have a chestnut to pull out of the fire for the Colonel with regard to one of the officers, that's the reason I'll go along—just leave it to Ludwick, he'll fix things painlessly for all concerned. This officer is an old timer, has given years of faithful service, although still young, but is now considered excess by the C.O. [Commanding Officer] because he can only handle certain jobs which are filled and the Col. doesn't want him hurt because of his good record, etc. In other words, he's sort of "burnt out" and being on the inside in such matters, I am the guy that does the dirty work.

My job is certainly varied enough; from carrying wounded occasionally off the field during action, organizing mule trains for medical supplies, confidant and psychiatrist for the boys that have gone through hell and have momentarily cracked, sanitary inspector and hard boiled SOB who makes the boys keep decent and healthy in spite of their lowered incentive to do so, to "inside man" for the higher-ups when they get "stalled"—and then, occasionally, I practice medicine on the side.

20 February 1944; Italy

... Now that we are situated in a rest area, our mail is coming through pretty well again, but I still haven't received any letters from you since the three that arrived on 14 February. They are the only three that I've received during the month of February and I am very much worried for fear that something has happened to you that prevents your writing.

I keep telling myself that it's just a coincidence, that a lot of your letters are held up somewhere and will come through all at once, but I don't always convince myself.

I get boiling mad, sometimes, at the way the army runs things. Here we've been at war over two years, and we're still in the shoestring class over here. I can't speak my mind on account of censorship, and that's the rub. Back in the early days of the African affair, one was not surprised that we had to take chances and undergo rough times because we were only the early "few" and had to spread ourselves thin over "big" jobs. I wonder if things are much different now? Surely they ought to be able to send some of us home and give some other "patriot" a chance to do his bit, but the "few" are still on the job, though many are still sitting at home, as far as I know, and the brass hats just scream when someone makes any move to ask for rotation or leave. You'd think that there were only a few divisions in the army and that if we weren't here that the world would collapse.

I wish someone in Washington would wake up to the fact that there's a war on, with men getting killed and maimed, with equipment being used and destroyed, and that it's likely to go on for some time. We might as well organize ourselves to take it in our stride, which means to me that there should be a well-organized system of leaves, furloughs, and transfer so that our experience could be divided amongst the others and so that our mental equilibrium could be kept at a maximum efficiency. Some of these birds seem to think that we've all just got to hold out a little longer and then it will all be over (isn't it wonderful) and we can ALL go home. To my mind, this is very short sighted. It would be much smarter to plan on a long war over here, and manage the personnel with that in view. In addition to that, it wouldn't be a bad idea to start thinking about the next war, also. It looks to me as though someone is trying to cure a bad case of tuberculosis in ten people by putting two of them to bed for five days. I'll sure be glad when we can get down to brass tacks.

The officers at Regimental Headquarters had a dance last night. I squired four nurses from a nearby evacuation hospital, and a Red Cross "gal" from the 5th Army Headquarters. I enjoyed the party very much. As usual, some of the boys got slightly inebriated, and I laughed pretty hard at their and our antics. Actually, they don't get as drunk as they pretend to be, and everything was under control. One of the officers, Maj. Kermit Hansen, from Omaha, has an excellent voice, has done some radio work with Ray Noble's orchestra and in addition, is a swell fellow and much more intelligent than one would expect a man with that history to be. We had quite a song session for a little while during the party, with some of the more liquid members of the party supplying the volume and the "hotcha" embellishments to the ending of the numbers. What a gang. We've been through a lot together, and they are a swell bunch of soldiers, but it's only a flimsy excuse to pass the time until we can get out of this mess and home where we all want to be.

We have a new puppy at the Officers' Mess. He's only about two weeks old. Capt. Thompson picked him up on the front lines and brought him back with us. About 12 of us officers are sleeping in a large room in the mayor's house and one night not long ago we were about ready to "purge" Thompson and his dog because the lonesome pooch "hollered" all evening. Finally, someone got up, picked up the pup, and threw him into bed, under the covers, with Thompson, who was blissfully sleeping through it all. There was quiet for the rest of the night. The pup got a good deal of feminine attention at the party last night. I think the pup is going to be called "Sad Sack," after the woebegone "GI" in the cartoons of that name. We aren't sure just what his ancestry is, but his face looks something like a St. Bernard right now. There is no keg of brandy around his neck, though.

Col. Gittler called on me this morning, called me out of church to tell me about some plans for the future. It seems that I'm going to lose some of my officers because they are cutting down on the number of M.O.s in an infantry regiment. They are also going to cut down in other ways. It's useless, I guess, to try to tell someone in Washington that you have to have MORE men than normal requirements to fight and carry supplies and wounded in and out of steep and rough mountainous country. In many situations that we've been in recently, it's required two to four men to do what one man could do on level ground. We won't need to worry about the higher-ups learning what the score is, they will, but what burns us a little is the cost that will have to be put up by the "GI" before they do.

I haven't seen Jack yet, but should be able to look him up this week. I don't know where he is located, so don't know whether I can find him in one day or not.

22 February 1944; Italy

... Last night we had a very distinguished (ahem) visitor for dinner at the Officers' Mess. She was and is Martha Gellhorn who is also Mrs. Ernest Hemingway. I don't know what she is doing over here, possibly getting "atmospheah" for a new novel, but she was running around talking to all the soldiers about the "exthperiences" in this teddible war. She is somewhat of a character, I guess, but we really (or rather, the rest of the boys at the mess) set her back on her heels. This gal is a fairly well-preserved blonde, she must be in her middle thirties, but has very long eyelashes and looks somewhat young (???). She had a "G-I" knit cap perched on her head "a la chic," and a very affected manner. She speaks English with all the broad "A's," etc., and she was really a riot for us. Major Burt Barr, from Oregon, who is one of our youngest staff members and who pretends that culture is the thing he most lacks, the Colonel, and Hank Hansen tore into the poor girl before she even got settled. I sat right across from her and the first thing the Col. said was: "This is Major Ludwick, he's a psychiatrist, you'd better be careful or he'll have you all analyzed." Well, I didn't say much during the conversation, but I could hardly restrain my mirth at the show the boys put on. The main topic of the evening was American women and the gal was gasping for breath after the first round. Everyone complained about the lack of beauty that was present in the American women over here, including the peroxide glamour girls that dance in some of the leg shows. This surprised her no end, because we've had some muchly advertised film stars, etc., at times over here. We all solemnly assured her that the Italian girl, although possibly somewhat dusty from taking only one bath in four months, was much more graceful in her carriage as she walked stately down the train with a keg of wine on her head. Poor Martha didn't know whether to believe us or not, and several times shook her head helplessly at our warped and benighted souls. Barr told her very solemnly that the 34th Div. was the great society of the "Unwashed." In the Feb. 7th edition of "Time," there is a review of Martha's newest novel, "Liana." Somehow, I feel that the review was most adroit, although I've never had the pleasure of scanning the book ... such is the life of a dough-foot. We tried to get her to stay all night with us, but she declined, not too firmly. She thought we were all horrid.

The above little interlude was most enjoyable to us, but it doesn't begin to lift us out of the slough of despondency that we're in due to our lonesomeness. We have a good time frequently for a short while, but it's always overshadowed by the fact that we are so far away from the good old U.S.A. and those that we love. Maybe that's the reason we sometimes are a little hardboiled with our visitors, although actually, we aren't as tough as we sound, which they probably recognize. I sure do wish *you* could walk in to dinner at the mess some night. You'd have all the boys hanging on the ropes in a few minutes instead of the opposite case that occurred last night. I couldn't help but compare her with you, and Miss Gellhorn was choked with dust at the starting line.

Our days are pretty "dull" right now. This is the first time that we've sat and done nothing for a long time. It won't last for long, of course, but always before when we were told that we were resting, we were actually putting in very full days training, with many classes and demonstrations. I ramble around this little town without much to do and I'll "sorta" be glad when the old routine begins again, as much as I dislike it. Sometimes I can't figure out how they're running this war. With what we know about how things are going over here, both on the southern front and at the beach head, it certainly looks messed up at times. Wish I could be more explicit, but I can't defy the censor too often. It seems to me that they need a few "savvy" boys somewhere along the line.

One of my men, the clown of the outfit, Corp. Voorhees from Des Moines, just walked into the front room of the house that we use as an office. The back room is occupied by the two gentle little old ladies who own the place. They are about 60 years old and look upon all of us as their "boys." Well, tonight they've cooked up quite a feed for us; it's some sort of a festival today for them, and Voorhees just said that we are all in the doghouse because he didn't provide any bread and because we didn't know what it was all about. When we were here in December, my orderly, Sam XXXXX, spoke Italian fluently and, of course, acted as interpreter, but Sammy got hit by artillery shell fragments about two weeks ago and is in the hospital with a broken leg (doing nicely) and so we have to use sign language and our very limited vocabulary to get along. The old dears jabber Italian at us right and left even though we tell them we don't understand.

23 February 1944; Italy

Dearest Jean,

It's raining again this afternoon, after a week of good weather, but it's a great day for me because I received your airmail letter written the night of 17 January, as well as two (count 'em!) Valentines, both mailed on 29 January. Hooray for everything! Right now I feel pretty good, but I'll begin to slip again in another day unless I get some more letters from you tomorrow. You'd think that after the months and years of our separation that the importance of your letters might gradually fade into the distance as this busy life of combat goes on about me, but Uh-uh, kid, it does just the opposite. I'm getting so that I need a letter every day, although I know that such is not possible if you do your job properly.

I hope this doesn't offend the censor. The paragraphs below may contain general statements that are not known to anyone who has never fought in battles, yet are common knowledge to anyone that has had anything to do with armies, either now or in years, centuries, and ages past. Human nature is the same today as it was in the days of the Medes and the Persians [two ancient Iranian peoples], the Greeks and the Romans, Napoleon, and other warrior tribes and leaders. In effect, my statements will contain nothing new and in fact contain truths that I believe the public will ultimately become acquainted with, and should become acquainted with, if we, as a democracy are going to win the war. I don't want you to talk about what I'm writing, however, as coming from an individual source, the unenlightened mass of people at home who vaguely imagine what combat is like will not understand it, nor possibly appreciate it. As a physician, I believe that I know whereof I speak because I was somewhat acquainted with, before the war began, the mechanisms by which the normal and abnormal human mind habitually act. Maybe I'm not as smart as I think I am, but that remains to be seen.

In the first place, the universal emotion experienced by all soldiers in real combat, unless they are mentally deficient, is fear. All notions of "glamour," "hate," "adventure," "thrill," etc., are rudely crowded out of a soldier's consciousness within a few minutes after he has first engaged in combat. He knows and realizes that the monster and deadly machines of modern war such as the artillery shell, the mine, the machine gun, the air bomb, are terrifying dragons with which he cannot himself manually cope. In other words, no matter how strong his biceps are, no matter how he can throw out his chest and shout "carry on," he cannot in the slightest influence the course of this artillery shell which might be coming directly for his foxhole and crush off his head … he has no shield with which to ward off the blow. It's just God's will, or some call it "luck," that determines whether he survives or not. He can do a few legitimate things about preserving himself, such as digging a better fox-hole, or creeping along a stone wall in the shadow instead of the light, but these are useless when the enemy is shelling an "area" for instance, with no particular individual in mind as a target, or with no actual observation of his person.

The soldier reacts to this situation in several ways, according to his mental makeup. There are a few really brave heroes who apparently are able to truly discard thoughts about their own safety and charge like a bull toward the dragon, but I seriously doubt that many apparent acts of heroism are accomplished without fear being present. The great majority of men, by dint of emotional control carefully instilled by mass suggestion (discipline), make a creditable showing in the face of grave danger. There are many, though, that do not. This fact is what the newspapers never publish. Before a battle, the sick calls are frequently large—men desperately hoping, in some cases, that they are too sick to be asked to die for their country. In every battle there are those soldiers who "disappear," can't find them anywhere, but show up again after the battle is over. There are those men who "crack-up" emotionally in battle, come right out and admit that they can't take it anymore, don't want to fight, and "what are you going to do about it?" Not infrequently, men change from one group to another. A soldier who has been able to make the grade for six or eight months, say, will begin to realize that he will be required to keep on running the gauntlet of percentages until he is (1) wounded, (2) killed, (3) captured, or (4) the war is over. As he looks back at what has happened to the bunch that started in with him, his outlook is not enthusiastic, to say the least. I've had men (medics, my own boys) tell me that they couldn't "go up there" anymore, because they'd just keep having to go up there until they died. Let me repeat that all this is nothing new as far as the history of the world is concerned. It has been present in all armies, as long as they have been made up of men.

Real military leadership, then, entails among other things, the keeping of large numbers of men at a gravely dangerous job which they (the men) intensely despise and genuinely fear. This is accomplished in a number of ways: by discipline (fear of court-martial, etc.), by appeal to pride in himself and the "fighting outfit" (wave flags here) he belongs to, by fear of the national consequences if we fail to be victorious, and others. Not all of these approaches will touch each man. Some have no fear of court-martial, would rather spend twenty years in a good safe prison (so they feel now) than risk further combat. Some are very humble and have no pride in themselves. Some think the outfit is punk and that the leaders are numbskulls, because to them, it's a "mistake" when they see only one of their buddies killed. Some are not convinced that things would be too bad if we all just went home, not realizing that in ten years Hitler could out build the British fleet, have 20,000 cross-Atlantic bombers, etc.

When the bravery (?) of the Russian soldier is held up to them, some say: "Yes, but he is fighting for his home," not realizing how lucky he is (the American) to have the same chance with his home and women folk and children safe. Another thing that enters in, is the soldiers' intelligence, literacy, and real belief in all the benefits of democracy. He sees the thousands of soldiers back at the bases who scarcely even know a war is on. He says to himself: "I've done my share, why can't those guys do some of this, too? I'd be glad to trade with them," but the trade never occurs. Also, he reads about all the things that are going on at home amongst the soldiers, how civilians are making the "terrible" sacrifices of giving up Pullman berths so soldiers can actually go on leave and see the home folks (Is there really such a thing?) and he sees the flag waving about Sgt. So-and-So who has moved to Seattle with his wife (How cruel!!!).

He reads the magazine advertisements about how the American soldier is the best equipped and fed soldier in the world (which he actually is), not realizing that in wars past, soldiers actually starved to death, or had to forage their own food, while today he is reasonably sure of one or two meals a day in combat. What he remembers as "good food" is steak and fried potatoes and that's what he thinks the soldiers at home are getting when the packing house advertisement pictures a luscious tray of food instead of the cold, nauseating, and greasy hash that he must eat in actual combat. (Meals in rest areas are pretty good, now, although they too were lousy in spite of all the ballyhoo, back in the early days on the other continent.)

Fortunately, our armies, and many units within those armies, are commanded by strong men who know their stuff, from a human standpoint. This is particularly true of West Pointers, who have made a profession of studying war and all its ramifications, who are drilled about just such things as I have been talking about. They are professional soldiers and have been taught from the first WHY discipline and leadership is necessary in order to hold together a mass of men under the conditions I have described. I once heard Gen. Bradley quoted as saying that it wasn't easy for a general to sleep when he was forced to order his men into combat (and many to their death), but that on the other hand, he had been building up a frame of mind to stand such tension by over thirty years of constant effort. I certainly take my hat off to the West Pointers.

They have been consciously and persistently trained to meet this very situation and they are doing a swell job. Many other officers, in fact most of them, have caught on to their philosophy, although each amateur must go through a certain period of battle seasoning before it dawns on him what these boys are driving at. Some of the newer and younger officers react much as the ordinary soldier does at first, and, of course, a few never get over it. With all the "Philosophy," though, there is still present that primitive emotion of fear, because they are human like all of us, and to say that you embrace that philosophy, is certainly not to free oneself from fear of his life.

Let us now turn to the attitude of the leaders, these men who are doing a job the magnitude of which few "laymen" ever BEGIN to realize. Although, these leaders (the Bn. & Regimental commanders, division commanders, etc.) are just as afraid for their own lives as the lowest buck private. They put on an attitude of just itching to get their hands on the enemy, of just wanting to get into battle, and of just being astounded that anyone would want to quit and go home at this stage of the game. However, I know that they, privately, are just as homesick as "G-I Joe" and long for the comfortable days of peace on a nice army post instead of the cold and mud—but you'll never get any of them to admit to it. They've given their lives to the profession of fighting and it would be like a doctor refusing to deliver a baby because he thought it wasn't a clean job, (and let the mother go hang), for them to break down and ASK to be relieved or to go home.

I'm firmly convinced that this attitude on the part of the leaders: this "enthusiasm" for the very thing that is distasteful and fearful to them, is the only one to take. It's contagious, and it's brave, and it's damned patriotic. After all, what kind of an army would we have if the leaders shrank back from combat and began to weaken about going home now or ever? It's the only attitude that I know of that will keep men plugging away at this horrible business in which we are now engaged. I think their wives understand this, although I know that they go through all the hells there are on this earth, just waiting for them.

I'm very proud of these guys whom I've seen in some pretty tough spots, and I mean TOUGH (I, myself, was just scared to death—and, incidentally, they were, too) and yet they clamor (in a quiet way) for more. These men are the real heroes of this war. You understand that I'm not eulogizing the West Pointers as a class alone, I'm eulogizing any leader, corporal or general, who takes the bit in his teeth, realizes the great problem that we have with human nature, and reacts as an aggressive leader. In other words, if you expect ANY men to stay and fight, there must be an example-setter to lead them on, and its American Army tradition to keep coming, in spite of hell and high water. The Germans are pretty good at this sort of thing, too.

I must confess that I am on this attitude as external armor, and it hasn't come quickly, or merely by argument, or easily. I've never talked with any of these leaders about this to any extent. It's my own opinion, forged through the crucible of experience (I know I sound H.A. [hard-assed?], but to reel off the stimuli that my brain has absorbed to arrive at this philosophy would take a book), and I realize that few can understand it who have not been though the mill themselves and have seen how men actually behave in battle.

For instance, the history books teach the public that we won the war of 1812 and let it go at that. They don't mention the details of military history. To them, all American Armies have been composed of "golden heroes." They don't know that in the battle before Washington, in 1812, that 18,000 Americans were put to route, ran, after suffering only SIX casualties at the hands of 3,000 regular British soldiers, and then the British walked in and burned and sacked (and here even my source of facts stops short) our Capitol. I wonder what happened to the women in this conquered city, back in 1812? Of course, we rallied, and circumstances changed, and we "won" the war because actually, Britain was greatly occupied elsewhere. They ought to put those things in the movies a few times. That's why I lambast Hollywood, because it gives our kids a distorted picture of ourselves.

Without patting myself too much on the back, I think that I've been one of the spark plugs in this outfit, to keep it fighting. I've leaned over backward to give every "G-I" a square deal from a medical standpoint, but I've been steadfastly hardboiled toward the fellow who is following the perfectly understandable human trait of wishing to hell that he could get out of here. I've prayed about this, that I might have the RIGHT judgment in handling the lives of men, and their destinies, and I've had to pray, because without "Outside" help, I couldn't take the responsibilities that I have.

And yet, I'm so darned homesick and lonesome for you, I hate all this suffering and killing, I want to come home to you NOW so much that sometimes I can hardly stand it. Maybe I've really done my share by now, who knows, but can I face myself when and if I see return? I think I'm about at the stage where I might face myself, with perfect equanimity, and say that I have done all right, with God's help, so far.

26 February 1944; Italy

In my last letter, I tried to show you something of the attitude held over here by the ones who will be the ones to win this war for us. I have been keenly observant (I think) of their attitude and have emulated their mental attitude toward overseas service partly through personal admiration, and partly through realization of my own responsibilities as an American … but I wonder, sometimes, if I haven't been carried away a little by my "hyper-scrupulous" conscience, if I have one. At any rate, I need very much your advice on the subject, for a very important reason.

In other words, I have felt recently, that maybe I have actually done my share or more, toward pushing the effort along; especially since I did not choose "arms" as my profession. This is a rather delicate subject to present properly.

The whole problem is this: I'm sure that I can get home, fairly soon, if I make a big enough "stink" about it, even get out of the service entirely. I have a true idiosyncrasy to quinine; and I actually have auricular paroxysmal tachycardia. This latter condition as you know, I've had ever since I can remember, and it hasn't really interfered in any way with the physical aspects of my life—and yet, it is cause for rejection from the armed forces, if I want to press it. The sensitivity to quinine could be played strongly for a transfer to at least a "non-malarial" theater, which might end up with my being transferred to England or home.

I've always thought, secretly, that Uncle Sam always takes care of his soldiers, that is, that within limits which are sometimes rather harsh, that we are all treated alike. And so we are, on general principles, but the army is so large and unwieldy at times, that there is many a slip b'twixt the ideal and reality. For instance, on this rotation deal: Any student of military history and operations know that there is a steady "leak-back" to the states of those who are wounded or who are sick. This is expected and planned for and, incidentally, when the whole force over here is considered, it's quite a large number. The average person doesn't realize this. The average person, including many "G-Is," wonders why 20% or so per year can't be rotated back to the states. To his way of thinking, that means that the armies over here would only have to be replaced in toto every 5 years. Actually, however, when you consider the large stream of wounded and sick that would go back also, the forces over here would have to be entirely replaced much sooner. I'm not quoting any figures, Mr. Censor, the entire statement is hypothetical.

It is because of the facts in the above paragraph that the actual rotation of healthy and normal men is so low and will always be low. It's a big enough job just to replace those overage, sick, wounded, and dead, etc.

Now we come to you, Jean. I've always thought that you certainly got a rotten deal when we were married. It wasn't my doing, this going off and leaving you the way it happened, but nevertheless, you've had a rough time of it alone right in the time of life when you should be the happiest. I think I'm fairly "tough" mentally, so that while I suffered a great deal from being away from you, and knew that you suffered also, I thought that we could stand it "for awhile," by "awhile" being longer, I think, than the average person thinks is reasonable.

Well, I believe that "awhile" has come and gone, probably. I can stand further punishment over here all right, principally because there's nothing else for me to do and also because I can still "take it," but how about YOU, darling? When I get to thinking that no other woman in American has been, with some exceptions, separated from a husband overseas longer than you have, I wake up suddenly to the fact of how cruel and heartless this has been on you. The exceptions to the above statement are the few women whose husbands WERE in Iceland, Hawaii, and such places when I sailed and who have not yet returned home, probably not very many; and the women who have husbands as prisoners of war.

So now the question: Shall I get home soon by the means that I've mentioned? I'm now at the stage where it's up to you. If you want me to come home now, and nothing else will do, if you think our relationship would in ANY way be strained by my staying overseas, then I'll get busy on the coming home from the "finagling" angle. I say finagling, because that's the way it seems to me in a way, and yet there are army regulations that permit and in fact allow for it. (Paroxys. tachy, etc.) I'm at the stage where my own conscience has been satisfied, if yours has, either way you answer. If you *know* that our love will continue to grow stronger as months of separation go by, as it has in the past, and if you in your deepest heart would be in any way ashamed of my working or shall we say "allowing" such a return, then don't hesitate to tell me.

I'm asking you for moral advice, because I believe that there is no one that I know of who has a more level head about such matters. Take your time about thinking it over and then let me know, with your reasoning in the matter. Don't take my personal wishes into account, just your own, and what you think is right between us and our country and God. You don't need a reminder to know that I love you more than anything else in the world and that my physical desire for you, for your kiss, to feel you close to me, to make love to you, is so strong that it will *never* be any other way, come hell or high water. I also know that I can't always make an unprejudiced decision because of it. I want to come home so badly that it isn't funny and I mean only to come home to you, but my conscience would never allow me to return just to accomplish my own selfish desire. It WOULD allow me to return, certainly, though, if I knew that this separation was destroying something in your life.

I suspect that maybe I shouldn't ask you these questions, that maybe I should be a little more debonair about the whole thing, make my decisions myself and expect you, as my wife, to abide by them. I would, except that "I y'am what I y'am," and you are what you are and that's the reason we got married. If I were married to an empty-headed siren, I'd not trouble you about such matters.

Yesterday I drove down to the big metropolis [Naples], which is about 40 miles from here. I went down to see if I could find Jack and to visit some of our medics who were wounded and who are in general hospitals there. On the way down I stopped at Rear 5th Army Hdq. and I looked over their roster of outfits like Jack belongs to, but they didn't have it on the list, so concluded that Jack was further south. I finally found his outfit listed at M.P. headquarters in the metropolis. It's in a town near where we first hit this country and was a considerable distance further on. It was just about dark before we found out where he was located so we didn't go on down, but started on back "home." It takes several hours to negotiate the road "home," and we didn't want to try to hunt over the strange countryside in the dark for Jack's outfit. We'll make connections one of these days, though. I wrote Jack a letter this afternoon, and probably we can get together by each coming part way. Incidentally, although disappointed at not being able to see him, I'm darned glad that he's located where he is because if I know rightly, he'll probably be engaged in doing the same thing he did in Africa instead of mixing it up with Jerry further north. I wouldn't communicate my reasons to him, but believe me, they are ample, with a capital "A" for his kind of outfit.

I must close and hit the mattress. For about ten days we've had a real rest, just sat around having as good a time as one can have in a desolate little Italian country hill town. I didn't get up until noon today. In a few days we'll get back on the early rise schedule, so I'll have to start getting to bed earlier "so's" I can get up in the morning and whip this medic outfit of mine back into shape.

27 February 1944; Italy; V-mail

… This letter was just interrupted by the appearance of Sgt. Xxxxxxx, one of my Technical Sgts. whom I evacuated with high blood pressure over a month ago. He's only about 25 years of age, a slim, yellow-haired boy from Milwaukee and a swell kid. He went through all the various hospitals and was boarded for return to the states, but after being flown to Africa, his papers got mixed up some way and he now turns up back here in Italy for "duty." These things make you tear your hair out once in awhile, the way the army works (?), but we are persistent and will send him to the hospital again. In addition to his bewilderment about what happened to him, when he arrived back here he received a letter from the girlfriend back home, the one he has always talked about, saying that she was getting married. He's a rough and tough guy, but his voice was a little husky when he smilingly mentioned that he was now a member of the "lonely hearts club." I just read her letter; it was a model of self-deprecation, one of the old "I hate to do this to you" things. It's a little rough, it seems to me, to have most of life's happiness stripped away from you, to daily run the risk of crippling and death, and then have someone plunder the strongbox where the last pearls of happiness are hidden back home, but guess I'm getting a little melodramatic. We soon learn the stern realities of life over here and I guess they apply everywhere, but I would raise heck for fifty years or longer if something like that ever happened to me. There is one situation to which I could not and would not adjust myself and I'll give you just one guess as to what that is.

Another little incident just came up. I've always told my boys to use their heads in regard to drinking. I've always told them when they reached the stage where they thought they "had" to throw a drunk, that they should come to me; that I'd arrange for them to be relieved of all responsibility for 24 hours, arrange for someone to look after them and maybe even provide the liquor. Well, one of the boys just took me up on the deal, so I "issued" his three ounces of the best rye whiskey and detailed a Sgt. to look after him for the day. The only trouble is that now that the ice is broken, I'm afraid there'll be a line outside the office in the morning. Such is life in the army.

28 February 1944; Italy

… I wrote you letters yesterday and the day before, but I'm warning you, that as much as I want to, I'll probably not be able to keep up the precedent. We are getting back on an "early-rising" schedule of training and the days are going to get full and a little hectic again. If you could train soldiers for combat by sitting in an office, I'd always be able to find time to write every day, but such is not the case.

Your story about the young girls back in the states was interesting, and new in a way, yet the problem is certainly present over here. For publication purposes, the authorities over here placed the metropolis off limits to soldiers except on business, because of typhus, but actually it was probably for the other reason [gonorrhea]. When men get desperate, that is, when they have none of the comforts that they once had, have no future that they can look forward to, see their buddy's twisted and mangled body next to them on the battlefield and know that it'll just be a matter of time, maybe one battle, maybe ten, before they are possibly a little lucky and just get wounded—when men get to that stage, they are hard to reason with. In fact, most of them that you talk to can't be reasoned with, especially the ones, as you mentioned, under 25, but it applies more or less to all of them. Some of the older ones may be a little smarter in avoiding the physical results of their "desperation," but to me, that's nothing to commend them about.

I, myself, certainly am normal when it comes to physical things, in fact maybe a little above the average, as you know. The fear of disease is entirely absent in me—if I as a doctor couldn't avoid that, I might as well start digging ditches; and there are plenty of "nice" opportunities over here. There are a lot of "nice" American girls over here who have been overseas a year or longer, are tired to death of the work and war, who are being taken for granted by the paunchy officers that they work with, and who would be a push over for an aggressive and persistent (and smoothly worked) campaign. They are very lonesome, tired, bored, and frustrated as they see their "physical" years slipping by with no hope of return home until "too late."

I'm no Casanova, but I think I've learned a lot about human nature—such knowledge comes pretty fast during periods when you see many people under stresses much greater than they'd ever experienced in peace time—and I've actually learned to smile and get a much bigger kick out of mixing with people than I ever had back in my "monk" days when I had pretty narrow ideas. So, if I had any real deep desire to "adjust" myself to our harsh environment, I could do it with practically no effort, and you would never know the difference. Your husband is a lot smoother along many lines than he was when he left you (at least he thinks he is).

And yet, no one can take your place with me, and I don't like to play the "smooth" game. I still think that it's worth the price, probably in many ways that I do not now understand, to set a standard and stick to it. I'll admit that I've been somewhat surprised at the large number, in fact the majority, of people that don't play the game, but it's never made me want to do likewise. Maybe I'm an "unadjusted fool," a "child," a "naïve simpleton," but I honestly like it that way, so what's it to anyone else? It isn't as simple in practice as it sounds, as you know. The old primitive urge comes again and again and I react perfectly normally to a pretty leg, a loose shirtwaist, or an inviting look, but there's something else that keeps my purely primitive instincts under control—it must be this thing that I now know to be rare in this world: real love, for YOU. I know that you would be the last person in the world to ask me, but I'm TELLING you, because I want to, that the last woman that I had sexual contact with was a beautiful, seductive, and loving girl on the night of December 30 in Oakdale, Louisiana, 1941. (It was "sort of" interrupted, as I clearly remember, by a telephone call.) Incidentally, now that I know what I know about overseas shipments, and the time wasted standing around, I curse myself for not telling them to go to blazes that night. I've thought of that many, many times, as I've thought of every time we were together.

29 February 1944; Italy

... I'm losing Lt. Spoo, the MAC officer that's been with me since early September, tomorrow. He's being transferred to another, different type of unit in the division, and I'll have to get along henceforth without such an officer. I sure do hate to lose him, because he's such an efficient officer and such a very likeable fellow, very good-natured, but very conscientious. He has gone through shot and shell many times to see to it that medical supplies reached our battalion aid stations properly. I've made some written recommendations that I think will please him, but can't divulge them until they are approved, but am hoping that there'll be a dash of color added to his uniform, as well as an increase in silver ware.

Several days ago, we were visited by the cartoonist, Bill Mauldin. Mauldin is a Sgt., I believe, now, originally came over with another Yank division and has been drawing cartoons for "The Stars and Stripes Weekly" for some time. You've probably seen his cartoons in that paper, the ones of the "dough-foot" named "Joe" who is always bearded. Some of his cartoons appeared in Life Magazine several months ago. He is the best cartoonist portraying real battle conditions that we've ever seen over here; his cartoons all bearing an unusual ring of authenticity that only could be imparted to them by his own experiences right up on the front lines. I suppose many of his masterpieces will never be understood by those at home, but we all "get" them over here. One has to participate in battle, know how things get mixed up, how men react, and what becomes important and what not important, to properly appreciate them. I understand that he has published a small book of his best drawings over here and I'm going to try to get a copy if at all possible.

A party to "end all parties" is scheduled for the officers tomorrow night. I have been requested to furnish 17 litter squads to handle the expected "casualties" of this "magnificent" social event. Someone thought up a rather clever invitation to send to the various hospitals to inveigle unsuspecting nurses to attend. It started out something like this: "The officers of the 168th Infantry Regiment and the 175th F.A. Bn., after completing a successful return engagement with Herr Schickelgruber's klop-headed fluff heads will, on the night of 1 March, 1944, throw one of the biggest and loudest social events of the season at such and such a place, etc."

There are two wine listings made, one "domestic," listing native wines and ending up with "aspirin" and "anacin" and "Sod Amtyol" and the other called "imported," which mentions Scotch, Manhattans, etc., ending up with a "Crème de Acetylene" concoction. It also mentioned something about barbecued beef cut directly off the spit, etc.

I haven't had anything to do with the arrangements, but it sounds good, all except the music. We are going to have an orchestra composed of elements of the band, many of whom have recently been up on the front line acting as litter bearers and whose close harmony as a result of rather indifferent and nervous practice in fitful gusts is simply atrocious. Usually, some of the officers invade the orchestra's seats and add some little touch in their own inimitable way, which makes the music even worse but everyone always has a good time. I don't have a date, so will stag the affair in the grand manner and will consider it my duty as guardian of the mental health of the regiment to pass on all the sundry gals present so that I can advise the boys the next morning as to the best approach for future operations. I sure will miss Maizie at such a party. I'm afraid you'd think the party a little rough, but it's all wholesome fun and tom-foolery and no one gets serious about anybody or anything.

The parties are fun in a way, but only by comparison to our everyday life. Personally, I'm sweating out the return to "everyday" life back home with Maizie Ludwick. Some of the guys over here think some of the nurses are not bad on the eyes, but they must have considerable myopia, or else have never travelled in Blackhawk [Waterloo, Iowa] country.

I hesitate, sometimes, to write you about our social events for fear that some people over there may get the idea that life is just one social whirl over here, but actually, it is much the opposite. When we are drawn back from the line, parties are about the only function that we can have, and the contrast between parties and combat is so great that the former loom in magnified dimensions, whereas at home we would be very much bored by the whole thing and you probably would have a hard time getting me to go to one (if you could stand them yourself) more than once. I'd rather go to Miami with you.

I love you very, very much, dearest, and only you. Surely, we are over the hump on this separation. It can't last forever. I pray that it will soon end and that, rather selfishly, we can watch while others go through what we've gone through.

6 March 1944; Italy

… Well, the last and biggest blowout that we have had since coming out of combat was pulled off Friday night. It was a huge, colossal, athletic and somewhat alcoholic success. We "engaged" the ballroom or banquet hall of a Duke that has a castle in the next little town [Piedmonte d'Alife.] The music was provided by the "Rhythm Majors," the dance band from the old outfit (133rd Reg.) that I used to belong to, and their style is still smooth. There was plenty of feed and beaucoup liquor and much enthusiasm. I stagged the party, drank less and danced more than most anyone else and had a swell time. One of the belles of the party lost her date somewhere in the melee and of course your husband ("Wreck" Ludwick), having always been used to associating only with the very best belles, escorted her home.

This last week we had the first canteen issue of Coca Cola that we've had since Swamp Island. We "finagled" some coke off a navy boat soon after we arrived on the other continent over a year ago, but that's the last we've had since the island days. It sure did taste good. We pay 10¢ a bottle for the first batch (3 bottles) and thereafter, 4¢ a bottle, apparently to cover cost of bottle losses and breakage. We're hoping that the ration will continue to be three a week.

Must close and let my 1st Sgt. get some work done on this machine.

10 March 1944; Italy

[In Castella? Foggia?]

… We've moved since I last wrote to you on 6 March. We are now situated in rolling mountain upland country, which is well cultivated. We are higher in altitude than we were, but the country is more level and much more prosperous looking. Once again, the headquarters section of the "medics" was lucky and we've secured a building in the little country town for use as aid station and office. We have electric lights going this evening and the little radio belonging to one of the boys is busy grinding out semi-classical music. It's pretty wet here, and the mud is gluey—gumbo, but the people around here tell us that the weather is very "unusual" and that the rains should stop pretty soon. It can't be too soon for us, because although we are nearer to Jack than where we formerly were, it's colder in this upland country.

I should be able to get down to see Jack pretty soon, possibly within the week. As you may remember, I tried to find him one day about two weeks ago, but wasn't able to learn the town where he is located until just about dusk. This time, when I can get away and things are running all O.K., I should be able to drive right to it. I'll certainly be glad to see him.

Several weeks ago, we had a visitor from a very important office in

Washington. He was over here on the special mission to get the "low down" on certain matters from the frontline boys. I told him some pretty straight facts which interested him very much; in fact, he stopped by my office after the conversation at the colonel's office and left a note for me saying that I was "on the beam," etc. I expect that most of it was "ballyhoo" on his part as he was a pretty good salesman himself, but nevertheless, it made me feel pretty good about it.

13 March 1944; Italy

[Silver Star award in Benevento, Italy, pinned by Lt. General Mark Clark. See photo page 20, and endnote vi for official commendation text.]

… I suppose this day should stand out as a big event in my life, but when I returned home from the little "outing," and found no mail from you, the bottom fell out completely. I can't tell you much about the "outing" except that together with a bunch of other fellows, I stood out on an airfield, met and shook hands with Lt. Gen., and received from him a small "token" [The Silver Star]. There were some reporters (Associated Press) present, as well as photographers. The reporter asked me my home address (as he did all the others), which I gave as 142 Graceline [Waterloo, Iowa], so maybe one of these days you'll see some highly exaggerated account of various doings over here by your long-absent husband.

I hesitate a great deal to talk about this, so many things can happen in the army in a short time, but I've recently (yesterday) learned for the first time DEFINITELY that I'll probably be showing up in the good old U.S.A. sometime "soon." Just what "soon" means, I can't say, but the way the schedule has been running, it will possibly be in the latter part of May, but might conceivably be slightly earlier or later. A lot of things can happen between now and then, as you know—but at least it's definitely past the hunch or rumor stage. I know that my name has been put on the list. I'll keep you posted as well as I can. You remember how long it took Mo Cohen to make it after he left the outfit, so it many take me just as long which would make it somewhat later before I can give you a private consultation out behind the Presbyterian Hospital.

16 March 1944; Italy

… Yesterday, I received a letter from Jack, written 6 March, in answer to the letter I wrote to him about two weeks ago when I tried to get down to see him. He is a Sgt. now, according to the return address on the envelope. He said that he had just returned five days previously from the hospital where he had been for ten days with malaria—said he was a pretty sick boy when he first went in to the hospital, but after they "knocked" his fever down, he said he felt much better and really had a nice rest for the remaining seven days. I'm going to try to get down to see him again within the next few days, otherwise I won't have the opportunity for quite some time.

I expect you to have charge of furnishing my office when I get back into civilian practice. You have the best taste in clothes of any woman I've ever known, and since taste is never restricted to one category, the job is yours whether you want it or not. The only trouble is that you'll probably be restricted to piecemeal "furnishings" of the office at first until I get a mob clamoring for my services. In addition, you might have to act as consultant occasionally, on lab matters, run the house, pilot me around in our plane, raise a family, be my mistress and otherwise sustain me in this troubled world. I'm not going to try to run your life, or anything, but I do believe that you probably won't have time to belong to the Thursday Afternoon Literary and Culture Society.

Must close, I'm late for supper now. I don't think that I'll be able to write you more than one more letter before a slight break will occur in my correspondence. Same old reason only this time it has a new twist to it. Might get a little nauseated due to the repeated effect of circular motion on the semicircular canals [sea sickness], but it won't last more than a few hours. The spray may blow in my face a little, but what's that to a guy used to the rain.

See you this summer, I hope and pray.

5

Winding Down

Anzio and Headed Home, March–April 1944

Anzio and Naples, Italy; Algiers, Algeria

> I know that a great many men who are now overseas will be strangers when they return, and their secret need for understanding and companionship will go unheeded. No rough, tough fighting American is going to admit that need, but it'll be there just the same, and its frustration will come to the surface in a variety of actions, reactions, and behaviors.... Darling—I'm going to need you very much when I get home.
> —22 January 1944, Italy

Orders came on March 11, 1944, for the 34th Infantry Division to move to the Anzio beachhead. According to journalist Sgt. Milo Green, a few days before embarkation, new recruits poured in from the States, presenting the task of absorbing and indoctrinating the men with no battle experience.*

Lud's 168th Regiment arrived in Anzio around March 19, 1944. Once again, they were not the invading troops, so did not land under fire although artillery could be heard a few miles away.

Letters: March 21–April 5, 1944

21 March 1944; Italy

[Anzio]

> ... I was very much disappointed that I didn't get to see Jack, because now I am prevented from calling on him by reason of several factors, including Jerry. I wanted to see Jack very much, to check up on him so that I could report to you

---

* The 133rd and 168th regiments were Iowa outfits in Northern Ireland, North Africa, and in Italy until the fighting moved into the Cassino sector. Then it began to change. The familiar Iowa faces of the original Iowa National Guard and the early draftees started to disappear. A lot of them were killed or seriously wounded. When the regiments embarked for Anzio, they were almost entirely new outfits. *Breakthrough Bn*, 222–229. *34th Inf Div Assoc.* (Winter 2016).

how he had recovered from the malaria, but guess it'll have to wait until we can reach each other by road again.

There isn't very much to write about here now. We are marking time before another deal, which will come off soon. I'm writing this letter in the small wall tent that we've put up as temporary aid station until we can move into a more permanent location. One of the boys strung up one of the lanterns so that it would shine over my shoulder, but at that, I still have to "feel" for the keyboard at times.

The big thing that's always on my mind, of course, is "coming home." As I've already written you in several letters recently, my name has finally been put on the list and all I have to do now is to sweat out the "campaign" over here until the orders come through sending me on my way. I "figure" that they won't come through until sometime in May or maybe June. Hope I can duck Jerry's little presents until that time comes around. I'll let you know when I leave the outfit, because when I do, you might as well quit writing since the long trek homeward is from one "replacement" center to another, and my mail address will be constantly changing.

On the trip up here I thought of you constantly and dreamed wonderful dreams of what we'll do when I finally make the grade of standing again on the soil of the good old U.S.A. If they pass that bill allowing overseas stripes on the uniform, I'll be able to wear quite a slew of them—will probably have to have my sleeve lengthened in order to have room for them all. I can now wear four ribbons over my left upper pocket on my blouse. I'll let you sew them on for me when I get home.

24 March 1944; Italy

[Anzio]

… Things are very quiet in this place, much to our surprise. The weather is getting warmer all along and there are fewer showers. It's always warmer along the coast, however, in the Mediterranean area. The quiet is almost eerie, because we had read a great deal about this "hot" place in the "Stars and Stripes" and news bulletins before coming here. I guess things were pretty hot at one time, and very probably will get that way again one of these days, but right now it's almost a "country club" war for us at Reg't'l headquarters, although the dough-foot out in the foxhole probably wouldn't agree with me. At that, though, his lot is much better than it was on the cold and rain-snow swept mountains a couple of months ago.

There isn't much to write about here, now, for several reasons. One of these is that in quiet times, even on the front, the business of war is so stereotyped that it soon gets monotonous. Another reason is that most of my thoughts during waking hours, are concerned with my expected departure home, however distant that may be. I realize that I'm babbling about coming home in every letter much like a four year old that has belatedly learned to talk, but it's that important to me.

Two patients just came up to the aid station tent where I am writing this letter, so I'd better close and take a look at them. I've lost my assistant recently. Capt. Drye is no longer with us, some way managed a lucky transfer into an auxiliary surgical unit. I would envy him very much and start raising hell myself again if I didn't know that my name was on the list from this regiment to come home. Guess I'd better be a good boy and keep quiet for a change.

27 March 1944; Italy

[Anzio]

... Recent advice from the censorship office permits me to tell you that I was on the Cassino front back in January and part of February. I imagine that you probably guessed as much or possibly that the papers told you what we were not permitted to tell at the time. That little fracas was quite a deal, all right, and for that matter, still is (see previous letters, can't mention the location of the outfit, must only mention personal experiences). None of my personal experiences were the kind that you'd write home about to a patiently waiting wife. I'll make it "Chapter 10" of my war memoirs when I get home. You'll probably get so tired of hearing about some things that you'll put a gag on me at bedtime every night, but that'll just get you in trouble because then I'll have to talk with my hands.

Did I tell you that Capt. Schuster, one of my medical officers, got the Distinguished Service Cross recently? He is quite a guy all right and is legendary in the regiment by now. You remember the article in Life Magazine about the story of "Ft. Schuster" that I mentioned back in December? That incident happened before he came to us, for which he received nothing but the publicity which was partially incorrect, according to him.

31 March 1944; Italy

... Your letter written 13 March (airmail) arrived here about noon, and I'm on top of the world again. I'm very glad that you were thrilled a little by the radio announcement—that's the kick I get out of such things.

It would be impossible for the whole unit, as mentioned in the clipping you sent, to come home, for several reasons, until the war is over, over here. One reason is that there are thousands (not many) of men scattered back along the trail from here to Casablanca in hospitals and in replacement depots on the way back to the outfit. In other words, while we have only a certain strength (number) of men here on duty and fighting, the number of men who "belong" to the outfit, i.e., are from the 168th, for instance, is much larger than that. It's a regular cycle: a replacement arrives, is wounded or takes sick, is evacuated, misses one or two battles, shows up for another battle, etc. Sort of a "shifting" population, only a few of which are boys that originally came over with the larger unit. Also, most of our men now are NOT from Iowa and Minnesota. The answer to the whole thing is to make the rotation faster, or at least to make it work the way it was originally intended.

I get browned off at this rotation deal every once in awhile. The regulation reads that any unit that has been overseas six months can rotate their percentage. That means that some outfits that have been over here just 6 ½ months are sending just as many boys back to the states as we are. Ho Hum, this IS the Army!!

I talked to Gittler several days ago. I've never seen him so depressed and discouraged. He said that Leslie was "about ready to crack," that he had been making some despondent statements, couldn't sleep nights, was taking some amytol, etc. I went over to see Leslie yesterday afternoon to check up a little and try to cheer him up. I found him his usual self, but very discouraged, said the only way to get home was to get himself wounded and that he hoped things got "hot" again soon. Of course, neither G. or L. are on the list that I am on, but I certainly know how they feel—I've seen too much. I don't believe he's doing all that G. says he is, though—L. is too smart for that. However, I wondered today if Leslie's wife ever saw any of the clippings by Gammack [Gordon Gammack—*Des Moines Register* journalist] that you said mentioned his name. If you can find them, send them to his wife (Mrs. Morris J. Leslie, xxxx xxxxxx, Brooklyn, N.Y.). I like Leslie very much and hate to see him suffer. I'm reasonably sure that both he and G. will get home "one of these days," but such meager assurance as that doesn't count for much when there are no definite prospects of going. Leslie has two little girls that he has many photographs of—shows me how they are growing almost every time we meet....

5 April 1944; Italy

... I can't say that I exactly foresaw just how you would reply (as you did in the "V-Mails"), but I'm tremendously happy, Jean, after reading the two letters. You made just exactly the right answer that YOU should make to ME, although I certainly didn't realize that when I wrote those two letters to you.

I'm bursting with pride that you, my wife, has both enough intelligence and enough social conscience to consider what effect any such action on my part would have on our happiness, BUT I'm also just as happy to know that deep in your heart you want to say "Yes," and that you want me home with you. I hope you can realize how much those letters have acted as "backer-uppers"—and they are towers of strength to me, and yet they have a fragile and feminine beauty that makes you endeared to me more and more.

After reading the letters, I know that you understand—that you aren't bitter and depressed, in spite of how the world has dealt with us so far. It's this knowledge that means so much to me. I knew that you were one in a million when I married you, but now I'm really beginning to appreciate you (Remember?) more and more. I'm very much in love with you, Jean.

Interviews: April 1944; Italy & Algeria

PL: When did you find out you were going to be finally sent home?

Dad: We were there in Anzio about two to three weeks before my commanding officer came to me and said, "Major, you have enough points and have been overseas 28 months, and you have other points, Purple Heart, Silver Star, etc.—you have enough points to be rotated home. Do you want to go?" And I said, "Yes!" The timing was lucky for me, I guess. I learned later that the battles in and around Anzio for the next four months were very intense and deadly.

I had a big bedroll, because I carried a mattress with me, one of those four-inch-thick cotton Army mattresses—no springs in it or anything. I could carry it with me and have those little perks of my own because I had six by eight trucks and six by six ambulances under my command.

I went by ship from Anzio down to where they had a Repo Depot, which was slang for "replacement people" at the fairgrounds at Naples, and that's where the incoming troops and the few of us that were being rotated out, were billeted. There were new soldiers coming into Italy all the time, every day, to replace the wounded, sick, and the MIA. They all had to go through this place. I was stuck there for about a week until I could get an empty "victory ship" going home.

PL: When did you finally get to see Jack Hoyer, Jean's younger brother?

Dad: I was stuck there in Naples for about a week or ten days until I could get an empty Victory ship going home and during that time, I commandeered a jeep and a driver. I was a Major, had a lot of ribbons, you know, so I could do that. We went down to Eboli, that's where Jack Hoyer, Jean's brother, was located. He was a Sergeant, serving in the 752nd Tank Battalion. Miraculously, I was able to find him and we spent a few hours together. He had adopted a little dog that he had gotten somewhere, I think in North Africa. We talked about a lot of things. I'd been through a lot—I had seen quite a bit of action and combat—14 battles and engagements with Rommel's troops, and had seen terrible wounds and tragic deaths, you know—and it was hard for me to talk about them and tell him what I'd seen. I forgot to tell him not to walk into any driveways after the fighting and always watch where you step.*

And so I visited with Jack and his buddies for a couple of hours. They all kind of ganged up around us, and we talked about the war. I think Jack was proud of my service and recall him saying something like, "This is my brother-in-law, he's a Major and has been through a lot of action and seen a lot of fighting." I think I showed them that you can survive bloody combat and get back home alive, because that was where I was headed in just a few days after serving on the frontlines for 28 months.

---

* "'Watch where you step,' [General] Clark's headquarters advised, 'and have no curiosity at all.' North of the Volturno [River], 'you could follow our battalions by the bloodstained leggings, the scattered equipment, and the bits of bodies where men had been blown up,' the 168th Infantry reported." Rick Atkinson, *The Day of Battle* (New York, N.Y., Henry Holt & Co., 2007), 253 [hereafter cited as *Day of Battle*].

After visiting my brother-in-law, I returned to Naples to the Repo Depot and in a day or two, I was put on a ship. There were about 30 other guys that were being rotated back and otherwise, the ship was empty except for the crew and the captain. We left Naples, and first went to Algiers. I got off at Algiers, and looked around town. And that was where, I had my camera with me, I saw a very well-dressed man. He must have been a wealthy Arab, with white flowing robes, white turban, and jewelry. He was walking down the street of Algiers, and so I just took a picture of him.

Boy, did he give me a dirty look, because the Muslims don't believe in photographs: that cameras steal your soul, or something like that. I didn't know that. But I was in uniform, and he realized I was an American officer of some kind, so he didn't call the police or anything.

I stayed in Algiers for a couple of hours and bought some beautiful rugs there, which we still have. I returned to my ship and I think we just sailed on out through the Straits of Gibraltar. A Victory ship can only go about ten miles an hour. And so, for 1,600 miles, it took us about a week or ten days to get home.

I was real glad I had that time with Jack Hoyer, because about a month later on May 27, 1944, he was killed instantly on his first day of combat, near Maenza, Italy. He was only 23 years old, and was buried in the American Military Cemetery in Nettuno, near the area of engagement.

It was a sad chapter in our lives and for our family. Jean and her fourteen-year younger sister, Joan, were devastated, as were their parents, Ben and Lenore Hoyer. In fact, I don't think Jean's mother, Lenore, ever recovered from that loss. The tragedy and heartbreak of war became even more personal after that. [See Appendix D for details of Jack Hoyer's death and a photo.]

April 14, 1944, Eboli, Italy: Jack Hoyer, Jean's younger brother, with the little dog he adopted while serving with the 752nd Tank Battalion. Photograph taken during Lud's last visit with him before being rotated home.

Letters: April 14–30, 1944

14 April 1944; Italy; V-mail

… I'm on my way home!!! I can hardly believe it, but it's true! I left the outfit day before yesterday and am now back at Division Hdq., Rear Echelon, after my semi-circular canals were exposed again yesterday. Tomorrow I will sever my connections with this division and will go to the first of many replacement depots there, to begin the long trek homeward.

As you can see from the above, my orders came through much more quickly than I expected. It was certainly a pleasant surprise, so hold on to your hat, kid, here we go.

This morning I borrowed a peep [slang for jeep] and driver and drove down to see Jack. We arrived about 1:30 p.m. and found him just loading up to go out on an all-night problem. The battalion executive officer arranged for him to stay in camp so that we could have a visit. I had lunch at Jack's kitchen and then we sat and talked until about 4:30 p.m.

Jack looks very fine, the best I have ever seen him. There are certainly no traces left of his malaria. He chided me a little for telling you about his malaria—said he received some five letters on the subject but, of course, was just kidding. He certainly has a swell outfit and the nicest camp I've seen in Italy. They've made the camp what it is, themselves. They have gravel walks, sleep on canvas cots in pyramidal tents, have their own hot showers and a kitchen with good cooks. Jack said they wouldn't let the boys out of camp very much, and that some of them were getting pretty restless but apparently he, himself, has been able to get away some by accompanying officers on business. He said he was within six to eight miles of Cassino, soon after we pulled back from that area, looking for me, but we didn't make the connections.

30 April 1944; North Africa
[Algiers?]

… Well, I can't say that I'm on any express train on the way home. In fact, it's a pretty slow outfit, as you might guess from the lack of progress that I've made since I last wrote.

I'm going back into town tomorrow to spend the day and probably the night. It's a beautiful city (where Glenn formerly lived) and there are many sights to see and stuff to do. It's certainly a wonderful feeling not to have any responsibility for troops or duties, and to be able to roam around without any deadline to make back at camp. The lack of transportation is a slight hindrance, but I'm a "doughfoot," so that doesn't make much difference.

You ought to see the handsome face of your husband right now. I have a nice mustache and beard, mostly trimmed, of course. I thought maybe I'd better prepare you for the shock. I'll probably shave it off about the time we get close to shore, so don't worry too much about it. Such is the life of an itinerant, ho hum.

This will probably be the last letter from overseas, so until the honeymoon begins, remember that I LOVE YOU.

6

Chronology of Military Service and Major 34th Infantry Division Events

December 2, 1940–November 12, 1951

- Camp Claiborne, Louisiana; Northern Ireland; North Africa; Italy
- Iowa National Guard and 34th Infantry "Red Bull" Division
- Medical Corps USAR 0-420498
- 133rd/168th Infantry Regiments—Battalion/Regimental Surgeon
- Active Duty: Feb 10, 1941–Jan 29, 1946

Author's Note: My father served with the 133rd Infantry Combat Regiment of the 34th "Red Bull" Infantry Division where he was a Battalion Surgeon in Northern Ireland, January 26 to December 22, 1942. He was still with the 133rd when deployed to North Africa, from January 3rd to the end of February 1943, when he was promoted and transferred to the 168th Infantry Regiment as its Regimental Surgeon. He continued to serve with the 168th through the end of the North African campaign and on into Italy, before finally being rotated home in May 1944.

This chronology of my dad's movement across North Africa and in Italy with the 133rd and 168th Infantry Regiments, has been pieced together using a wide range of historical resources: U.S. Army Military documents, firsthand testimonials and books, clues from my father's wartime letters, and my recent trips to North Africa and Italy to retrace his routes, encampments, and battlefields. Although I was able to corroborate most of the dates and general areas of my father's wartime locations, (I have listed those sources here), there are some unnamed locales referenced in my dad's letters where I could only make an educated guess as to the exact village or camp location, based on the evidence at hand. Therefore, I cannot guarantee the absolute accuracy of a few locations mentioned in this document.

Iowa National Guard: Dec 1940–Dec 8, 1941

- **Dec 2, 1940: Iowa National Guard**—Commissioned as 1st Lt., Medical Corps (M.C.), Waterloo, Iowa.

- **Feb–Dec 1941: Camp Claiborne, Louisiana**; Battalion Surgeon—intensive training and maneuvers. Feb 10, 1941, 34th Infantry Div was mustered to Federal Duty; the 34th ID was composed of soldiers from the states of IA, MN, ND and SD.
- **Aug 11–Oct 1, 1941:** Louisiana Maneuvers at Fort Polk, Louisiana, which is about 10 miles east of Leesville, LA, and circa 30 miles north of DeRidder, LA; built in 1941, to support an Army preparing to do battle on the North African, European and Pacific fronts. Soldiers at Polk participated in the Louisiana Maneuvers which were designed to test U.S. troops preparing for World War II. The Maneuvers gave Army leadership the chance to test a new doctrine that stressed the need for both mass and mobility. Sixteen armored divisions sprang up during World War II after the lessons learned during the Louisiana Maneuvers were considered. These divisions specialized in moving huge combined-arms/mechanized units long distances in combat.
- **Oct 11, 1941:** married Jean Hoyer in Alexandria, LA.
- **Dec 7, 1941:** Pearl Harbor bombed; living in Oakdale, LA, with Jean; Lud in 133rd Regiment Medical Detachment, 1st Battalion.
- **Dec 8, 1941:** war declared; arrived in New Orleans for guard duty.
- **Dec 23, 1941:** returned to Camp Claiborne, LA, to prepare for shipping out, destination unknown.
- **Dec 31, 1941:** loaded onto a troops train in New Orleans to Fort Dix, New Jersey.
- **Jan 4, 1942:** arrived at Fort Dix, NJ, a permanent Army post since 1939; during and after World War II the fort served as a training and staging ground during the war and a demobilization center after the war.
- **Jan 14, 1942:** 133rd Infantry Regiment/1st Battalion boards the *Strathaird* (reconfigured British passenger ship) and sails from New York to Northern Ireland (destination unknown at the time—the first American combat troops sent to Europe).

Northern Ireland: Jan 1942–Dec 22, 1942; 133rd Inf Div, 1st Bn.

- **Jan 26, 1942:** arrived in Belfast, Northern Ireland, at Dufferin Quay; contingent strength was 4,058—medical personnel total of 41 officers, 42 nurses, and 322 enlisted men; ~ 1,000 troops traveled by truck convoy to Castlerock, ~ 52 miles north of Belfast and encamped there for ~three months; places visited/stationed: Armagh, Caledon, Castlerock, Coleraine, Dogleap-Limavady, Londonderry (Derry side is water side), Port Stewart, Portrush, Tynan Abbey.
- **May 28, 1942:** assembled in vicinity of Caledon, Northern Ireland, for intensive training and maneuvers.
- **June 1942:** American troop strength in NI highest peak of year: 41,205 (http://www.history.army.mil/reference/ireland/irechr.htm).

- **Oct 1942:** one week of "Tropical Medicine and Hygiene" training in London at University of London, London, England.
- **Nov 11, 1942:** promoted from 1st Lieutenant to Captain.
- **Dec 22, 1942:** 133rd moved from Northern Ireland to Liverpool, England.
- **Dec 23, 1942:** sailed from Liverpool, England, for Oran, Algeria, (North Africa) aboard the *Empress of Australia*, and participation in Operation TORCH.

North Africa: Jan–Mid Sept, 1943; 133rd/168th Regiments of the 34th Infantry Division

- **Jan 3, 1943:** landed at Port of Oran at Mers El Kabir dock area in Operation TORCH—marched to Assi Ben Okba, ~ 10 miles east of Oran and "billeted" for about a week; moved to a barracks in central Oran (vicinity of Lavayssiere), previously occupied by Black Senegalese French troops; light training; stayed about one month.
- **Jan 16, 1943:** in place (Arzen?) overlooking Mediterranean in Tlemcen, Algeria, area; in a block of Moorish buildings that served as the Artillery Barracks; training for a few weeks; war in Tunisia at a standstill (*Paulus Diaries*, p. 86).
- **Jan 30, 1943:** movement order to region of Maktar-Pichon, Tunisia; snowstorm (*Paulus Diaries*, p. 89; also report by Division Surgeon, Ludwig Gittler).
- **Feb 7, 1943:** 133rd moved by motor convoy east towards Tunisia, over the bitter cold Atlas Mountains to the vicinity of Maktar to relieve the French units in sector south of Fondouk Pass and east of Hadjeb-el-Aioun; pulled into Maktar in the night; bitter cold and snowy; turned south toward the road that ran from Tebessa to Kairouan where about midway between, came upon Fondouk Pass in Tunisia.
- **Feb 16–24, 1943:** Battles of Kasserine/Faid Pass Area; 34th Infantry Division arrives 16–17 February at Sidi Bou Zid; 168th Regiment's first major engagement w/enemy; many casualties and pushed back over 50 miles from positions west of Faid Pass; loss of 106 officers including ten physicians and 1,747 enlisted men, mostly from Iowa; Germans capture about 1,000, including the regimental surgeon, Major Fred Beaumont, and most of the regimental headquarters; "...most of the medical detachment of the 168th and the collecting company of the 109th Medical Battalion would become POWs."
- **Feb 17, 1943:** 133rd's first contact with Rommel's highly trained Afrika Korps at Hadjeb El Aioun, southwest of Fondouk; in minor skirmish off to the side of Faid/Kasserine Pass; turned back the enemy at Kef-el-Amar (Le Kef) Pass.
- **Feb 15–28, 1943:** Combat Medical Badge paperwork: "Served as Surgeon, 1st Battalion, 133rd Infantry Regiment, 34th Infantry Division in combat beginning 15 February 1943 and ending 28 February 1943 in the vicinity of Sbiba, near Sbeitla, Tunisia, North Africa"; this engagement was known as the "Defense of Sbiba Gap" (or Battle of Sidi Bou Zid).
- **Feb 24, 1943:** Kasserine retaken by Feb 24, 1943; German forces withdraw

6. Chronology of Military Service and Major Division Events

from Kasserine Pass; Col. Frederic B. Butler takes over as 168th Regiment's Commanding Officer and reorganizes regiment in vicinity of Ain Beida; requisition for 1,645 replacements in unit; Lud now with 1st Bn. (of 133rd) to temporarily to help out; address changes Feb 28, 1943, to 168th Regiment; in defensive position at Sbiba Feb 22–March 26? (*109th Gold Star Museum*).

- **Feb 28, 1943:** 39 officers and 904 enlisted men transferred into the 168th regiment.
- **Mar 1, 1943:** Lud transferred to 168th Infantry Division as Regimental Surgeon and commanding officer of medical detachment; "was possibly in the little deserted town of Sbiba, where the regiment set up its headquarters for over three weeks during the lull in battle caused by a stretch of rain and mud which made activity on either side virtually impossible" (*Brickbats*, p. 152).
- **Mar 26, 1943:** move from defensive to offensive position; 168th moved through El Kef pass to area of Hadjeb El Aioun for surprise attack on Fondouk.
- **Mar 26–Apr 10, 1943:** two Battles of Fondouk Pass; Tunisia: 1st attack at Fondouk: "just make a lot of noise"; half-hearted assault (*Army at Dawn*, p. 468); 2nd battle at Fondouk: April 8–10, 1943, objective taken; 583 total casualties at Fondouk (*109th Gold Star Museum*, p. 19); turning point of war; 168th had learned a lot of lessons; defeat of Germans in Kairouan area and capture of a large amount of enemy material (*168th—Volunteer Citizen Soldiers of SW Iowa*).
- **Apr 11–25, 1943:** two weeks of intense remedial training and repair with Col. Butler after Fondouk; near Hadjeb, then to snowy cold Maktar; Bizerte is the objective (*Paulus Diaries*, p. 111; 34infdiv.org/history).
- **Apr 23, 1943:** 168th moves east to vicinity of Beja.
- **Apr 29–May 2, 1943:** The Battle for Hill 609—Sidi Nsir Station, Tunisia; after Fondouk, went on to capture of Hill 609 in the final Axis collapse in Tunisia; hard fight, many casualties (*Paulus Diaries*, p. 114).
- **May 2, 1943:** 168th "in reserve"; the next Allied objective was capture of Bizerte and Tunis.
- **May 5–9, 1943:** Lud earns Purple Heart at Eddekhila, Tunisia; 168th taking the lead in last major battle of the NA campaign; thousands of German prisoners taken; "The division drove the enemy from the last mountain defense positions in the vicinity of Eddekhila, thus forcing the Germans and Italians into the open Tunisian plain where they were at the mercy of the Allied forces" (*The Gallant Fight*).
- **May 7, 1943:** Tunis and Bizerte taken.
- **May 9, 1943:** Eddekhila area—last day of combat for the men of the 168th in the Tunisian campaign; at that time, they were about fifteen miles from Mateur; assemble in a bivouac area about two miles northeast of Eddekhila; the last week of fighting in Tunisia brought in 50,000+ prisoners for a total of 350,000–400,000 (*Paulus Diaries*, p. 117) prisoners into Allied custody, a flood which all but swamped the victors (detention center near Mateur); the 2nd Battalion (including F Company) helped guard some of the prisoner of war compounds.

- **May 15, 1943:** the enemy surrendered and the battle for North Africa was over; month's rest and training for 168th between Bizerte and Tunis; billeted in olive grove near Bizerte and staged the 1st Division to invade Sicily.
- **May 28, 1943:** Tunis, Tunisia; sightseeing ancient ruins in Carthage.
- **June 6, 1943:** commissioned as Major (from Captain) of Medical Corps.
- **Late July/Early Aug 1943:** move 800 miles west from Bizerte to Sidi Bel Abbes, Algeria (home of the French Foreign Legion) for training; Col. Butler insisted on rigorous physical and combat training; probably where the troops contracted Infectious Hepatitis A from contaminated well water.
- **Aug 17, 1943:** moved again; about a ½ mile from sea on a bald and dusty hill overlooking the Mediterranean, a few miles from the large city where the Villa was located [Oran?]; rough bivouac area.

Italy: Late Sept 1943–May 1944; 168th Regiment of 34th Infantry Division

Overview: The 168th crossed the winding Volturno River three times in October and November 1943, and after a 5-day bloody battle, took Monte Pantano before being relieved, 9 December 1943. In January 1944, the Division drove into the Gustav Line, took Mount Trocchio after a bitter fight, pushed across the Rapido River, attacked Monastery Hill, and fought its way into Cassino, being relieved 13 February 1944. After rest and rehabilitation in the small mountain village of Sant'Angelo d'Alife, they landed on the Anzio beachhead 25 March 1944, maintaining defensive positions until the offensive of 23 May, when it broke out of the beachhead, took Cisterna, and raced to Civitavecchia and Rome.

- **Sept 25, 1943:** 168th [from Oran] landed peacefully, 30 miles south of Salerno, Italy, near Paestum at Foce del Sele; marched ~9 miles inland to staging area near Battipaglia; training and organization; set up Hepatitis A camp for ~200 very sick soldiers.
- **Sept 28, 1943:** first contact with enemy at the Calore River, near Montemarano.
- **Oct 1, 1943:** Naples falls.
- **Oct 9, 1943:** Pompeii.
- **Oct 13, 1943:** first Crossing of Volturno near Limatola, resulting in capture of Caiazzo and Marciano Hgts.
- **Oct 19, 1943:** second crossing of Volturno at Dragoni; capture of Dragoni, Capriati Lete and Sava River Valleys.
- **Oct 21–24, 1943:** "resting," after having secured the 168th objective; the Hdq. Sect. of the Medics is now housed in a small mill at one end of a town of about 2,000 population.
- **Oct 27, 1943:** the 168th and Company C move down the valley west of Alife—may relieve the 133rd; the plans are in the making for a big-scale attack to include a third crossing of the Volturno (*Paulus Diaries*, p. 163).

6. Chronology of Military Service and Major Division Events 201

- **Oct 28, 1943:** the 168th and 135th attack in the morning to clean up the valley west of Alife to Pratella (*Paulus Diaries,* p. 163).
- **Oct 31, 1943:** the 133rd and 168th are pushing on well on either side of the valley above Pratola (*Paulus Diaries,* p. 164).
- **Nov 1, 1943:** battle has slackened somewhat for 168th/133rd; well along in the hills heading down the valley (*Paulus Diaries,* p. 164).
- **Nov 4, 1943:** third crossing of Volturno River near Roccaravindola, in vicinity of Venafro; ground thick with mines and booby traps; heavy casualties and evacuation difficult; capture Hill 400; wet clothing and boots, miserable, agonizing cold; 168th to be relieved soon.
- **Nov 14–24, 1943:** rain, mud, mud, mud!; bridges out on Volturno; 34th Div doing nothing and no plans; vehicles stalled in mud everywhere (*Paulus Diaries,* pp. 168–170).
- **Nov 18, 1943:** one week off to repair and resupply??; still in farmhouse with fireplace.
- **Nov 25, 1943:** 168th Regiment moved back on line (*As You Were,* p. 59).
- **Nov 27, 1943:** third crossing of Volturno; in vicinity of Venafro; ground thick with mines and booby traps; heavy casualties; evacuation difficult; capture Hill 400; wet clothing and boots, miserable, agonizing cold.
- **Nov 29–Dec 4, 1943:** Battle of Monte Pantano; counter attacks and heavy casualties; Lud earns the Silver Star for "gallantry-in-action" on Mt. Pantano, Italy; north anchor of German Winter Line captured. (1st Bn. 168th received the Distinguished Unit Citation for action on Mt. Pantano.)
- **Dec 8–17, 1943:** the Battle of San Pietro just south of Monte Cassino and half way between Naples and Rome; major engagement; von Ripper etching.
- **Dec 8–14, 1943?:** relief of the division; 168th coming back across river to its relief area (Alife) (*Mud, Mules, Mtns,* pp. 174–176); 76 consecutive days of contact with the enemy.
- **Dec 13, 1943:** Ludwick and Leslie present at the medical conference in Piedimonte. (*Paulus Diaries,* p. 177).
- **Dec 14–24, 1943:** 168th relieved for rest; in Sant'Angelo d'Alife; many go to rest camp ~fifteen miles east-northeast of Naples at Caserta, King Victor Emmanuel's "summer palace" (*As You Were,* p. 50).
- **Dec 22–26/27, 1943:** at officers' "rest camp" at Hotel Minerva in Sorrento, Italy, overlooking the Mediterranean.
- **Dec 29, 1943:** Col. Fred B. Butler transferred out of 168th; will become Brigadier General; Col Mark Boatner, Jr., replaces (West Point classmate of Butler's).
- **Dec 29, 1943:** the 168th moves to replace 36th Div in the Mignanao Valley (San Pietro-Infine and St. Vittore area, generally southwest of Mt. Pantano) and attack Jan. 1st or 2nd (*Paulus Diaries,* pp. 180–181); beginning of approach to Cassino.
- **Jan/Feb 1944 Summary:** Cassino Front; the 34th Div drove into the Gustav

Line, took Mount Trocchio after a bitter fight, pushed across the Rapido River, attacked Monastery Hill, and fought its way into Cassino, being relieved Feb 13, 1944; after rest and rehabilitation, it landed on the Anzio beachhead March 25, 1944.

- **Jan 1–16, 1944:** Venafro Camp; very tough going; almost 400 litter bearers being used—not enough; snow, wind, and rain—everyone wet and cold; 133rd in the high mountains running above Venafro approaching Cassino; longest litter carry trail, up to 12 miles, for evacuation of the wounded in the history of the American Army, organized by Major Morris J. Leslie, of the 133rd; 168th attacks Mt. Trocchio.
- **Jan 10–12, 1944:** the 168th and 135th are pushing on for limited objectives past Mt. La Chiaia & Trocchio that dominate Cassino approaches; attack on and capture of Cervaro, a village that overlooks Cassino three miles away; 168th received War Dept. Unit Citation for this ferocious battle (*Paulus Diaries,* p. 185).
- **Jan 15–Jan 23/24, 1944:** 168th still in village where it stopped; fairly quiet.
- **Jan 20–22, 1944:** Gari River battle; capture of Mt. La Chiaia and San Vittore, which unhinged key position of German Winter Line; almost 2,000 casualties, deaths, missing-in-action.
- **Jan 24–Feb 15, 1944:** 168th close to/at Cassino.
- **Jan 27, 1944:** 168th launches a ferocious river [Rapido] crossing attempt in the area of Pratella; Germans flood the river banks; tanks and vehicles bogged down in thick mud but the infantry forged ahead into the minefields; under fire and w/o tank support, the 168th had to retreat; further attempts failed.
- **Jan 30, 1944:** the 168th breaks through to take some high ground above Cassino; prisoners taken; moderate casualties (*Paulus Diaries,* p. 191).
- **Feb 8, 1944:** 168th moves to attack Cassino from the south; the 133rd continues to fight in the city.
- **Feb 11, 1944:** 168th attacks the Benedictine (Monastery) Hill—did not go well; plans for the 34th to be relieved by the 4th Indian Division in a day or so (*Paulus Diaries,* p. 195).
- **Feb 15, 1944:** the 168th relieved; 133rd to stay in Cassino (*Paulus Diaries,* p. 196).
- **Feb 17–27, 1944:** rest and respite from frontlines for ~ 10 days; back in desolate little Italian mountain village where they were in December 1943/Jan 1944, Sant'Angelo d'Alife; next village over was Piedimonte d'Alife; living in house owned by two elderly sisters; Naples, 40 miles away; looking for Jack.
- **Feb 21, 1944:** Martha Gellhorn (Mrs. Ernest Hemingway) visits 168th.
- **Feb 28, 1944:** back to training schedule to prepare for action.
- **March 1, 1944:** Exercise "Blowout," huge party after 1st Cassino battle; at Piedmonte d'Alife, Duke's Palace.
- **March 13, 1944:** Benevento—awarded Silver Star by General Mark Clark.
- **March 18, 1944:** Anzio-bound aboard LST (*Paulus Diaries,* pp. 205–6).

6. Chronology of Military Service and Major Division Events

- **March 19, 1944:** arrive at Anzio-Nettuno beachhead; go to bivouac area and dig in; at Cisterna and vicinity?
- **March 22, 1944:** 168th to relieve the Parachute Regiment of the Special Service Force (*Paulus Diaries,* p. 206).
- **March 23, 1944:** 168th goes into the line replacing the 15th Inf Reg (*Paulus Diaries,* p. 206).
- **March 25, 1944:** 168th completes the relief; no future plans (*Paulus Diaries,* p. 207).
- **April 12, 1944:** relief for rotational return to the United States from the Anzio-Nettuno Beachhead.
- **April 21, 1944:** first available ship from Anzio to Naples to the "Repo Depot," awaiting departure; visited Jack Hoyer (752nd Tank Battalion) in Eboli.
- **May 21, 1944:** arrives back in U.S.
- **May 27, 1944:** brother-in-law, Jack Hoyer, killed in action on his first day of combat with the 752nd Tank Bn, by incoming artillery from the hills outside of Maenza, Italy.
- **June 19, 1944:** Camp Butner, near Durham, NC: Eastern Personnel Reassignment Center; interview and PX; awaiting reassignment; continuing monthly $ allotments: "$250 to Jean, $90 to mother."
- **June 28, 1944:** assigned to 8th SvC, ASFTC, Camp Barkeley, TX; AG 210.31 Med Res.
- **Sept 29, 1945:** four mo leave of absence granted at Camp Crowder, Carthage, Missouri; to Waterloo on Jan 29, 1946.
- **Jan 29, 1946:** date of separation from Active Duty; Camp Crowder, MO.
- **Nov 28, 1947–Nov 12, 1951:** Army Reserve.

7

Walking Wounded

During the battle of Monte Pantano, Italy in late November/early December 1943, my father treated and evacuated injured men from his unit under a curtain of heavy artillery fire. The rough terrain and extreme weather conditions required miles-long litter relays to transport the most seriously wounded down the treacherous, almost impassable trails to the nearest Aid Station. There were also the "walking wounded," injured soldiers who could still walk, guided by my father and the litter squads to safety.

The term "walking wounded" was traditionally used in conflict to describe those who sustained low-priority injuries and were still ambulatory. However, now we know this designation also applies to a much wider group of victims who suffer from the collateral damage and psychological toll of war. Innocent civilians and bystanders, military families and, of course, combatants returning home, can all suffer from the lifelong, devastating emotional scars of war. These casualties are often not counted.

After their first major skirmishes with German troops in North Africa in February of 1943, many American soldiers suffered from "combat fatigue," now referred to as Post Traumatic Stress Disorder, or PTSD. Although the 34th Infantry Division had trained in Northern Ireland for nearly ten months prior to engaging with the enemy in North Africa, they were very young, inexperienced, and ill-equipped for actual live combat.

In these early conflicts at Kasserine and Fondouk Passes, in North Africa, "psychiatric reactions" were responsible for 20 percent of all battlefield evacuations, and ran as high as 34 percent. These numbers of "casualties" were unacceptable and marred a Commanding Officer's unit record. Something had to be done. As Albert E. Cowdrey noted in his book, *Fighting for Life,* "Battles began to last for days, then for weeks or months, forcing men to spend seemingly endless time under fire. The body's fight-or-flight mechanisms, designed by nature for use in brief emergencies, instead were evoked over long periods by the constantly impending danger of injury or death."

In 1951, Pulitzer Prize winning journalist and Associated Press staff writer Relman Morin wrote that "During World War II, 640,000 American soldiers cracked up from mental or emotional causes and became unfit to bear arms. These men were not 'crazy.' Nor were they 'cowards' in the absolute sense that they were totally incapable of controlling fear. Nevertheless, they were casualties, as surely as though each one had been hit by a bullet." Psychiatric casualties were indistinguishable from men who had been physically wounded—unable to function or fight, and paralyzed by fear. Their rehabilitation took more finesse.

Our family refers to my father's story about his unusual treatment method for dealing with these psychological casualties of war as "The Magic of Oatmeal." He seemed to instinctively know that unlike the physically wounded, soldiers suffering from combat fatigue became worse, not better, as they were moved farther to the rear. To effectively rehabilitate these men, they needed to be treated with compassion at the frontlines and kept *with* their unit. If they were evacuated and replenished with inexperienced replacement soldiers who lacked emotional ties to their new comrades, the result could make matters worse for the rest of the regiment. Also, because combat replacements were in such high demand, many of these soldiers, suddenly shoved forward to the frontlines, had not even finished basic training or qualified in their mastery of elementary weaponry, as well as being in poor physical shape and often overaged. Therefore, it was in a regiment's best interest to keep as many original unit members together as possible.

Perhaps Lud's novel and compassionate approach to treating PTSD was due, in part, to his own father's influence: Major Arthur L. Ludwick, Sr., M.D., who had been trained as a neuro-psychiatrist (or "alienist" as it was then called) and spent more than twenty years in civilian life treating patients with "nervous" and mental disorders.

1919 Carlstrom Field, Arcadia, Florida: Major Arthur L. Ludwick, Sr., M.D., center, one of our nation's first trained flight surgeons, with World War I pilots and biplane.

After joining the army during World War I in 1917, he became one of the country's first trained flight surgeons in the Army's Aviation Corps, graduating in 1918 from the newly opened School of Flight Surgeons and its Aviation Medicine Research Laboratory at Hazelhurst Field, Mineola, New York, and began treating "nerve-shocked" aviators, our nation's earliest and most daring pilots.

In December of 1918, amidst the great Spanish Flu epidemic, Capt. Arthur L. Ludwick, Sr., along with his wife and young son (my father), was transferred from Love Air Field in Dallas, Texas, to Cooperstown, New York, where the Mary Imogene Bassett Hospital was nearing completion. The U.S. Army had determined that the hospital's bucolic setting in upstate N.Y., along with the neurological expertise of hospital founder Bassett, would be an ideal location for convalescing aviators.

As a psychiatrist in civilian life and with flight surgeon training in the Aviation Corps of the U.S. Army, Captain/Dr. Ludwick was the logical choice for directing the treatment of these "stale" and traumatized World War I pilots. He believed that the majority of medical problems these flyers had were related to morale, fear, anxiety, and other emotions that interfered with their performance as pilots.

In one of his hospital reports, Ludwick Sr. noted:

"These 'Birds' are hypersensitive, quick-headed, reckless, and superstitious."*

And so, prior to its opening to the public-at-large, the new Bassett Hospital was turned over to the military for the treatment of "shell-shocked" aviators. At that time, it was assumed that flyers' neuropsychiatric disorders were a result of concussions suffered in artillery barrages and/or lack of oxygen in the open-air cockpits of the era's primitive bi-planes. However, this was not always the case. "Stale" aviators, whether they had engaged in actual combat flights or not, often faced terrifying challenges in the open cockpits of their flimsy planes.

Captain Ludwick Sr. had a sophisticated understanding of nerve shock, what we now refer to as PTSD, and how it should be treated, recommending a complete break from military discipline and talking freely with patients about their traumatic experiences.

Over a hundred years ago, Ludwick Sr. pioneered the use of a new and unconventional rehabilitation method now referred to as "psycho drama," where the distressed pilots wrote, staged, and performed in short re-enactment plays depicting their frightening and dangerous flight experiences. One such play, "The Eyes of the Army," was presented to neighboring communities in and around Cooperstown, New York, during the summer of 1919. In one particularly dramatic scene, an actual fuselage of an old army plane dropped onto the stage from the loft above, and in it were two aviator patients. This "special effect" stunned audiences and became a well-publicized attraction for subsequent performances.

"Captain Ludwick was promoted to Major on July 21, 1919, and assumed

---

* John S. Davis, M.D. *Bassett Hospital in Cooperstown, New York: 200 Years of Health Care in Rural America* (New York, NY: Bassett Healthcare Network, 2017), 61. [Hereafter cited as *Bassett Hospital*]; Ludwick Family Archives.

command of the Military Hospital. On August 30, he reported in a memorandum to the Chief Surgeon, Air Force Service, that 335 cases had so far been treated in the hospital, including 327 plane crash survivors."*

I can't help but think my dad's familiarity with his father's compassionate and innovative treatment of PTSD during World War I laid the foundation for his own approach to the "combat fatigue" he treated in North Africa and Italy: taking traumatized, young soldiers from the frontlines back to his aid station for a few days, and giving them the personal attention and counseling they needed.

Group/talk therapy sessions, in a circle of camaraderie with bowls of hot oatmeal, proved to be highly effective. The simple acknowledgment of a soldier's "normal" feelings of fear during combat, the opportunity to share those feelings with those who were fighting beside him, and bonding with unit members in a more personal and non-judgmental way resulted in the majority of these "combat fatigue" soldiers returning to service on the frontlines within a few days.

My dad's references to depression and fear in his letters are poignant and significant. They remind us of the hidden, uncounted injuries of war—the invisible wounds that veterans carry into their postwar lives that can affect families for generations to come.

Soldiers who return home from war physically unscathed are not necessarily injury-free. Their latent emotional scars can percolate for years, eventually bubbling up into a toxic brew as debilitating as a serious physical injury; or, they can manifest in more subtle ways that erode relationships with loved ones, friends, and colleagues, adversely affecting their quality of life. Either way, the dues are a high-price for membership in the not-so-exclusive "Walking Wounded" club.

Shortly after World War II, in one of the biggest projects conducted by the military, to study and investigate why there were so many cases of PTSD during World War II, two distinct factors emerged that led to some major reforms in officer training:

1. About 60 percent of the breakdowns occurred before the men ever were in combat. They occurred during training.
2. A direct ratio existed between the percentage of neurosis cases in a division while it was in combat, and the number of men killed and wounded by enemy fire. In other words, the more "psychos," the more gunfire casualties.

The Army concluded that good leaders are made, not born.

An essential component in command and leadership training had nothing to do with tactics, weaponry, or administration. Rather, it is the relationship among officer, soldier, and the given situation confronting them. Today, officers are educated to know that:

---

* *Ibid.*, 58.

1. A member of the infantry reaches his/her peak of mental and physical efficiency at about 90 days in the battle line. After that, it begins to decline.

2. A combat fatigue case should not be sent home or even very far away from his own unit. S/he can be used in a necessary/non-combat job before returning to combat.

3. Absolute obedience to a commanding officer is essential, but a soldier in the American army will perform far better if s/he knows the purpose and meaning of an operation and how it fits into the larger picture.

4. Officers are now encouraged to treat each woman/man as an individual, call the person by name, and take a personal interest in each person's welfare. If this can't be done in larger units, it certainly can be done at the company and platoon level, which is where battles are won. Officers today are being taught many of the things that chaplains have known for years—basic psychology, the ordinary things that motivate a soldier, the things that worry him/her, how to talk to and reason with them, and acknowledge the soldier's hard work and important contributions to the unit as a whole.*

Over the course of Lud's 28 months overseas, his frustration with the Army's bureaucracy and entrenched, inefficient "systems" compounded, as did his own bouts of depression and homesickness. However, he felt a deep obligation and determination to maintain a certain level of equanimity in front of his men; after all, he was responsible for their psychological well-being, as well as their physical health, and wanted to set a good example; but many of his letters expressed the constant struggle with despair as the war dragged on and the number of days in combat accumulated.

My father, himself, may have suffered from PTSD, whose effects were manifested in more indirect ways after the war. His quiet and subdued manner could have been, in retrospect, low-grade chronic depression, obsessive compulsive disorder, and/or melancholy that interfered with his ability to really "let down" and have fun. Yet, these behaviors may have also been merely a reflection of his true nature, shaped by being an only child of older parents, growing up during the Great Depression, and losing his beloved father at the age of sixteen.

During the war, Lud gently counseled his men and was a pillar of courage and strength on the frontlines; yet, where did *he*, an officer, go for his own support, comfort, and encouragement? Who helped him process the horrors of war and the seemingly random selection of who lived and who died? Obviously, his letters to my mother were an outlet for his frustrations, but not necessarily for his constant fear and anxiety. Most likely, he did *not* recount the many harrowing incidents and emotional trauma of war after arriving home, but whose effects he would always carry with him.

In email communications during the last few years with several other families whose fathers served alongside my father, there was a common theme: the postwar

---

* Relman Morin, AP staff writer and veteran war correspondent, "U.S. 'Lost' 640,000 in World War II Because of 'Psycho' Casualties; We Guard Against Repetition," Fort Benning, Ga. *The Montana Standard* (newspaper), July 3, 1951.

legacies of the brutal wartime conditions in North Africa and Italy revealed the hidden costs of war, not only for those who suffered physical and psychological wounds from combat experience, but also for their families back home, both during and after the war.

One soldier's family shared their father's postwar writings about the relentless and intense enemy shelling on the Anzio beach head:

> How can I describe four months of living with a lump in my throat every minute of the day and night? ... [with] the constant wear and tear on the nervous and emotional system, I believe I reached the point where I would have welcomed a disabling wound, just to be able to escape honorably from further exposure, but no such luck....
>
> ... I learned after a few days, that one could get a few winks [of sleep] in between the messengers of hate. It was just a matter of acclimation, for which one had to pay a price ... a price that only a psychiatrist could measure ... a price that might require a life time to pay ... a price that often showed its effect long after the war was over, but not forgotten.

The far-reaching trauma of combat still reverberates today, and continues to be a troublesome and largely unaddressed issue in our nation's military history. What lessons have we learned from the past and how do we mitigate the terrible after-effects of war? Is this even possible?

Collateral Damage

After my dad's death in February 2008, I began the enormous task of sorting through all he had saved, filed, and catalogued throughout his lifetime. Because I lived out of town and spent most of my time tending to the needs of my 91-year-old mother when I visited, it was slow going. But by November 2008, I had gathered together an assortment of World War II photos and postwar letters that Dad and his "Sidekick," Lt. Morris J. Leslie, had exchanged. Through this curating process, I began to more fully understand the significance of "Leslie" as part of my dad's war saga; I was determined to find his family and send them the tangible evidence of our fathers' deep connection.

I searched the internet for an obituary of Dr. Morris J. Leslie with no luck. Surprisingly, there were no references to this man, almost as if he had never existed. The 34th Infantry Division Association Newsletters were still being sent to my dad, even after his death in 2008. I was on the verge of cancelling the subscription when, on a hunch, I contacted the organization to see if it had any "Leslie" family members on its mailing list. It did, giving me an address for a "Joyce Leslie" in New Jersey, the only "Leslie" in their files. Could this be Dr. Leslie's wife? I had to know, so I sent the following letter via "snail mail."

November 5, 2008

Dear Joyce,

I am looking for a relative of M.J. Leslie, M. D., who used to live and practice family medicine in Brooklyn, NY. "Les" served with my father overseas during

WWII and they became close friends. Les and Dad shared a genuine fondness and respect for one another that is very evident in the letters they exchanged after the war. I also have several photos of Lt. Morris J. Leslie from WWII that my dad took and captioned. He mentioned "Les" many times in his letters home during the war.

In the summer of 1956, my family took a trip back east to New York and visited a family that I now realize was the Leslie family. I have some fond memories of this trip, but I was only seven years old. I have photos of the Leslie family and mine on top of the Empire State Building.

If you are related to Dr. Leslie and would like to have copies of the letters and photos of him that I have, I would be happy to send them to you. Old letters and photographs, like these, are so precious—I would never just throw them out without first trying to locate the family of my dad's beloved "Sidekick," Lt. Leslie.

Sincerely,
Peggy Ludwick

Three days later, I received this email from Joyce Leslie:

November 8, 2008:

"Dear Peggy,

I just received your letter and am so excited and happy to hear from you. I'm in tears! I am the daughter of 'Les' and we did, indeed, live in Brooklyn. My name is Joyce Leslie. I believe that I remember your visit with us in the 1950s. I was about 13 years old then.

My sincerest condolences on the recent passing of your father. My Dad died in February, 1965 from a coronary. He was only 56 years old. I miss him terribly to this day. I have desperately tried to find anyone who knew my dad, which is why I keep up my Associate Membership with the Gold Star Museum. My dad served in the 133rd Regiment of the 34th Infantry Division for 4½ years during WWII.

Peggy, I would absolutely LOVE to have the letters and the photos that you referred to in your letter. I will treasure them forever. I would be very happy to pay for the cost of mailing them to me.

I can't tell you how overjoyed I am to hear from you. I am in tears and so happy. Thank you so very much for contacting me. I hope to hear from you again soon."

Sincerely, Joyce Leslie

This was to be the beginning of an intense and emotional nine-year relationship between two daughters, on opposite coasts of the country, whose heroic fathers shared the extreme conditions of combat and subsequent camaraderie that lasted a lifetime. My email friendship with Joyce was intimately forged through highly personal and revealing exchanges, all based on the common bond of our fathers and their war experiences, as well as our own deep sense of loss.

Joyce suffered from severe rheumatoid arthritis and was pretty much housebound. She wedged a pencil into her deformed and crippled hand to type with the eraser head, "one stroke at a time," as she would say. She was a bit of a loner and recluse, and wrote that our correspondence was a lifeline for her.

She shared a lot about her father's medical practice, their close relationship as father and daughter, and most importantly, about the devastating effects of PTSD on her entire family:

Peggy,

WWII had a profound and devastating effect on my dad. My mom said that he was a totally different man when he returned after 4½ years on the front lines in the European Theatre. He weighed 125 pounds when he came home vs his normal weight of about 155 pounds. The way your dad described my dad [in his war letters] was not the dad I came to know. He was NOT a happy, clowning-around man—just the opposite, in fact. He was very serious, moody, brooding, short-tempered, and suffered from severe headaches.

He would sometimes sit in silence for a long time in a dimly lit room. I know he wanted to talk about the war, but nobody wanted to hear it, except for me, and I was just a kid. I often asked him about the war and he would tell me about things that happened (avoiding the worst, of course). He mentioned your dad's name many times....

He was very difficult to live with in many ways, but I adored him and he was wonderful to me. He took me fishing and horseback riding. My parents had a difficult marriage and finally separated about two years before my dad died in 1965. His life was changed forever by the war. I am just now beginning to understand what my mother was referring to.

I want to thank you so much for the letters and photos that you have sent to me, which I treasure so much, and for our email conversations. I've "talked" to you about things that I have NEVER discussed with anyone else, ever. You have shed light on my dad that I never was aware of before. Perhaps I will help you to better understand your dad, as well. Joyce

Sadly, Joyce died of uterine cancer in fall 2017. Although she and I planned to meet in person at some point, it did not occur. We still had so much to say to one another and many questions to ask and answer. My dream was to collaborate on some type of writing project about our fathers and their war experiences, but we ran out of time.

* * *

Growing up, I was very sensitive and attuned to the undercurrents of my parents' marriage and what was unspoken. Personality wise, they were very different from one another. In a letter my dad wrote to an old medical school friend, he referred to my mother as "...a lovely woman of great beauty and intelligence—fiery, but kind." *He* was quiet, an intellectual introvert, with a dry sense of humor and wit; *she* was vivacious, social, and full of energy. She enlivened his life and he grounded hers. But their predisposed differences could create misunderstandings and tension in their relationship.

Although they were married for 67 years, I remember the slamming of kitchen cabinet doors, periods of icy distance, and both of them withdrawing into themselves after an argument for days or even weeks at a time. They were definitely devoted and loyal, rigidly bound by their marital vows—but at times, they could be punishing and unforgiving towards one another, often resulting in a thick silence that was suffocating. I never knew how long that gloomy quiet would last. At times, I felt it was something I needed to help "fix."

Was my parents' poor communication with one another a result of being so mismatched, or was it a dynamic that grew over time? Or, perhaps it was the product of their upbringing and generation? After reading through all my dad's war letters and my correspondence with Joyce Leslie, I began to wonder if my parents' 28 months of separation at the beginning of their marriage was its own kind of trauma? Did those early years of anxiety, uncertainty, and being apart create a chasm so wide and deep that it was next to impossible to establish real intimacy once they were reunited? Perhaps, additional time together as newlyweds might have given them the opportunity to learn more about each other's emotional "style" and needs?

It was my observation that my mother expected my father to read her mind and anticipate what she needed or wanted, and he was never able to guess what that was. The cues were not given *or* received.

Jean specialized in "the sulk," which then became an impenetrable barrier to further inquiry by my dad. "The 'Sulker,'" according to author Alain De Botton, who writes about love and relationships, "both desperately needs the other person to understand and yet remains utterly committed to doing nothing to help them do so. The very need to explain forms the kernel of the insult: if the partner requires an explanation, he or she is clearly not worthy of one."*

Successful love, according to De Botton, is not just a feeling but a skill that generously invites each partner to share their story—to give each other a manual for how the other works and better understand their own behaviors. It's a teacher-student dynamic that flips both ways. My parents were smart, well-educated people, but lacked this kind of emotional intelligence. And their lack of experience with any previous romantic relationships of their own, or living parental role models from which to learn, may have also been contributing factors. Now, as an adult, I recognize the current of anger and resentment running below the surface of their marriage. Over time, it built a dam as formidable as the Grand Coulee.

However, my father's war letters home to my mother revealed a very different couple from the one I had experienced as my parents. I was astonished by my dad's passion and deep love for his wife of just two months and the heartache of their 2½ year separation. Now, I wish I had known more about their beginnings that eventually *did* sustain them throughout their uneven marriage, and that I could have had more compassion for the conflicts I observed. After reading Dad's letters, I came to realize I had been presumptive in passing judgment on my parents' marriage without

---

* Alain De Botton. *The Course of Love* (New York, NY: Simon & Schuster), 2016, 63. [Hereafter cited as *Course of Love.*]

a better understanding of the times in which they'd lived and the hardships they endured.

Dad's letters were, of course, only half of my parents' early love story. During the war, Lud was unable to keep Jean's letters, the contents of which would have been a fascinating read, providing a better understanding of the two as individuals and their new dance as husband and wife.

As my parents moved into their 80s and 90s, I noticed their increased appreciation of and patience with one another. A lifetime of familiarity, habit, and steadfast support became reassuring and consoling as they dealt with failing health and greater dependency on one another. I realized that their commitment and dedication to each other *was*, indeed, unflinching and resolute. And, despite their vast differences, they persevered in their marriage.

I can only wonder how and when this ardent and seemingly adoring young couple evolved into the parents I came to know. Was there a gradual erosion of openly expressed affection between them over the years, part of the natural progression of a marriage; or, did it begin soon after my dad returned home from war? They had only lived together two months when he left to serve overseas. The "honeymoon" period was most certainly still in effect when he finally returned home; but then, after 28 months of separation, was their reunion awkward? Were they somewhat estranged? Was it a joyful but also disappointing transition back into "normal" life?

A note in one of my dad's wartime pocket journals reads:

"J afraid we'll be strangers." Perhaps, their marriage became its own casualty of war?

8

Epilogue
Return and Readjustment

"None of us can ever know the value of our lives, or how our separate and silent scribblings may add to the amenity of the world, if only by how radically it changes us, one by one."
—Mary Karr, *The Art of Memoir*

Finding Home

November 2007

The Columbia River's deep pewter shimmered as we drove alongside it to the nursing home. Its dark, sinister beauty had always frightened me. As a little girl, I was repeatedly warned to never swim in it—strong, dangerous, and unpredictable undercurrents had claimed hundreds, even thousands of lives. At dinner, my dad periodically announced news of another unfortunate drowning and he most likely kept track on one of his hash-tag charts somewhere.

He kept meticulous records for almost everything: the number of shaves with a single razor blade; how many tachycardia (rapid heart-rate) incidents he'd had that month; dates when the furnace filter was last changed; the purchase dates and prices of clothing, carefully printed with a laundry pen inside trouser waistbands and shirt collars; lists upon lists and seemingly random entries in his small red leather pocket notebooks—names, phone numbers, addresses, bicycle lock combinations, a myriad of things to remember and keep track of yet miraculously retrieved when needed, even years later. Carefully logging the details of his life became a ritual.

As we crossed the river bridge, I was reminded that the powerful body of water flowing underneath had been the reason my parents settled in Wenatchee, Washington, in 1945. It was a small, tidy city of about 15,000 people, spread along the western bank of the "Mighty Columbia" River. It spanned the length of a narrow fertile valley and up the foothills, dotted with scores of blooming fruit orchards, all irrigated by the Cascade Mountains snow-pack that eventually made its way to the river. A large wood-carved sign in the shape of an apple and painted red sat at the town's north entrance, proudly proclaiming that *this* was "The Apple Capital of the World."

In October of 1945, when my father was discharged from active duty with the Iowa National Guard, he and my mother loaded their 1939 Oldsmobile Coupe with everything

8. Epilogue

they had, including their five-month-old son—my older brother, Jack—asleep on a mattress in the back seat. Heading west, they embodied the modern version of the early pioneers' optimism and adventurous spirit, seeking a new beginning and a place to call home.

They had a short list of locations to explore: Boise, Idaho; Spokane, Washington; Bend, Oregon. These places boasted plenty of sunshine, four good seasons, and had lower counts of ragweed pollen, to which my dad was terribly allergic. His hay fever had become almost debilitating in the Midwest—for several months of the year, his runny nose might drip onto a patient or contaminate a field of treatment.

After visiting Spokane in eastern Washington, they traveled west on Highway 2 through large expanses of golden wheat fields and over dry, rolling hills. As they wound their way down from the high plateau of Waterville, they caught their first glimpse of the Columbia River, near Orondo. Such an enormous resource of water, in my dad's innate wisdom, would most likely become the foundation of economic stability for generations. They turned left, followed the river to Wenatchee, and that was that.

And so it was, and still is. The Columbia River's formidable, fast-moving water has been the lifeline to a rich agricultural valley, irrigating row upon row of apples, peaches, pears, cherries, and grapes, a tapestry of ever-changing colors against the brown scrub foothills of the Cascade Mountain range. Almost as important, the massive force and energy of that river would eventually turn enormous steel turbines, providing abundant hydroelectric power and the cheapest electricity rates in the country. Wenatchee, a hidden gem in the shrub-steppe of central Washington, was poised for growth. It would be the perfect place to raise a family and build a medical practice for a young, eager physician.

"Say, Ahhh."

When Dad retired from his career as a family doctor in 1989 at age 76, the Washington State Medical Association honored his fifty-plus years as a full-time physician. In a front-page story by the local newspaper, *The Wenatchee World*, Dad fondly referred to the practice of medicine as "an old friend."

For him, becoming a family physician was more of a calling than a profession—a comfort, as well as the primary foundation of his identity. Moreover, it was a deeply personal tribute to his beloved father who had also been a general practice doctor.

Dad was an incredibly hard-working, devoted physician who took care of generations of families. He was one of the last remaining independent doctors who still made house calls and would often accept homemade goods from patients who couldn't pay their bill: breads and pies, hand-knit sweaters, freshly caught salmon, overnight hunting horse-pack trips. When visiting a patient, even in the middle of the night, he would dress in shirt, tie, and sports coat to maintain his professional appearance. "Patients need to trust you," he said. He always carried a fresh tongue depressor and pencil flashlight in his shirt pocket, even at home, as neighbors and friends would often knock on the back door for medical advice or treatment of a minor ailment. Living two hours away in Yakima, Washington, as a new mother, I was the recipient of one of his "ultimate" house calls in the middle of the night, to check on my sick baby with a high fever, his first grandchild. Now that's what I call devotion to his patients—and, of course, to family.

As a small-town doctor on call 24/7, Dad worked long hours: early morning surgeries, patient appointments in his office until 5:30 p.m., house calls and hospital rounds in the evenings after dinner. The practice of medicine was a way of life, not just a profession. We couldn't count on him to take us to a movie, attend a dance recital, music program, or even a backyard barbeque with friends. Doing anything together as a family depended entirely on his availability, which was always an unknown. I spent a lot of time just *waiting* for him, looking through the wavy, leaded-glass dining room windows of our Red Apple Road home for a glimpse of his car coming up the street—and ultimately, listening to the kitchen clock tick, "too late."

For recreation, he played golf a few times a year—and he and my brother would occasionally go on one- or two-day hunting/fishing trips, hosted by one of his grateful patients; but those kinds of activities were never open to my tagging along.

Though I didn't spend much recreational time with my father, I *did* work in his medical office for several summers, starting at about age twelve. I answered the phone, filed charts, logged payments, and performed other simple clerical tasks while also getting an up-close-and-personal view of running a medical practice—in particular, how long patients were kept waiting in his office waiting room.

Dad was notorious for spending an inordinate amount of time with each of his patients, something for which he never apologized. He thought it was important for the patient to understand their illness, often drawing simple sketches and diagrams to explain how the human body worked and why/how the symptoms were being manifested. He believed that the *psychology* of treating a patient and collecting a thorough medical history, including details of their life circumstances, led to a more successful treatment

1956, Wenatchee, Washington: Dr. Arthur L. Ludwick, Jr., in his medical office.

outcome. It truly was an art form that we don't often experience today, given "modern" medicine's coded time constraints. The fact that Dad was able to maintain and grow a thriving medical practice, attests to the loyalty of his patients and the quality of care they received.

Sometimes, he would take me to the ER to see a patient, make hospital rounds after dinner, or go on a house call. Those times with my father, as his "assistant," are seared into my memory: helping hold down a screaming, wriggling toddler in the ER while he fished out a live earwig from her inner ear; a dark and dingy dining room permeated by the smell of cooked cauliflower; an African American family's home filled with strong vibrant colors and framed photos of places and people I didn't know about.

A couple of times we visited an overly warm trailer on the outskirts of town. Madeline, with her lovely English accent, was in her 50s and had serious heart problems. She was a "welfare" patient, and often paid my father with beautifully hand-knit ski sweaters that both my brother and I wore through the years.

Dad carefully listened to her chest with his stethoscope as she sat on a worn plaid couch, naked from the waist up. I had learned from him that placing the head of a stethoscope on bare skin was crucial for capturing every nuance of a beating heart. Still, seeing another woman's bare breasts other than my mother's, and in the presence of my father, was a bit of a shock. My cheeks burned.

Lud did a little bit of everything: tonsillectomies, hernia repairs, appendectomies, pinning hips, pediatrics—and he delivered more than 2,000 babies. He was a gifted surgeon, with one year of surgical residency plus wartime experience, but did not specialize in this medical discipline. Instead, he did as much surgery as he could on his own, but also referred patients to his surgeon colleagues for more advanced/technical procedures. He usually assisted in these surgeries, becoming the preferred surgical assistant for many complicated surgeries.

We had a somewhat unusual relationship as father and daughter. One morning, while driving me to school in the fourth grade, he told me all about sex in his clinical yet informative way. He set my broken leg when I was twelve and pierced my ears when I was in college. When I left for college, he stocked a fishing tackle box with everything I'd need to treat myself and 60 sorority sisters in case of minor illness: thermometer, antihistamines, antibiotics, band-aids and steri-strips, Unguentine ointment and Neosporine, cough syrup and decongestants. As a Bacteriology and Public Health major, I was able to swab a sore throat and culture it in the lab to rule out a strep infection. Once, noticing a roommate's symptoms of frequent urination and extreme thirst, I diagnosed her onset of diabetes with a simple blood glucose test. Slipping into the lab to do a discreet pregnancy test or check a blood slide for mononucleosis became routine, although I sent those with a fever to the Student Health Center. Mostly, I treated common colds, allergies, coughs, and skin rashes, sometimes in consultation with my dad over the phone. Towards the end of my pregnancy with my first child, he sent me a four-page typed letter about the virtues and techniques of breast-feeding. He taught me well.

At my dad's nursing home, where he lived for three months before his death in 2008, there was a non-stop litany of caregivers—from the shower attendants to the dining room servers to the nursing staff—who would affectionately remind him that he had delivered their mother, or father, or brother, or sister. They felt some kind of very loyal, generational connection to him.

His patience, calm, and unhurried manner evoked a deep trust within his patients and families—and they were devoted to him. They believed him and believed *in* him. He *always* told the truth even if, at times, the news seemed harsh or unpleasant. His loyal office staff adored him, as well, becoming their own family over the years. A small, hand-printed framed sign hung in his office that said, "Take care of your office, and your office will take care of you."

At his retirement party in December of 1988, one of Dad's favorite patients, Katherine K., wrote:

"Dr. Ludwick,

After 39 years as your devoted patient, you may think I might have difficulty in coming up with my favorite memory, but I knew right off the bat what it would be! I was seven months along with my first of nine successful pregnancies. I was getting nervous about what was going to happen when it was time for the baby to be delivered. You spent a whole hour describing verbally and with diagrams the normal delivery of a baby from my arrival at the hospital until I would leave. You also described some out-of-the-ordinary ways in which babies are delivered. My mind was so relieved and filled with confidence that when my waters broke at home, I just followed the instructions you gave me two months before and told everyone else what to do and away we went to the hospital! Your final words of instruction on that day have always remained with me: 'Put your trust in God first, then in yourself, and then in me!'

And, I'll never forget the time I called you at home about 6:30 p.m. (after office hours) and told you I was afraid to go through the night without you seeing Teresa, Joe, and Steve, who were suffering from asthma due to allergies. You were taking Jean to the theater that evening, so you came by the house on your way and gave the ailing children a shot. About 10:30 p.m., you called from the theater and asked if someone would be up about midnight. You were afraid Joe, who was most ill, would not last through the night on that one shot and you wanted to give him another one on your way home from your outing. I've never heard of such dedication and I know I never will. There's only one Dr. Ludwick!"

Lud studied for the American Academy of Family Physicians (AAFP) board exams in 1970, at age 57, after practicing medicine for more than 30 years. DNA and penicillin hadn't yet been discovered when he was in medical school, 1932 to 1936. Much of the material on these exams was technical rather than practical, so he was at a disadvantage. He didn't *have* to put himself through this scrutiny and certification, but felt it was important to designate the practice of "Family Medicine" as its own unique specialty and to prove that he was well qualified. In 1970, he was in the first group of AAFP Diplomats to become board certified.

Some might have thought my father was a little peculiar, but to us, his idiosyncrasies were standard practice. Our house was filled with used surgical scrub brushes and sponges, recycled into a variety of uses: hair brushes, window sill props to prevent the shades from banging in the evening breeze, kitchen sink scrubbers, foot scrapers, soap holders, or whatever. He didn't like to waste anything. He had a fit when he discovered there was no window in the newly remodeled doctors' lounge at the community hospital, and voiced his disappointment to the administration. "Surgeons need to see some daylight and the outdoors when they've been operating for hours and need a break," he argued. Lo and behold, in the ensuing months, a window appeared in that doctors' lounge, complete with a sign above it: "Ludwick's Lookout."

Over the years, Lud maintained a variety of unorthodox treatments for particular ailments. One was his cure for a serious nosebleed. He kept a package of salt pork in his office and home refrigerators for just such occasions. If a patient came in with a bad nosebleed, Lud stuffed the nostril with a small roll of the salt pork, which naturally cauterized the ruptured blood vessel and usually stopped the bleeding. There was a notebook full of such remedies for medical students, "fellows," and/or new physicians joining the practice, as part of their orientation.

My father strictly adhered to a low fat/salt diet, which he adopted after his father died unexpectedly of arteriosclerosis in 1930 at the age of 57. No cheese, salt, cream, or butter, an egg just once a week, non-fat powdered milk with meals. He never felt the need to do aerobic exercise due to the fact that since childhood, he had regular spells of Paroxysmal Atrial Tachycardia or "PAT," where his heart rate would speed up to ~150 beats per minute until he pressed on his carotid artery to stop it. "Just like running a mile," he'd say, with his signature deadpan delivery.

The Jean and Lud I Knew

My mother's idyllic early childhood took a significant turn when she was eight years old. While playing with her five-year-old sister, Marjorie, on the grassy meridian in front of their home in Virginia, Minnesota, a drunk driver swerved up over the curb, instantly killing little Margie and narrowly missing my mother, Jean. It was said that after this traumatic incident and terrible loss, Jean's mother, Lenore, began drinking heavily—mostly in her kitchen in the afternoons with the parish priests. This "escape" would often continue into the evenings, after the priests returned to their parsonage for dinner.

In the late 1920s and early '30s, there were no Alcoholics Anonymous groups or treatment centers for addiction to alcohol. Alcoholics were sometimes banished to a mental health sanitarium if a family could afford the long-term room and board; but this "therapy" was more of an asylum than a rehabilitation facility, with patients often heavily medicated.

Alcoholism was considered a character flaw and a family disgrace. In what might have been a last-ditch effort to save their marriage, her parents had one more child, Joan—14 years younger than my mother. Jean took little Joanie everywhere with her around town—on dates, to high school basketball games, long walks in the baby carriage, and grocery shopping. A year or two before my mom died at age 95, she wondered out loud if maybe the town thought the baby was hers.

As successful and accomplished as my mother became in life, she was also a wounded child who grew up in a small Minnesota town, carrying the dark deep secret and shame of having an alcoholic parent. She had very little contact with her mother, Lenore, after leaving for college and felt terribly guilty "abandoning" her baby sister, Joan. Her father, Ben, eventually moved south to Duluth, taking young Joan to live with him and his elderly, deaf Danish mother, Petrea Hoyer. He became a social worker and, out of necessity, placed Joanie in a series of Catholic boarding schools until she came of age. The last time the Hoyer family gathered together was in Duluth in June 1944, for young Jack Hoyer's funeral after he was tragically killed in Italy during World War II. In 1952, my mother received a phone call that Lenore had died. I was four years old and knew nothing of my grandmother.

Jean never shared details of her family life with Lud while they were courting. He knew something was amiss, but didn't want to pry. Her adored younger brother, Jack, attended their small private wedding in Alexandria, Louisiana, in 1941, and miraculously, Lud was able to rendezvous with him a few times during the war. Their father, my beloved "Grampa Ben," was always an important part of my childhood and our family life over the years, but there was never any mention of Lenore.

I remember having a conversation with my mom when she was about 94 years old, four years after Dad died, wanting to know more about *her* mother and childhood. She had blocked a lot of it out and became upset at my questioning. In fact, she asked me to stop "badgering" her. She was proud to be a "survivor," not dwelling on or even recognizing her emotional scars and their effects. But on that evening in 2012, at age 94, with a child's quivering chin, she painfully revealed that as a young girl, *no* one—no teacher, neighbor, friend, or family member, had ever asked *her*, "Are you okay?" The "problem" was kept private by *everyone* and buried in a deep hole of shame and denial.

In 1951, when my brother was six and I was three, my mother contracted polio and was quarantined in a hospital room for a month. I remember waving to her from the hospital parking lot and sobbing. Jack and I had to be taken in by neighbors and my dad was beside himself with worry. Eventually, Mom recovered with no serious paralysis and "bounced back" by starting the first therapeutic swim program at the local YMCA.

Jean was a dynamic civic activist and leader involved in local and state Republican politics, serving on many community boards and appointed to the Washington State Board of Community Colleges by then-governor Dan Evans. In 1976, she ran for public office, becoming the first woman in Washington State to be elected as a Public Utility District (PUD) commissioner. She served diligently on the Chelan County PUD board for twelve years, six as president. With two dams on the Columbia River, the PUD's hydroelectric power was a multi-billion-dollar business that required a lot of time, study, and policy-making. She took the job seriously and pored over the thick packets of information sent before the weekly board meetings. She asked good questions and challenged the status quo. During her tenure, she was instrumental in the planning and completion of six beautiful "Hydro Recreation Parks" on the Columbia River, her name forever emblazoned on the bronze plaque at each park's entrance.

Mom not only canned all the fruit growing in our yard, but picked it as well, even into her 90s. Her energy was boundless, often starting a batch of apricot or plum jam at 11 p.m. Instead of organizing closets or drawers at home, she'd go hit a golf ball and at one time was the oldest active golfer at the Wenatchee Golf and Country Club. At age 94, she renewed her driver's license and drove towards 96.

Although my mother and I butted heads for most of my life, I am forever grateful for the last five years we had together after my father's death in 2008. As our parent-to-child roles reversed, she softened and apparently, I grew up. During those "post–Lud" years, we both shifted into a space of acceptance—and beyond. I valued her cheerful, "can-do" attitude as her body deteriorated and her short-term memory failed. And she more freely expressed her love and appreciation for me in a way I had not experienced before. Yes, she truly *needed* me at that point in her life—but apparently, I also needed her. And as much as I had yearned for a different kind of mother during my formative years, here we were—very much together at the end of her life and showing each other the best we had to give to one another.

Mom's longevity afforded me the time and opportunity to acknowledge and witness her strength and determination to make the most of what life had given her. The full impact of the losses she experienced as a child, adolescent, and young adult culminated into the realization that like my father, she too was a valiant and proud survivor of life's traumas.

* * *

My father was a deeply religious man in a quiet and personal way. He never preached or evangelized, but his faith in God was a constant and vital source of strength and guidance throughout his life. I believe it was forged into steel during World War II when he felt he should have died many times in battle, but finally became resigned to the fact that the Lord had another plan for him. Before bed every night, he would kneel on one knee beside his bed, hands clasped and head bowed in prayer. Many times growing up, and even as an adult, I witnessed this intimate and reverent ritual of my father's which always reminded me of his humility and devotion to a Higher Power.

Lud was thrifty and practical, recycling and repurposing everything he could before finally throwing it away. He patiently repaired what was broken, worn or torn, darned his own wool socks, sewed on lost buttons, patched hoses and bicycle tires. When he pulled on his faded blue zippered jumpsuit, we'd all groan, because we knew the impending repair job would take *forever*, given his slow and methodical pace. But the job would always be done right and last forever.

He was so meticulous and deliberate in everything he did, it eventually evolved into a degree of Obsessive Compulsive Disorder, OCD—and I'd occasionally point this out to him:

"Dad—I'm pretty sure you're OCD," I'd say in moments of frustration and impatience. He'd wryly respond with, "Don't you want your surgeon to be OCD?" He had a point, I guess, and even seemed proud of this eccentricity; after all, it had saved lives and served him well.

He usually wore long sleeves and always a wide-brimmed hat in the summer to protect himself from the harmful UV rays of the sun. During the last few years of his life, when the family gathered at our summer place on the shores of glacier-fed Lake Chelan, he'd spend his time indoors studying the World Atlas, or looking something up in a book or medical journal. "Dad," I'd say, "Come outside with us and have some fun." His standard reply would be, "This *is* fun to me. I'm having a good time right here." And, it was true. Glancing up occasionally from his reading and witnessing the comings and goings of his children, grandchildren, and friends was entertainment enough.

I came to realize that in my father's world, indulging in recreational/fun activities was not only unnecessary, he may even have considered it somewhat selfish and frivolous. For him, the idea of *pleasure* was fraught with connotations of triviality and an unwarranted waste of precious time. When I told him about a friend who had just climbed Mt. Rainier, he asked: "Why would anyone ever choose to purposely put his life at such risk? They've obviously never been shot at in a fox hole." The vestiges of losing his father at an early age and experiences during World War II, still were a presence in his life.

Dad did, however, take up sailing in the 1970s, purchasing a small sail boat that he kept 45 miles away from Wenatchee at Lake Chelan. I think it was the quiet and physics of sailing that appealed to him. Family members and a few close friends would occasionally take turns going out with him for a "quick sail," privately dreading the possibility of sudden strong gusts and choppy water, or even worse, the wind dying down to nothing at all. Being stuck in the middle of the huge lake for a couple of hours with my dad, trapped on his little boat patiently waiting for a breeze and listening to his corny jokes, was not necessarily on our "fun" list. He'd rarely resort to using the single paddle to get back to shore, demonstrating the more important principle of patience to not rush or unnecessarily intervene—another one of his life lessons.

As serious as my dad could be, he was also known for his dry sense of humor and perfect timing in the delivery of a long rambling joke's punch line. Around the dinner table at a family gathering, or as a speaker at some community organization's event, he'd have carefully prepared to lead off his comments with a well-curated anecdote that always drew a hearty laugh and collective groan from the audience. Having made his home in Wenatchee, Washington, the "Apple Capital of the World," prompted him to take a box of Washington State apples to his University of Kansas Medical School reunion, lamenting how difficult it was for a doctor to make a living where he lives. (You know, "An apple a day keeps the doctor away?")

He could carry a tune and liked to sing, although his musical repertoire was limited to the Big Band orchestras, Mitch Miller's sing-alongs, and KU fight songs. He got a kick out of tapping out a tune with his fingers on top of his big, bald head, moving his mouth into various "ohs" to shape the notes; or cupping his hands to blow a song through the make-shift reed of his thumbs, controlling the pitch with three of his fingers. And he was a fluid, rhythmic ballroom dancer. At my parents' dance club that met four times a year, Dad always had a line-up of women waiting to dance with him. Most of the husbands merely swayed back and forth without moving much; but Lud skillfully steered his partners all around the dance floor in whatever dance step the music dictated. It was a challenge and thrill to follow him.

As a little girl, Dad taught me how to properly ballroom dance by having me stand on top of his polished wing-tipped Florsheim shoes, as we'd glide across the kitchen linoleum floor. Dancing with him continued into my young adulthood, most likely to prepare me for the first dance at my wedding. What a disappointment it was to learn that most of the boys I slow danced with in high school and college didn't know how to waltz, fox trot, or swing—they just stayed in place and swayed a bit, barely moving their feet. It was boring. Wasn't dancing all about moving around the dance floor to the rhythm of the music?

After I graduated from college with a degree in Microbiology and Public Health and pursued postgrad studies at Stanford Medical Center in Palo Alto, California, my dad's annual birthday present to me became the latest volume of *The Merck Manual*. First published in 1899 as a small reference book for physicians and pharmacists, "The Manual" grew in size and scope to become one of the most widely used comprehensive medical resources for professionals and consumers in referencing symptoms and possible disease diagnoses.

In the fall of 2000, when my father was 87 years old, I took him on a ten-day trip back to his family roots in Missouri and Kansas. After picking up our rental car in Kansas City, we visited all his old homes, schools, and ancestors' gravesites throughout the two states. Along the way, I used a small hand-held recording device to ask him questions about his childhood, family history, legends and stories that had been passed down over the years. They were now all securely preserved on tape, which I eventually transcribed into a draft document over the course of a few years. Little did I know at the time, but this was to be the beginning of my years-long project to honor my father and his remarkable life.

My dad's birthday present to me that year was a new *Merck Manual* with this inscription, written with blue fountain pen in his beautiful flowing hand:

To Peggy, in commemoration of her birthday 6 Oct 2000 and of our great trip back to Missouri & Kansas at that time. With much love, Dad.

* * *

Whether in medical school, on the battlefield, or in the operating room of life, my father embodied his favorite quote from Calvin Coolidge: "Nothing in this world can take the place of persistence. Persistence and determination alone are omnipotent. The slogan, 'Press On,' has solved and will always solve the problems of the Human Race."

And his personal slogan that enabled him to overcome all obstacles in life with honor and dignity: "*Success* is doing something you don't want to do, and doing it well."

The Last Battle

As a physician, Dad spent plenty of time in nursing homes making rounds and visiting his elderly patients in the evenings after dinner. Years before, his 82-year-old mother, struggling with memory loss, was eventually moved out of her apartment in Wenatchee to such a facility. One night she went missing and was found collapsed along the nearby irrigation canal. "Heart Failure" was the autopsy report, but Alzheimer's is what stole her mind and quality of life. This scenario may have been playing in my father's mind as we drove to the Mountain View senior living facility.

My mom and brother, Jack, had gone ahead to finish setting up Dad's room. Although it was a "private," it was small and dark with barely enough space for the basics: a dresser, recliner, a small bedside table, and the hospital bed—the only available private room in one of two skilled nursing facilities in town. The building was old and understaffed with patients in wheelchairs parked in front of the nurse's station for much of the day. They were slumped over asleep or mumbling words, asking—no, *calling, pleading* for help. It was disturbing and heartbreaking.

But, as we crossed the bridge and headed toward the nursing home, tiny shreds of relief and hope crept in—maybe it wouldn't be so bad after all—Dad would get the constant care he needed, more social interaction with a wider range of people, and my 90-year-old mother would be able to get some rest and take better care of herself. At least that was what I kept telling myself.

For the next few months, my mother devotedly visited my father twice a day, bringing his favorite homemade soups and oatmeal cookies. Eventually, he struck up a nice friendship with a married couple, Earl and Margaret Bird, who shared a room next to his. They ate their meals together in the dining room and talked about their lives, when prompted. Margaret had been a practicing registered nurse in Waterville, Washington, almost as long as my dad had been a doctor, so they had much in common. During my frequent visits, I came to know the Birds well, and kidded Margaret and Dad that they should set up office hours to treat the patients in their wing of the facility. They laughed at this, but I could see the wheels turning in my dad's head at the suggestion. For decades, he had carried his meticulously packed doctor's bag with him at all times, "just in case." I have to admit, I briefly considered bringing it to his room, all ready to go.

Early one morning, just three months after my dad entered the Mountain View nursing home, he was found collapsed in his room, on his knees between the bed and chair. My brother was certain he'd been praying. I think he rang the bed bell for help in the early morning hours due to some kind of cardiac incident, or needing assistance getting to the bathroom, and no one showed up in time. Regardless, he was gone, and I so wish someone had been there to hold his hand as he slipped away. If I were there, I would have whispered his sweet farewell to me whenever we parted:

"Be good, and if you can't be good, be careful."

9

Behind the Lines
A Daughter's Reflections

We "...don't write in order to be understood; we write in order to understand."
—C.S. Lewis

"What's remembered, lives."—Jessica Bruder, Nomadland

"History is a symphony of echoes heard and unheard. It is a poem with events as verses."
—Charles Angoff, journalist

Ironically, it was only *after* my dad died that I was able to more fully appreciate what a remarkable man he was and realize that I had squandered precious time when I was with him. I spent much of my life trying to show him who I *wasn't* and how different we were, instead of just *being* with him, asking more personal questions, and getting to know him as someone other than my father. I was often exasperated by his conservative and narrow views of the world and frequently challenged his political, religious, and societal beliefs. I had come of age in the late 1960s/early 1970s during the Civil Rights/Women's Rights movements and the Vietnam War. I lived, worked, and did postgraduate studies in California, and was convinced that times had changed, while my dad had not. I was certain that most of his opinions were outdated, old-fashioned, and obsolete. Our lifelong, intense debates were lively and sometimes heated, but were always respectful. He patiently listened to my rants, gently replied with his own thoughtful responses and questions and now, I realize, often gave more of an inch than I.

The father I grew up with is the man I so arrogantly *thought* I knew; but after reading his notes and letters written as a young man, I came to know him in a completely different way. I was given a second chance to experience him as the complex person he was, separate from his role as my father: the grief-stricken sixteen-year-old boy who unexpectedly lost his father at a tender age; the determined and completely focused college and medical school student; the responsible head-of-household son; the faithful and supportive husband, courageous combat officer, and beloved physician.

His writings and all that he saved became the tangible remains of his voice, evidence of what mattered to him and providing glimpses into his interior life. They helped me make better sense of how he came to be the father I knew, providing me the opportunity to pull back a curtain with a different vista.

There was an emotional tethering that intensified as I sorted through all of my father's archives. Paradoxically, through the tactile act of writing down his stories and excerpting his hundreds of letters and notes, I discovered we were more alike than I ever imagined or dared to admit. My own long letters, compulsive lists, analyses of every issue and situation, detailed notes and expansive files suggest that I *am*, indeed, my father's daughter.

Most importantly, through my father's eloquent letters home to my mother during World War II, I was given the gift of imagining them both as the people they once were, *before* my existence. In so doing, my own internal landscape shifted and expanded, shaping their presence and now, absence, with softer edges. Seattle writer Scott Driscoll notes, "Death ends a life, not a relationship," and in discovering my parents as a young couple very much in love, my connection with them changed.

* * *

As poet Marilyn Nelson writes, "...our stories are what we are—that's all that we are; learning how to understand ... and what they teach us and can teach others. This could be the very essence of our existence here."

I wonder how *our* children and their children will come to know and remember us? As much as I hope treasured family stories will be lovingly told and passed down through generations, I'm also skeptical. In today's frenzied and demanding world, with family members often scattered geographically, the spoken word is a fragile strand that could easily break. In our "modern," technological times with most communication so transient through emails, texts, Facebook, Twitter, and Instagram posts, all of which disappear over time, what *will* remain of us? Photos that live on our cell phones and computers with no identification of who's who, will quickly disappear into oblivion. How will families get a glimpse of an ancestor's image, unique character, challenges, triumphs and stories; of their fears, passions, life choices and what mattered most to them? And ultimately, is any of this important and will anyone really care?

Is a life then, what you've done—or what you've saved, treasured, and kept? What do the remains of a person's life and what they leave behind say about who they were? The material and physical collections of a family member's cherished objects, photos, journal entries, and letters, have the capacity to live beyond a generation or more and provide insight and understanding, if we take the time to look—and contemplate. Physical archives can be handled and pondered, sorted and considered over a period of time, sometimes providing clues to how we came to be who *we* are. These kinds of deeper connections to the roots of our family trees can corroborate what we already *think* we know about our family's past; but they can also expand our perspective, understanding, and appreciation of complex family relationships and the cultural influences of time and place.

Connecting the dots from previous generations can be illuminating as we dare to learn more about family stories and their clues to what we know about ourselves. Our ancestry defines us in large and small ways and our ancestors still have an effect on us. We're a mosaic of not just their DNA, but of their life choices, as well. Where we go in life is heavily influenced by where our ancestors have been. Knowing where we're from can guide us to where we're going.

Unfortunately, this interest and curiosity often comes later in life, as we confront our own mortality. It wasn't until I was in my early 60s that I began to more seriously explore my parents' beginnings and their individual family histories—and consider that collective impact on my own family. Fortunately, both my parents lived well into their 90s, giving me the gift of time to begin the process of sorting through and untangling generations of family patterns and dynamics.

Old family photos provided an immediate and strong sense of connection. Now, when I look at photos of my Danish great-grandmother, Petrea Hoyer, I see some of myself there. Standing next to my great-grandfather John Hoyer, outside their two-story clapboard house in Duluth, Minnesota, her arms crossed over a starched white apron—or with friends at a typical Scandinavian picnic in the community cemetery—she looks and feels familiar. I often find myself naturally settling into her very same cross-armed stance. Seeing this in an ancestor, whom I never met, gives me a sense of continuity and grounding. Our shared DNA has manifested itself in a way I recognize and makes me wonder what other traits we have in common. It changes the way I see myself—not just as the unique entity I think I am, but also deeply connected to my past and part of the cumulative sequence of those who came before me.

2003 Winthrop, Washington: Jean and "Lud" Ludwick at the wedding of their grandson, Josh Henretig.

9. Behind the Lines

The massive paper trail of my father's life has been a priceless gift. Author and historian Walter Isaacson, in his brilliant biography of Leonardo da Vinci, notes:

> Paper turns out to be a superb information-storage technology, still readable after five hundred years.... Five hundred years later, Leonardo's notebooks are around to astonish and inspire us. Fifty years from now, our own notebooks, if we work up the initiative to start writing them, will be around to astonish and inspire our grandchildren, unlike our Tweets and Facebook posts [524].*

As humans, we all grapple with similar life challenges: fear, uncertainty, compromised choices, mistakes made, unrequited love, regrets, hopes and dreams. It's surprising how even a stranger, in sharing his/her own story and vulnerabilities, can provide consolation and reassurance—and help one feel not so alone. This kind of random connection can be comforting and transforming. My hope is that this book will provide that kind of link with readers.

Maria Popova, in her book, *Figuring*, postulates, "History is not just what happened, but what survives over time."

My father's experiences on the frontlines of World War II and his letters home remain alive, providing timeless insights into the nature of love and war—two of human history's most enduring themes. Their soft yet steady pulse still throbs with quiet wisdom and remarkable relevance. I am, indeed, astonished and inspired.

---

* Walter Isaacson, *Leonardo da Vinci*, New York: Simon and Schuster, 2018; Maria Popova, *Figuring*, New York: Vintage, 2020.

Appendix A

Silver Star Commendation

The Silver Star is the third-highest military combat decoration that can be awarded to a member of the U.S. Armed Forces. It is awarded for gallantry in action:

—While engaged in action against an enemy of the United States;
—While engaged in military operations involving conflict with an opposing foreign force;
—While serving with friendly foreign forces engaged in an armed conflict against an opposing armed force in which the United States is not a belligerent party.

Actions that merit the Silver Star must be of such a high degree that they are above those required for all other U.S. combat decorations but do not merit award of the Medal of Honor or a Service Cross (Distinguished Service Cross, the Navy Cross, or the Air Force Cross). *https://valor.defense.gov/Description-of-Awards/*

The text of Major Ludwick's original Silver Star Commendation:

<u>CONFIDENTIAL</u>
HEADQUARTERS 34TH INFANTRY DIVISION
UNITED STATES ARMY
APO-34
CWR/LAB/rc

27 January 1944

201.—Ludwick, Arthur L. (Off)
Subject: Award of the Silver Star.
To: Major Arthur L. Ludwick, 0420498, 168th Infantry Regiment.

Thru: Commanding Officer, 168th Infantry Regiment

Under the provisions of AR 600–45 and as announced in General Order Number 6, Headquarters 34th Infantry Division dated 25 January 1944, a Silver Star is awarded to the following named individual:

<u>Arthur L. Ludwick</u>, 0420498, Major, 168th Infantry Regiment. For gallantry in action from 30 November 1943 to 4 December 1943 at Pantano, Italy. Major Ludwick, upon his own volition, left the Regimental Aid Station when evacuation of the wounded had been slowed down due to heavy fire, and went forward to Pantano, Italy, to reconnoiter a shorter and easier route of evacuation for the wounded. For five days he made frequent trips to the assault companies and supervised and coordinated the evacuation of the numerous casualties. During his trips to Pantano, Major Ludwick personally carried medical supplies to the front lines and rendered aid to the wounded men on the battlefield. On 4 December 1943, when casualties had been very heavy among the frontline units, Major Ludwick personally, and in the face of grave danger, led four litter squads up Mount Pantano to the forward positions of the Second Battalion and supervised the removal of three wounded men. He remained, with one litter squad, at the unit's position, which was under intense enemy fire. During this time a soldier was seriously wounded, but in spite of the intense fire, Major Ludwick went forward from his position, administered aid to the wounded man and supervised his evacuation. Due to his initiative and tireless efforts, many lives were saved that otherwise might have been lost. Major Ludwick's courage and bravery were highly meritorious and a credit to the Armed Forces of the United States. Entered military service from Waterloo, Iowa.

CHARLES W. RYDER,
Major General, U.S. Army, Commanding.

Appendix B
German Treatment of American POWs

Col. Thomas D. Drake, Commanding Officer, 168th Infantry Regiment. *Confidential War Department Report* (6 September 1944); Factual Account of Operations of 168th Infantry, from 24 December 1942–17 February 1943. The Battle of Kasserine Pass was the first major engagement of American troops with the German Army. The following account refers to the capture of over 1,000 soldiers of the 168th Infantry Regiment in North Africa at the Kasserine Pass battle and their treatment as POWs, by the Germans: [As a result, Captain A.L. Ludwick, M.D., became the 168th's Regimental Surgeon, replacing the 168th's Major Fred Beaumont who became a German Prisoner of War.]

The column had become somewhat disorganized in marching and at this point proper approach formation was taken up. When the returning men attempted to cross the road into the foot hills of El Haidra, a machine gun opened up on the right column from the hills as a German motorized column came up the road. The enemy stopped and started leaping from their trucks, while enemy tanks immediately began encircling the American column. One U.S. plane flew over at this point and opened fire on the column. Our men, with surging morale, thought it was the promised air support, but it apparently was a lone night fighter a little late getting back from its mission. One German truck was hit and set on fire. Colonel Drake immediately deployed his mixed command and opened fire with the weapons that they had. By this time there were about 400 men in the command and not more than half of them were armed. Col. Drake asked for volunteers of an officer and men, the officer to lead the group of men to a knoll in their rear as the German Infantry was running to circle them. First Lt. William Rogers, Artillery Liaison Officer of the 91st Armored Artillery, volunteered to lead the twelve men and urged them to follow him. They gained the desired ground, a little knoll in the desert, and they were able to hold the enemy off for about an hour. At the termination of the hour, Lt. Rogers and all of his men had been killed.

The Germans brought up several tanks, all of them with yellow tigers painted on their sides, and opened fire. They also set up machine-gun positions and supplemented that with rifle fire. While they were doing this, their infantry completely encircled the small American force. After three and one-half hours of fighting, American fire power diminished and then practically ceased as the men were out of ammunition or had become casualties. Finally, a German armored car bearing a white flag came dashing into the American circle. Colonel Drake ordered his men to wave the car away. When the car failed to respond, he then ordered his men to fire upon the German car. Some of the men began to fire, but others could not as they had no ammunition and so began surrendering in small groups. German tanks came in following that vehicle without any negotiations for surrender. The Germans had used the white flag as subterfuge to come inside the circle of defense without drawing fire. Their tanks closed in from all directions, cutting Col. Drake's forces into small groups. The men who did not surrender were killed by the Germans.

... Col. Drake was arrested and taken to German Divisional Hqs where the German General immediately came forward to see him, drew up at attention, saluted and said, "I want to compliment your command for the splendid fight they put up. It was a hopeless thing from the start, but they fought like real soldiers." ... The German Commander promised Col. Drake that all the American wounded would be cared for and that he could leave American medical personnel to properly look after them, but immediately upon Col. Drake leaving the field, the American medical personnel were carried off as prisoners and the American dead and wounded were left to the ravages of the Arabs who proceeded to immediately strip the dead and wounded and to beat insensible those wounded who protested to the stripping of their clothes. The American prisoners were assembled in a group and under guard were marched back that afternoon and night along the road to DJ Lessouda. Those Americans who were slightly wounded or who became ill because of fatigue, lack of food and water and could not keep up with the column were ruthlessly bayonetted or shot. Many were walking barefooted because the Arabs had taken their shoes from them under the supervision of the German soldiers.

Prisoners-of-war

a. The men had been left to be systematically robbed by the German soldiers and some junior officers for a period of about a half hour. During this time, pockets and kits were thoroughly searched, often at the point of a rifle or bayonet presented at the unprotected belly, while watches, rings, pocketbooks, pens and all valuables were ruthlessly seized. The men were then formed in a column of fours, officers at the head, and started to the rear. Three German tanks brought up the rear of the column, which was flanked by armed guards, waiting to strike, bayonet or shoot, any who for any reason struggled.

b. All day they marched through desert sands with unrelieved thirst almost unbearable. Col. Drake appealed to the German Commander in the name of common humanity to give the men a drink of water, but was met with the statement, "We only have enough for our troops." Near midnight, they were finally halted for the remaining hours of darkness. The men were herded into a circle in the open desert and there practically froze in the piercing cold of the African night. They didn't receive their first food for five days.

Appendix C
Capt./Baron Rudolph Charles von Ripper and His "San Pietro, Italy, 1943" Etching

*"In the battered town of San Pietro,
the medics had set up a First Aid Station."*

"Rudolph Charles von Ripper has been described as part John Wayne, part Ernest Hemingway, and part Vincent Van Gogh. His fascinating life included so many breathtaking adventures and hair-raising experiences that it reads like a work of fiction." In 1943, CPT von Ripper was assigned to the 34th Infantry Division as a War Department artist in North Africa just prior to the division's Italian campaign. He was born in 1905 in Klausenburg, a provincial capital in the Austro-Hungarian Empire. As a young man, he served with the tough French Foreign Legion and also fought in the Spanish Revolution with the anti–German Republican forces. With a family history of artists, statesmen, and soldiers, he studied at the art academy in Dusseldorf and in 1929 married fellow artist Dorothea Sternheim.

In 1933, when Hitler seized control over Germany, von Ripper and his wife emigrated to Paris. He hated the Nazi party philosophy. Von Ripper was from Austrian nobility and the Nazis had confiscated his family's holdings as well as killing several of his immediate family members. Later, he fought in Spain during the Spanish Civil War where he was wounded and became partially disabled. He decided to move to the United States due to the Nazi's domination of Europe and after Pearl Harbor, he immediately volunteered for the U.S. Army. However, due to his previous injuries, he was accepted only as a combat artist.

While serving with the 34th Infantry Division in North Africa and Italy, in order to obtain "eye-witness" subject material, he at first accompanied reconnaissance patrols. He demonstrated superb combat skills on these assignments and received permission to personally lead patrols of his own. He distinguished himself in combat, often behind the German lines; was awarded two Silver Stars and two Purple Hearts; and was credited with killing sixty-three Germans, thereby avenging his family's losses.

He was considered "one of the greatest combat artists in the world, with a dramatic and emotionally charged style that deeply impacted the viewer." The etching,

1943 San Pietro, Italy: "In the battered town of San Pietro the medics had set up a First-Aid station." CPT/Baron Rudolph Charles von Ripper, combat artist (von Ripper etching; Ludwick family archives).

Hitler Plays the Hymn of Hate, appeared on the January 1939 cover of *Time Magazine* that named Adolf Hitler, "Man of 1938."

—(Ret) LTC Michael J. Musel, *The 34th Division's Fighting Artist—CPT Baron Rudolph von Ripper,* 34th Infantry Division Association Newsletter (January 2008); and *Rudolph Charles von Ripper: Soldier and Artist* (Iowa Gold Star Military Museum, Camp Dodge, Johnston, Iowa).

Appendix D
John "Jack" Vail Hoyer

My mother's younger brother, John "Jack" Vail Hoyer, was killed near Maenza, Italy on May 27, 1944. Jack is mentioned in the *History of the 752nd Tank Battalion*, written by an officer of the 752nd, shortly after the war ended:

JOHN "JACK" VAIL HOYER
752nd Tank Battalion

"T/4 John V. Hoyer and T/5 Donald C. Barrett, both of the Assault Platoon, were the first men of our unit killed in action in an area about 45 miles southeast of Rome and 30 miles east of Anzio. Caught outside their vehicle when the Kraut counter-battery fire came in from the vicinity of Maenza, the boys were killed by air-bursts from the enemy 88s. Five other members of the platoon were wounded by the same shelling which occurred at around 1600 hours."

In a letter to Jack's parents, Ben and Lenore Hoyer, Capt. Harold V. Wright, an officer of the 752nd Tank Battalion, wrote:

Dear Mrs. Hoyer,

Your letter of July 6 reached me last night and I don't think it would be possible for me to be too busy to write to the Mother of a man in my outfit who has given his life for us and our country. I am sure that it is difficult for you to realize the justice of your son, Sgt. John Hoyer, to be taken away. It is impossible for even me to realize any justice for war and

John "Jack" Vail Hoyer, June 21, 1920–May 27, 1944, 752nd Tank Battalion, killed near Maenza, Italy on his first day of combat.

only because we were forced to defend ourselves and our principles that we had to fight. In battle some lose their lives while others are spared, even when they are side by side. The reason for that cannot be explained by us.

Your son was killed instantly in combat on May 27, as the War Dept. has notified you. His unit had been in action on that day only a few minutes when they were subjected to enemy artillery fire. The men all went for cover and thought they were in a safe place until shells began bursting in the air above them. One shell burst directly above Sgt. Hoyer and he died immediately. I cannot tell you the number of men lost or injured that day, but all men who were not killed immediately were carried to the hospital within a very short time and most of them are back with our unit.

All the officers and men of this unit had much respect for Sgt. Hoyer and his ability, willingness, and character were above the average soldier. It was a loss to us as well as to you when he was taken away.

You should have received letters from some of the men closest to your son. I remember Major Ludwick from his visit to Sgt. Hoyer just before his return to the United States. I have received a letter from him and answered it. Hope it has reached there before now. Please give him my regards.

I sincerely hope that the information that I have given is some comfort or has answered some of your questions and that nothing is contained that might offend you.

With best wishes to you, the Mother of a fine, upright and intelligent boy who has paid the supreme price of war, and to his family and friends. I know your suffering has been greater than his!

Sincerely,
Harold V. Wright, Capt. Inf.

And this touching and heartfelt letter from Jack's close friend, Sgt. James M. Corry, Jr.:

Hq.Co 752 Tk. Bn
APO 464—c/o PM-NYC
28 June 44—Italy

My Dear Mr. & Mrs. Hoyer:

I must introduce myself. My name is James M. Corry, Jr. I was John's platoon Sergeant. We were the best of friends and had shared the same tent for almost a year.

It seems to me that I have known you people for some time. John spoke of his family so often. In my own imagination I have been on numerous hunting & fishing trips with John and you.

John and I had a lot in common. That is to say our likes and dislikes. We shared the same faith, enjoyed sports and liked good beer. We both got a bit philosophical over our vino. Of all the fellows in the outfit I enjoyed talking to John the most.

It grieves me to have to write this letter. I just don't know how to express myself. There is so much I would like to say and write but I lack the eloquence.

Due to circumstances and regulations I cannot write all I would like to. If God wills it I will communicate with you after the war and let you know where, when and just how it happened. This will be all I can say about John's death until the time that censorship is lifted.

We, that is our platoon, was pinned down by three (3) self-propelled 88's. The fellows and I took cover in a dry creek bed. John was about 50 yards down from me and around a slight bend. His Sgt., Tony Borgen, came up to the Lt. and I and said one of the boys in his crew was hit bad. It was John! Death was swift and merciful. As we boys say, John never knew what hit him. We all say a prayer that if we get it, we will get it in the same quick way. They had us under direct fire and shells were coming in like rain. I am very fortunate and indeed thankful that I am alive.

Words fail me when I try to tell you how much we miss your son. He is still with us. Fellows like John are not forgotten. We have partially avenged him but we are not through yet. If I have the opportunity to return to Rome, I will have a mass said for him in St. Peters.

My home address is—

I would appreciate hearing from you.

Sincerely yours,
James Corry

Appendix E

34th Infantry Division Buddies

(Mentioned in Interviews, Letters, Photo Captions, and Military Papers)

***indicates special friends; NI = Northern Ireland; NA = North Africa

- **Lt. Johnnie Agnes** (photo, NI)
- **Lt./Capt. Kenneth "Chappy" Ames**: 34th Infantry Division Chaplain; Winnebago, MN; was asked to contact family upon return to States
- **Sgt. Bill Andrews**: killed; 27 March 1944 letter
- **Capt. "Buck" Armstrong**—dentist; in Italy (12 Dec 1943—letter)

*****Glen Ayres**: see letter: July 6, 1943, NI

*** **"Ace" Balliet**: dentist; Medical Assistant in NA

- **Barone**: canteen officer and unit "bootlegger"; Lud's roommate in 133rd Infantry, NI
- **Maj. Burt Barr**: from Oregon; (refer to 2/22/44 letter re: Martha Gellhorn.)
- **Col. Beam**: Washington University, St. Louis; NA hospital

*****Major Frederick Beaumont:** (Council Bluffs, IA)—POW; 168th Regimental Surgeon that was captured by Germans along with over 1,000 soldiers of unit at Kasserine Pass debacle on February 13, 1943.

- **Corp. Bickford:** March 1943 168th Inf Medical Training Schedule, NA.
- **Col. Mark Boatner**—CO of the 168th Inf in Italy after Monte Pantano; took over from Col. Fred B. Butler; Civil War historian; Lud respected and admired him; buried in Penrith Plantation, LA.
- **Sgt. Bucher**: March 1943, NA and December 12–26, 1943, Italy 168th Inf Medical Training Schedules.
- **Capt. Burdick:** from Des Moines, IA

*****Brig General/Col. Frederic B. Butler**: CO of 168th in NA & Italy; older, white-haired, West Point grad in top 10% of his class; stern; "The Great White Father" (TGWF); my dad greatly admired and felt close to Col. Butler; he reminded Lud of his own beloved father, who had died suddenly when Dad was only 16; was regarded as a "father figure"; Fred Butler and my dad corresponded for several years after the war; from San Francisco, CA.

- **George E. Carlson:** Cedarhurst, NY; Lud would look up family after rotation home.
- **John Castell**—16 Nov 1942: went to hospital for surgery—a cervical sympathectomy for Reynaud's Disease; *"I sure hope it works for John as he is a fine fellow and has a wife and two kids back in Fairfield. I don't suppose the effects of the operation will be determined for several to six months or so. I wonder if he has told his family anything about it. He is very quiet, and is just the type to keep mum over the whole thing."*
- **Albert Caves:** driver in NA and Italy; lived in NM 25 yrs, then moved back to Eddyville, IA area; died in 1988.
- **Col. Clark:** In Gittler's Hdgts office.

***Col. Fred G. Clarke, Jr.:** wife, Mildred; Waterloo, IA; *"...Col. Clarke sure was and is a prince of a man. He is a rare person, always quiet & gentle, yet possessing an inner strength that commanded respect and admiration. I sure like him very much."*—became "acting" battalion commander on Mt. Pantano—Knob 1.

- **2nd Lt. (MAC) Ross Cline:** Lud's photo caption: *"My 'first Sgt.'; Tech Sgt until a week ago when he got his commission as 2nd Lt. MAC and was transferred to the collecting company. He was the best non-com I've ever had, always on the ball. From Des Moines, IA."*

***Capt. Moses Cohen:** Lud's 2nd Bn Surgeon in NA; June, 1943: see photo caption.

- **Pat Cloughessy** from NYC, NY "My supply man."
- **Alvin Colbus** (Cannon Company)
- **Capt. Thomas E. Corcoran:** Medical Officer with the 168th Regiment; captured by the German army after the Kasserine Pass debacle in NA; wife, Florence; from Rock Rapids, IA

***1st Sgt. George W. "Bill" Crowell**: Tunisia/Italy; 1987 34th Reunion; from Des Moines, IA; corresponded with Lud after the war

- **Capt. James C. Drye:** December 12–26, 1943, Italy 168th Inf Medical Training Schedule; medical assistant; transferred in March 1944 to 109th Medical Battalion (*Paulus Diaries*)
- **Col. Duggan:** In Gittler's Hdgts office

***Col. Ray Fountain:** CO of 133rd in NA; Iowa National Guard officer; a former federal bankruptcy referee in Des Moines, IA.

- **Col. Arthur S. Fourt, M.D.:** 34th Inf Division Surgeon; from Melbourne, IA; served in both WWI and WWII.
- **Sam Friedman** (Asst to Col Hougen in JA section)

- **Jack Giffin** (Betty): Waterloo, IA; At Station Hospital at Keesler Field/School of Aviation Medicine at Randolph.
- **Dr. Rex Allen Gish:** 9/19/17–10/20/2000; born in Lawrence, KS; doctor in Waterloo, IA? U.S. Navy during World War II; son, Kiffen Gish, reported his father suffered from severe PTSD.

***Major Ludwig Gittler:** Dr. in Fairfield, IA; born in Bendzin, Poland, May 12, 1898; Iowa National Guard; 133rd Reg Surgeon and Division Surgeon of the 34th Infantry Division; Capt. Morris J. Leslie replaced him as 133rd Reg Surg in NA, 1943;

- **Capt. Grallap:** photo caption from NI.
- **W.S. Green:** Des Moines, IA; will call on wife

***Sgt. George William Green**: from Johnston, IA—later Des Moines; he was Lud's sergeant and they kept in touch over the years. George and his wife visited Jean and Lud in Wenatchee, WA in 1990.

- **Lt. Col. Greenfield:** (5/20/42, NI): "passed overage mark and transferred out of regiment this week."
- **Hank Hansen:** dinner with Martha Gellhorn; (see 22 February 1944 letter)
- **Maj. Kermit Hansen:** from Omaha; sang at dance 2/20/44; "excellent voice and a swell fellow."
- **Lt. Spec. Sgt. Heissner:** March 1943 168th Inf Medical Training Schedule, NA.
- **Capt. Horowitz:** Lud's Medical Assistant in 133rd and 168th, NI & NA; March 1943 168th Inf Medical Training Schedule, NA
- **Capt. DeBe (D.B.?) Johnson**—desk job with Glenn Smith.
- **Nelson Jones:** "Pappy" Trussell's right hand man.
- **Major Karns:** Reg Surgeon of the 135th; "...a darned good man..."
- **Maj. Kelso:** did sanitary inspection of *Empress of Australia* with Lud.
- **Lt. Kenworthy:** March 1943 168th Inf Medical Training Schedule, NA
- **Capt. Korostoff:** March 1943 168th Inf Medical Training Schedule, NA
- **T/4 Knoeller:** March 1943 168th Inf Medical Training Schedule, NA
- **Col. Langdon**
- **Lattrell (commanded Cannon Co.)**
- **Capt. Russell Law:** in 168th; went to school at Iowa State.
- **Capt. Le Fon:** March 1943 168th Inf Medical Training Schedule, NA

***Lt. Lupton:** Roommate on *Empress of Australia*; with 133rd in NI.

- **Joe Mackey:** photo caption from NI.
- **Capt. McClymont:** photo caption from NI.
- **Capt. Miller** (photo, NI)

Appendix E

- **Sgt. Miller:** March 1943 168th Inf Medical Training Schedule, NA.
- ***Lt. Col. Robert Moore:** World War II hero mentioned in *An Army at Dawn;* member of 168th Regiment; see 5 July 1943 NA letter.
- **Capt. Moorman:** Dec 12–26, 1943 168th Inf Medical Training Schedule, Italy.
- ***Corp. Hubert "Hub" Mott:** Lud's jeep driver in NI & NA; from McKinney, TX where Mott had a dry cleaning business; ran the laundry "rackets" service in NI (see 31 Oct 1942 letter); "my right hand man—one of the boys I brought over with me to NA from the 133rd in NI and who has been one of the few boys who never showed any reluctance to go into some 'jams' that we got into in combat"; in fact, Mott carried a gun under his jeep driver's seat, which proved life-saving in several situations; promoted to Sgt. Technician.
- **Bob Neely**
- **Capt. Noerman:** March 1943 168th Inf Medical Training Schedule, NA
- ***Dr. Arch "Hefty" Olson:** Physician in Waterloo, IA. Jean worked for him during the war; gave Lud an air mattress to sleep on overseas.
- **Col. Dick Parker**
- **Pete Peterman** (wife Alice)
- **Lt. Spec. T/4 Pierce:** Dec 12–26, 1943 168th Inf Medical Training Schedule, Italy.
- ***Will Power:** V-mails to Lud dated 5/29/43 & 8/20/43 from Box 2140 Cape Town, South Africa; single; pharmacist who worked for Lilly Drug Co.? in Waterloo?; good friend.
- **Larry Powers**
- **Chaplain Quinlivan**—Chaplain with 168th in NA; postwar (1948) doing parish work in Watertown, NY.
- **Jack Rathbone** (Marcia)
- **Rhythm Majors Band:** dance/orchestra band embedded with 133rd Infantry Regiment in NI, NA, and Italy.
- **Capt. Bob Rion**
- ***Lt. Robinson (Robbie):** killed w/133rd in NA; had been with Dad in LA and NI.
- **Sgt. Rogers:** Dec 12–26, 1943 168th Medical Training Schedule, Italy.
- ***Maj. Ed Rohlf:** Dr. Edward L. Rholf, (9/13/10–1969); served in Algeria and Tunisia w/Lud; from/lived in Waterloo, IA; U of Iowa Med School, '37; "…premature demise at the early age of 59, while still feeling the effects of malaria, malnutrition, and battle fatigue from his intensive military service." (in obituary)
- **Col. Rouse:** ~ Sept/Oct 1943 rotated home.
- **Lt. Martin Rudoy:** see 24 February 1943, NA letter
- **Capt. Schiffrin**, dentist at aid station at Sbiba, Tunisia.

- ***Capt. Emile Schuster**: Medical Officer, joined 168th in December 1943; *Life* Mag story w/ Mary Martin on cover (*Life Magazine*, October 25, 1943, 17–19. "The Story of Fort Schuster.") *He came to me when we were in sort of a tight spot* [Mt. Pantano], *and believe me, he is a dinger. Quite a boy, as you'll read from the story. There are many things I'd like to tell you about our "deal" together (the Life Magazine story happened before he came to us) on the top of the mountain in our last engagement.* [Mt. Pantano] *We get along very well together. It's sort of a shock to find someone like that at times. You'd better get set for some tall stories when I get home.* Earned the Distinguished Service Cross. (12 March 1944 letter)

- ***Dr. R. Glenn Smith**: wife, "Mid"; from Cedar Falls; as a First Lieut, best man/matron of honor at Jean and Lud's wedding in Alexandria, LA, October 11, 1941; Glenn lived in estate in NI.

- **Kenneth Snyder**, "non-com"; in Italy; from Leon, IA; March 6, 1944—rotated home; Lud asked him to call Jean when he got home.

- ***Lt. Barney Spoo**: Lud's Medical Administrative Corps officer; in farmhouse in Sant'Angelo d'Alife after Pantano; *MAC officer that's been with me since early September; likeable, conscientious, swell fellow.*

- **Capt. Harry ("Hank") Thompson**: Div AG, Asst to Col. Dee White; picked up two-week old puppy on frontlines, brought back to Officers' Mess.

- **Major Henry ("Pappy") L. Trussell, Jr.**

- **T/4 Vickery**: Dec 12–26, 1943 Medical Detachment 168th Infantry Medical Training Schedule in Italy.

- **Corp. Voorhees**: from Des Moines, IA; the "clown" of the outfit

- **Lt. Nadine Wagner**: Allen Hospital, Waterloo, IA. Served with the 12th General Hospital unit from Chicago in North Africa and Italy, 1942–1944?

- ***Capt. Marvin E. Williams**: was in the 168th with my dad; kept in touch after the war; he met his wife, Lt. Adeline H. Simonson, a nurse anesthetist, during the war and they were married in Italy; I've been in touch with son, Marvin E. Williams, Jr., for several years. We attended the 2016 34th Inf Div Association Reunion together at Fort Dodge, Johnston, IA.

- **March 4–10, 1943 Medical Detachment 168th Infantry Medical Training Schedule in NA lists these instructors:**
  Capt. Armstrong, Capt. Cohen, Capt. Horowitz, Lt. Kenworthy, Capt. Ludwick

- **Dec 12–26, 1943 Medical Detachment 168th Infantry Medical Training Schedule in Italy lists these instructors:**
  Capt. Armstrong, Corp Bickford, Sgt. Bucher, Sgt. Crowell, Capt. Drye, Sgt. Green, Sgt. Heissner, Capt. Kenworthy, T/4 Knoeller, Capt. Korostoff, Capt. Le Fen, Major Ludwick, Sgt. Miller, Capt. Moorman, T/4 Pierce, Sgt. Rogers, Capt. Schuster, Lt. Spoo, T/4 Vickery, T/4 Wry.

Bibliography

Brackets [...] and **boldface** indicate
bibliographic abbreviations used in footnotes

Ankrum (Ret.) Lt. Col. Homer R. *Dogfaces Who Smiled Through Tears: An Outstanding Chronicle of Heartbreaks, Hardships, Heroics, and Humor of the North African and Italian Campaigns.* Lake Mills, IA: Graphic Publishing Co., 1987. [***Dogfaces***]

———. *History of the Iowa National Guard: The 34th Infantry Division in WWII.* Online resource; website: https://www.iowanationalguard.com/History/History/Pages/World-War-II.aspx [***History of IA Nat'l Guard***]

———. "The 34th Infantry Division in World War II." *The Iowa Militiaman*, Spring Quarter 1991. https://www.iowanationalguard.com/History/History/Pages/World-War-II.aspx [***IA Militiaman***]

Ashcraft, Howard D. *As You Were: Cannon Company; 34th Infantry Division,168th Infantry Regiment, World War II.* Parsons, WV: McClain Printing Company, 1990. [***As You Were***]

Atkinson, Rick. *An Army at Dawn: The War in North Africa, 1942–1943.* Volume One of the Liberation Trilogy. New York.: Henry Holt and Company, 2002. [***Army at Dawn***]

———. *The Day of Battle: The War in Sicily and Italy, 1943–1944.* Volume Two of the Liberation Trilogy. New York: Henry Holt and Company, 2007. [***Day of Battle***]

Berens (Ret.) Col. Robert J., *The Red Bulletin: 34th Infantry Division Association Newsletter.* Online resource; website: http://www.34ida.org/association/newsletters.html. [***34th Inf Div Assoc***]

———. "Pantano," *Army: WWII at 5,* 1993. *[see above]*

———. "Von Ripper," January 2008. *[see above].*

Buch, Sandra Paulus. *Mud, Mountains, and Medicine: The WWII Diary of E.W. Paulus, M.D.* Ashland, OR: Hellgate Press, 2009. [***Paulus Diaries***]

The Center for American War Letters. Online resource; website:. https://www.chapman.edu/research/institutes-and-centers/cawl/index.aspx

Combat Chronicles of U.S. Army Divisions in World War II. U.S. Army Center of Military History, Washington, D.C. Online resource; website: https://history.army.mil/html/forcestruc/cbtchron/cc/034id.htm [***U.S Army Military History***]

Cowdrey, Albert E. *Fighting for Life: American Military Medicine in World War II.* New York: The Free Press (Macmillan, Inc.), 1998. [***Fighting for Life***]

Davis, John S. M.D. *Bassett Hospital in Cooperstown, New York: 200 Years of Health Care in Rural America.* Cooperstown, NY: Bassett Healthcare Network, 2017. [***Bassett Hospital***]

De Botton, Alain. *The Course of Love.* New York: Simon & Schuster, 2016. [***Course of Love***]

Drake, Col. Thomas D (GSC). "Headquarters 34th Infantry Division, U.S. Army: Confidential War Department Report, Factual Account of Operations 168th, 34th Division, from 24 December 1942 to 17 February 1943." April 2, 1945 (copied from files at Fort Dodge, IA). [***War Dept Report***]

Fifth Army at the Winter Line: 15 November 1943–15 January 1944. U.S. Army Center of Military History, Washington, D.C. 1990. https://history.army.mil/books/wwii/winterline/winter-fm.html [***Winter***]

Gammack, Gordon. "Iowa Outfit Grimly Held Peak in Italy." *The Des Moines Register,* March 8, 1944. Original newspaper article in Author's possession. [***Gammack: Pantano***]

———. "The Story of Cassino Is Glorious But Sad." *The Des Moines Register,* March 12, 1944. https://www.newspapers.com/image/130598889/?terms=gordon%20gammack&match=1Original newspaper article in author's possession. [***Gammack: Cassino***]

———. "Had to Carry Wounded Men For 12 Miles." *The Des Moines Register,* March 13, 1944. https://www.newspapers.com//image/130599069/ Original newspaper article in author's possession. [***Gammack: Relay***]

Green, Sgt. Milo L. *Brickbats from F Company,* Capt. Paul S. Gauthier, ed. Grosse Pointe, MI: Gauthier Publishing Co., 1982. [***Brickbats***]

"History of the 752nd Tank Battalion." Online resource; website: http://digicom.bpl.lib.me.us/ww_reg_his/60/. [***752nd Tank***]

Hougan, John. *Attack, Attack, Attack: History of the*

Famous 34th Infantry Division. Nashville: Battery Press, 1979. [**Attack**]

Kelly, Orr. *Meeting the Fox: The Allied Invasion of Africa from Operation TORCH to Kasserine Pass to Victory in Tunisia*. Nashville: Battery Press, 1979. [**Meeting the Fox**]

Kerner, Johm A, M.D. *Combat Medic: World War II*. New York: J. Boylston & Company (iBooks), 2002. [**Combat Medic**]

Lang, Will. "Life's Reports: The Story of Fort Schuster," *Life Magazine,* October 25, 1943, 17–19. Online resource; website: https://books.google.com/books?id=BVcEAAAAMBAJ&pg=PA17&lpg=PA17&dq=STORY+OF+FORT+SCHUSTER#v=onepage&q=STORY%20OF%20FORT%20SCHUSTER&f=false [**Life *Mag: Ft. Schuster*]

Lehman, Sgt. Milton, Staff Writer. *Stars and Stripes Weekly:* "U.S. Regiment Discovers Price of Hilltop in Italy." ~December 1943 or January 1944. [a military weekly newspaper published overseas and distributed to U.S. troops during WWII. [**Stars & Stripes**]

Lengel, Ed (PhD). Best Books on WWII in North Africa. The National WWII Museum. New Orleans, LA. Online resource; website: https://www.nationalww2museum.org/wwii-reads-north-africa [**WWII Museum**]

"Lessons Learned in Combat, November 7, 1942—September 1944." Headquarters, 34th Infantry Division, U.S. Army. 33–34. Online resource; website: https://archive.org/details/LessonsLearnedInCombatBy34thInfantryDivision-nsia/page/n25/mode/2up [**Lessons Learned**]

Lewis, Col. Walden S. *History 133rd Infantry, 34th Infantry Division*. Gorizia, Italy, September 29, 1945. 1–13. Online resource; website: http://34thinfantry.com/history/history-133rd.html, http://www.34ida.org/ [**133rd History**]

Majdalany, Fred. *The Battle of Cassino*. Boston: The Riverside Press Cambridge, Houghton Mifflin Co., 1957. [**Battle of Cassino**]

McCarthy, Sgt. Joe. "Iron-Man Battalion," *Yank Magazine (European edition)*, Vol. 1, No. 38, Dec. 22, 1944, 2–5. [**Iron-Man Bn**]

Morin, Relman. "U.S. 'Lost' 640,000 In War II Because of 'Psycho' Casualties; We Guard Against Repetition." *The Montana Standard,* July 3, 1951. https://www.newspapers.com//image/349905290/

"Mud, Mules, and Mountains." U.S. Army Center of Military History publication, 87–89. Online resource; website: https://search.usa.gov/search?query=Mud%2C+Mules%2C+and+Mountains&affiliate=cmh&utf8=%E2%9C%93 [**Mud, Mules, Mtns**]

Musel (Ret.) LTC Michael J. "The 34th Division's Fighting Artist—CPT Baron Rudolph Von Ripper," *34th Infantry Division Association Newsletter,* January 2008. [***von Ripper 34th Inf Div Assoc***]

———. "Rudolph Charles Von Ripper: Soldier and Artist." Iowa Gold Star Military Museum, Camp Dodge, Johnston, Iowa. Online resource; website: https://www.goldstarmuseum.iowa.gov. [***von Ripper Gold Star Museum***]

Narrative History: 109th Medical Battalion, U.S. Army North African Campaign. Gold Star Museum, Camp Dodge Iowa, 8 November 1942–15 May 1943. [**109th Gold Star Museum**]

Rampaart, MAJ Peter B., U.S. Army. *34th Infantry Division in North Africa, 1942–1943, A Monograph*. School of Advanced Military Studies US Army Command and General Staff College, Fort Leavenworth, KS. 2019 https://apps.dtic.mil/sti/pdfs/AD1083645.pdf

"Red Bull Attacks—The Big Picture: Mt. Pantano." YouTube, 11:30. Online resource; website: **https://www.youtube.com/watch?v=gAJisos2fCg** [***Mt. Pantano YouTube***]

The Red Bull in World War II, Oct. 23, 1944, 1–4. Online resource; website: http://34thinfantry.com/history/history-133rd.html [**Red Bull**]

Rutherford, Ward. *Kasserine: Baptism of Fire*. New York: Ballantine Books Inc., 1970. [**Kasserine: Baptism**]

Salvage Sailor. U.S. Militaria Forum Post. https://www.usmilitariaforum.com/forums/index.php?/topic/11032-wwii-typewriter-question/&tab=comments#comment-99244. January 28, 2008.

Senn, T/5 James Pierce Senn, edited by Joe H. Camp, Jr. *A Ride with the Red Bulls: An Ambulance Driver's War in the Mediterranean Theater*. North Charleston, SC: CreateSpace Independent Publishing, 2016. [***A Ride with the Red Bulls***]

Skelly, Patrick (transcriber). "Narrative History, 109th Medical Battalion United States Army, North African Campaign 8 November 1942–15 May 1943." 2002. n.p. [no page #s]

"They Stopped Us At Cassino." *Life Magazine,* April 10, 1944, Vol. 16, No. 15, 27–43. [**Life *Mag: Cassino*]

34th Infantry Division Association online resource; website: 34infdiv.org/history/109medbntxt

———. "The Story of the 34th Infantry Division." 34th Infantry Division Association. Online resource; website: 34infdiv.org/history/34narrhist.html, n.p. (no page #s)

———. "133rd Infantry Regiment—WWII Narrative History." 2009. n.p. Online Resource; website: 34th Infantry Division Association. Online resource; website: 34infdiv.org/history/133narrhist.html

"Trail of the 34th 'Red Bull' Infantry Division in WWII." Chart/graphic. *34th Infantry Division Association* poster/map.

"Up the Deadly Boot: The Italia." Video. A&E Television Networks, 1997.

U.S. Army, 109th Medical Battalion Narrative History: North African Campaign. 8 November

1942–15 May 1943." (copied from files at Fort Dodge, IA). [*109th Narr History NA*]

Whitehead, Don. "34th One of 'Most Fought' Divisions: Italy Campaign Role Revealed." *The Des Moines Register*, December 7, 1943. [***Whitehead: Des Moines Register***]

Wilkinson, Col. Richard F. *The Breakthrough Battalion: Battle of Company C of the 133rd Infantry Regiment, Tunisia and Italy, 1943–1945*. Self-published; Printed by McNaughton & Gunn, Saline, MI, 2005. [***Breakthrough Bn***]

Wilson, Richard. "The Gallant Fight of the 34th Division in The North Africa Campaign," *The Des Moines Register and Tribune*, 1943. [***Gallant Fight***]

The WW2 Medical Detachment. WW2 U.S. Medical Research Centre. Online resource; website: https://www.med-dept.com/articles/the-ww2-medical-detachment-infantry-regiment/ [***Med Research Ctr***]

Index

Numbers in ***bold italics*** indicate pages with photographs and illustrations

Afrika Korps 63, 68, 78, 198
Agnes, Lt. Johnnie 240
aid man (medic) 80, 167, 180
Algeria: Algiers 64, 194, 196; Assi Ben Okba 69; Black Senegalese French troops 69; landing at Mers El Kabir 68, 198; landscapes 72; living conditions 69; Midea 70; Operation TORCH, 66–69; Oran 64, 68, 70, 127; Relizane 70; sanitary conditions 69; Sétif 70; Sidi Bel Abbes 103, 127, 200; Sucaras 70; Tebessa 70, 198; Tlemcen region 72, 198; *see also* North Africa
Allied forces 65–66, 69, 71, 98, 142, 162, 164, 199
American Academy of Family Physicians (AAFP) 218–219
Ames, Lt./Capt. Kenneth "Chappy" 240
Andrews, Sgt. Bill 240
Arabs: 82, 109, 120, 133, 135, 234; culture/customs 89–91, 111, 194; language 91, 111; medical treatment 89–***90***, 111–113; *see also* North Africa
Armstrong, Capt. "Buck" 148, 240
An Army at Dawn (book) 11
Army Aviation Corps 206
Atlantic Ocean 36–37, 40, 60, 70
Atlas Mountains (North Africa) 67, 77, 198
Avenger Field (Sweetwater, TX) 78
Ayres, Glen 114, 240
The Axis 104, 119

badminton 59
Balliet, Dr. "Ace" 73, 240

Barone 62, 240
Barr, Maj. Burt 174–175, 240
Barrett, T/5 Donald C. 237
baseball 45–***46***, 107
Bates, Lt. Roy L. 88, 156
baths/showers 30–32, 52, 55, ***73***, 76, 149, 159, 162–163
battalion/regimental surgeon: duties 41, 104, 126, 155, 167
Beam, Col. 240
Beaumont, Maj. Frederick 79–80, 111, 198, 233, 240
Bend, OR 215
Berlin, Germany 94, 110, 142
Bickford, Corp. 240
Biloxi, Mississippi 34
bivouac 11, 30–33, 103, 107, 119–120, 199–201, 203
black-outs 58, 99, 110, 137
Blackhawk Medical Society (Waterloo, IA) 124
blood supply 78, 87, 165–167
Boatner, Col. Mark 158, 201, 240
Boise, ID 215
Botton, Alan De 212
Bradley, Maj. Gen. Omar Nelson 97, 178
"brass hats" 116, 130, 154, 162, 168, 172; *see also* bureaucracy
Brickbats from "F" Company (newspaper column) 24, 99, 160
British Army/Navy 24, 36, 38, 43, 45, 52–54, 58, 60, 63–64, 66, 69, 92–93, 95, 101, 103, 108, 114, 125, 153, 161–162, 177, 179, 197
British 4th Indian Division 161–162
Bucher, Sgt. 240
Burdick, Capt. 96, 240
bureaucracy, U.S. Army: 43, 46, 50, 60–61, 107, 154, 159,
163, 165, 169–170, 172–173, 175, 180–181, 192, 208
burros 90–91
Butler, Brig. Gen./Col. Frederic B. 81, 86, 88, 103–104, 121–122, 129, 141–143, 145–146, 158, 199–201, 240–241

camera 16, 52, 54, 194
Camp Claiborne, LA: 23–39; duties as a battalion surgeon ***24–25***; Lake Valentine 33; living conditions 27–28, 30; Louisiana Maneuvers ***24***, 197; Red River ***24–25***; training at 28, 31, 39, 101; *see also* Louisiana
canteen/supplies 41–42, 44, 62, 123, 186
Carlson, George E. 241
Cassino, Italy: abbey/monastery ***160***–162; approach 155–157, 162; battle ***160***–162, 168, 191, 195; casualties 161–162; Cervaro 162; city ***160***–161, 165; Highway "6" 142, 160; living conditions 146–147, 156, 168; Rainbow Coalition 162; weather 94, ***160***, 168; *see also* Italy
Castell, John 241
Caves, Albert 241
censorship 2, 5, 7, 9, 12, 40–41, 43, 45, 49, 64, 81, 95, 108, 131, 151, 169, 172, 175–176, 180, 191, 239
Chelan County Public Utility District (PUD) 220
Christmas 54, 60, 62–65, 76, 137, 140–141, 146, 148, 150–154, 157–159, 165, 167–168
chronology of military service and major 34th infantry division events 196–202

249

Index

Churchill, Winston S. 148
Clark, Col. 61, 73, 241
Clark, Lt. Gen. Mark W. 19, **20**, 162, 241
Clarke, Col. Fred G., Jr. 241
clearing stations 87, 100, 167
Cline, 2nd Lt. (MAC), Ross 241
clothing 159; *see also* trench coat
Cloughessy, Pat 241
Cochran, Jacqueline 78; *see also* Ludwick, Jean Hoyer
Cohen, Capt. Moses **105**, 187, 241
Colbus, Alvin 241
collecting companies/stations 28, 80, 87, 100, 167, 198
Combat Medical Badge (CMB) 87
Cone, Marvin 36
Coolidge, Calvin 223
Corcoran, Capt. Thomas E. 111–112, 241
Corry, Sgt. James M. 238
Crowell, 1st Sgt. George W. "Bill" 241

D-Day 66
dances **44**, 58, 62, 65, 123; *see also* parties
dates 45; *see also* dances; parties
de Botton, Alain 212
Declaration of Independence 61
Delta Upsilon Fraternity, KU 13
depression 61, 106–107, 147, 149, 171, 192, 207–208; *see also* PTSD
Des Moines Register (newspaper) *see* Gammack, Gordon
The Desert Fox 6, 63
desk jobs 165, 171
Distinguished Service Cross 191
dive bombers 31, 68, 99
"dough-foots" 154, 167–169, 174, 184, 190, 195
Drake, Col. Thomas D. 79, 81, 233–234
drinking/drunk 182–183, 186
Drye, Capt. James C. 170, 191, 241
Duggan, Col. 73, 241
duties of a Battalion/Regimental Surgeon 41, 104, 126, 155, 167, 172

Eisenhower, Gen. Dwight D. 97
Emergency Medical Tag (EMT) 80, 188
HSS *Empress of Australia* 64–65, 68
England: Liverpool 64–64, **67**; London 23, 38, 62–64; Northwich 63–64; *see also* London School of Hygiene and Tropical Medicine

family practice physician: 218; practice of medicine 6, 10, 13, 14, 23, 61, 124, 136, 140, 172, 187–188, 209, 211, 215–219; *see also* American Academy of Family Physicians (AAFP)
fear 60, 76, 80, 85, 88, 161, 176–178, 183, 204–208, 227, 229; *see also* PTSD
Field Surgical Units/Forward Head Injury Unit 161
5th Army 16, 145, 160–161, 168; Rainbow Coalition 62
5th Army General Hospital 60–61, 163
1st Armored Division 101
fishing 45, 211, 216, 238
fitness 61, 116, 119
flight surgeon 12, 205–207; *see also* Ludwick, Dr. Arthur L., Sr.
food: 58–60, 74, 92, 106, 108–109, 112, 116, 137–138; army rations 44, 69, 99, 106, 116, 141, 145, 156, 186; oatmeal 84–86, 205; Thanksgiving 140–141
Ford car 91
Fort Dix, NJ 5, 36
Fountain, Col. Ray 85–86, 241
"4-F'ers" 148
Fourt, Col. Arthur S., M.D. 25, 88, 111, 241
Fourth of July 13–14, 48, 55
foxholes 66, 93, 97, 106, 137, 141, 145, 161, 164, 168, 177, 190
France: Dunkirk 38; farmers 101; Foreign Legion 103, 200, 235; girls 116; Navy 69; 75 cannons 100; Vichy government 66, 69
Friedman, Sam 241

Gallaher, George L. 47
Gammack, Gordon 145–146, 156, 192; *see also Des Moines Register*

Gellhorn, Martha *see* Hemingway, Mrs. Ernest
German Army 6, 24, 36–39, 63, 66, 69–70, 79–80, 82, 84, 92–93, 98, 188, 101–102, 104, 111, 119, 127, 135, 138, 142–147, 151, 154–156, 160–162, 165, 179, 198–199, 233–235; 88 cannons 79–80, 93, 239; Gustav Line 142, 162; Navy 69; Winter Defense Line 142, 156, 160, 201; *see also* "Jerry"
German measles **44**
Gish, Dr. Rex Allen 242
Gittler, Maj. Ludwig 38, 61, 73, 88, 91, 109, 113, 117–118, 138, 161, 163, 173, 192, 198, 242
God 5, 49–50, **105**, 115, 130, 149, 165, 177, 179, 218
Gold Star Museum 210, **236**
golf 13, **34**–35, 216, 221
Grallap, Capt. 242
The Great Depression 13, 16, 39, 208
Green, Sgt. George William 242
Green, Sgt. Milo L. 24, 99, 160, 189
Green, W.S. 242
Greenfield, Lt. Col. 242

Hansen, Hank 173–174, 242
Hansen, Maj. Kermit 173, 242
Harvard (doctors) 61
Hebrew amputation 46; *see also* surgeries
Heissner, Lt. Spec., Sgt. 242
Hemingway, Mrs. Ernest 174–175
Henretig, Josh **228**
Hepatitis "A" 127, 129–130, 133, 147
Highway "6", Italy 142; *see also* Cassino
Hitler, Adolf 23, 49, 82, 104, 107, 140–141, 146, 148, 177, 235–**236**; *see also* "Uncle Hoiman"
Hollywood, ideas of 39, 49, 66, 72, 75, 97, 153, 179
homesickness 10, 125, 149, 169, 171, 178–179, 208; *see also* loneliness
Horowitz, Capt. 42, 113–114, 242
horses 47–48, 90, 155
Hoyer, Ben 13–14, 46, 59–60, 76, 139, 154, 167–168, 194, 220, 237

Hoyer, Jean Katherine 5, 13, *26*
Hoyer, Joan Vail 56–57, 106, 194, 220
Hoyer, John "Jack" Vail 12–13, 34, 91–92, 94, 111, 119, 141, 148, 164, 168, 173, 181–182, 186–187, 189–190, 193, *194*–195, 203, 220, 237
Hoyer, Lenore Vail *194*, 219–220, 237
Hoyer, Petrea 220, *228*
human nature 10, 176, 179, 183, 229

ingenuity 6, 39, 52–*53*, 54
Iowa National Guard ("Iowa Boys") 5, 7, 15, 23, 35, 48, 79, 136, 142, 156, 191, 214
Ireland, Free State 44
Italy: Anzio 189, 193, 209, 237; Apennine Mountains 136, 147; Benevento 145–146, 187; bridges 134–135; Caserta 150, 201; Cassino 142, 155; Castella 186; casualties 156–157; Cervaro 158, 162; Eboli 193–*194*; Foggia 186; German Winter Line 142; Highway "6" 142; Italian Campaign 100; Italians hating Germans 135; landings 127, 134, 136; landscapes 133–134, 136, 140, 142; Limatola 127, 134; Liri Valley 160; living conditions 134–135, 137–138, 140, 147–149, 151–152, 156, 164, 168, 170–171, 175, 186; Monte Marrone 142; Monte Pantano 141–146, 204; Naples 149–150, 193–194, 181; Piedmonte d'Alife 186; Pompeii 131–*132*, 200; Rapido River 130, 148, 160–161, 200, 202; Rome 142, 160, 237; rural culture 134; Salerno 127; Samuccro 156; San Pietro 146, 235–*236*; San Vitorre 155–157; Sant'Angelo d'Alife 136, 148, 150, 161, 170–171, 200, 203, 244; Sicily 66, 97–98, 100–101, 119, 200; Sorrento 152; southern Italy maps *66*, *128*; Venafro 156; Vesuvius 153; Volturno River 8, *127*, 129–130, 134, 140, 151, 165, 193; weather 131, 142, 150, 155–156, *160*, 164, 168, 170, 186; *see also* Cassino; Pantano, Monte

"Jack" *see* Hoyer, John "Jack" Vail
Japanese 5, 35
jeeps 9, 12, 37, 39–40, 52–*53*, 68, 82, 92, 99–*102*, 115, 131, 155–156, 159–*160*, 172, 193
"Jerry" 131, 134–140, 158, 168–169, 182, 189–190; *see also* German Army
Jerusalem 91
Jesus 91; *see also* God
Johnson, Capt. DeBe (D.B.) 242
Jones, Nelson 242

Kansas: Hertzler Clinic, Halstead 23; Lawrence 13; Overland Park 13; *see also* University of Kansas
Karns, Major 159, 242
Kelso, Maj. 65, 242
Kenworthy, Lt. 242
Korostoff, Capt. 242
Kesselring, Gen. Albert 161; *see also* German Army
King George VI 65
Knoeller, T/4 242

LaMarr, Hedy 57
Langdon, Col. 242
Lattrell 242
laundry/dry-cleaning service 12, 30, 32, 62, 109
Law, Capt. Russell 242
Le Fon, Capt. 242
Leslie, Joyce 209–211
Leslie, Lt./Maj. Morris J. "Les," M.D. 12, 16–*17*, 18, 42–*46*, 52, *54*, 59, 61–62, 65, 73, 138, 155–156, 163, 192, 209
letters/mail/packages 9–11, 41, 56, 76, 130–131, 133, 137–141, 149, 157, 167–168, 175, 227; letter writing 15, 47, 50, 135, 168, 172, 183; *see also* typewriter; V-mail
Life magazine 57, 184, 191
life motto *20*, 224
litters 143; bearers 143, 145,155; drills 28; relay stations 155–156
London School of Hygiene and Tropical Medicine 63
loneliness 10, 27, 28, 41, 44, 64–65, 76, 123, 125, 149, 157, 164, 169, 171–172, 174, 178–179, 184, 208; *see also* homesickness
Look Magazine 139
Louisiana: Alexandria 15, 24, 34, 197, 220; Baton Rouge; Caney 31; "chiggers" 26–27; Dequincy 30; DeRidder 32–33; Evans 31; Fort Polk 26; Kisatchie National Forest 33; Lake Valentine 33; landscapes 27; Louisiana Maneuvers; Merryville 45; New Orleans 35–36; Oakdale 34–35, 197; Red River *24*; rural culture 27; *see also* Camp Claiborne, LA
Love Field, Dallas TX 206
Ludwick, Dr. Arthur L. Ludwick, Jr. *17*, *20*, *25*–*26*, *34*, *38*, *70*, *73*, *96*, *102*, *105*, *132*, *216*, *228*
Ludwick, Arthur L. Ludwick, Sr. 12–13, *205*–207
Ludwick, Jack 21, 215, 224
Ludwick, Jean Hoyer 12, 136, 224, *228*; flying/pilot's license 14–15, 29, 77–78, 188; work 124, 136; *see also* Hoyer, Jean Katherine
Ludwick, Margaret Gallaher (mother) 13, 41, 47, 76, 95, 106, 130, 151
Lupton, Lt. 40, 61, 242

Mackey, Joe 242
malaria 64, 98, 106, 180, 187, 190, 195
marriage 181, 185–186, 213
Mass General Hospital 61
Mauldin, Sgt. Bill 156, 184–185
McClymont, Capt. 242
Mecca 112
medical aid station 16, 25, 28, 31–33, 39, 42, 46, 85–*90*, 93, 95–*96*, 99–100, *102*, 105, 109–112, 114–115, 117, 121, 122, 135, 138, 140, 146, 151, 165–167, 184, 186, 190–191, 204, 207, 232, 235–*236*, 243; medical treatment of civilians 31, *90*, 111–112, 135, 149
medical officer (duties) 73, 96, 150, 154
medical technologist 14, 77
Mediterranean 190; Ocean 37, 72, *105*, 112, 120, 122, 141, 198, 200; Theater 1–2
Merck Manual 223
Mexican War 35–36
military history 176–179
military leadership 158, 207
military transportation: ambulances 28, 31, 37, 57, *70*, 82, 87, 93,

99–100, 112, 146, 155, 167, 182, 193; amphibious "ducks" 127; lighters 68; "peeps" 159, 195; trucks 35, 82, 129, 193; *see also* jeeps
military weaponry: anti-tank 39, 70, 109, artillery fire 9, 20, 31, 66, 79, 97, 99–100, 110, 114–115, 127, 129, 131, 134–136, 145, 147, 161, 163, 165, 175–176, 189, 204, 206, 238; bazookas 79; 88 cannons 80; French 75 cannons; grenades 142; howitzers 136; machine guns 39, 98, 129, 143, 164; mines 98, 101, 138, 201; mortar fire 19, 143, 145, 161; multi-barreled rockets 129; pistols/rifles 39, 142; Stukas 68, 93, 145; tanks 39–40, 68, 79, 98, 103, 134, 160, 165, 202, 233
Miller, Capt. 242
Miller, Sgt. 242
Minnesota: Duluth 14, 220, 228; Eveleth 14; Lake Esquagama 13; National Guard, Virginia 13, 219
Missouri 15, 203, 223
money/financial affairs 41, 115–116, 121, 124, 139, 148
Montgomery, Gen. George 63, 92
Moore, Lt. Col. Robert 114
Moorman, Capt. 243
morale 2, 88, 133, 148, 161, 185, 206, 233
mother (role of Army) 66, 81, 91, 140, 238
Mott, Sgt. Hubert "Hub" 12, 62, 121–122, 130, 139, 151
movies 39, 49, 45, 51, 60, 75, 118, 149, 171, 179, 122
mule trains 155–156, 172
musette bag (field rucksack) 143–*144*
music 41, 62, 74, 109, 153, 172, 185–186, 222; *see also* Rhythm Majors Swing Band
Muslims 194
Mussolini 104

Neely, Bob 243
New York (state): Brooklyn 16, 59, 209–210; Mary Imogene Bassett Hospital, Cooperstown 206; New York City 16, 209–210
Newsweek magazine 154
91st Armored Artillery 233
Noerman, Capt. 243

North Africa: camels 90; campaign 66; children 82, *113*; farming *113*; final victory in Tunisia 71; landscapes 72–73, 95, 104, 107, 118–119, 125; living conditions 72, 76–77, 92, 82, 111, 118, 120; Operation TORCH 1, 64, 66, *67*–69, 198; Oran 64, *67*–69, *70*–71; Suez Canal 37; The "Villa" 72, 76, 82, 111, 121; weather 72–75, 92, 94–95, 108, 114; *see also* Algeria; Arabs; Tunisia
Northern Ireland 6, 37–38, 40, 110, 119, 153, 163; Belfast 37–38, 57; British Hospital 42–43; canteen supplies 42, 44; Castlerock 40, *42*, 44; Coleraine, County Londonderry 40; culture 41, 47–49; farming 47–48, *56*; Free State 44; landscapes 47, 51, *56*; living conditions 40, 43, 48–49, 51–53, *54*–*55*; Orange Hall 45; quarantine *44*–45; training 39; Tynan Abbey *54*–*55*; Ulster 44, *56*; women 42, 45; *see also* Swamp Island
Norway 36
nurses 74, 173; *see also* Red Cross

obsessive compulsive disorder (OCD) 221–222
officers' clubs 57–58, 122–123, 182, 190, 207
Olson, Dr. Arch "Hefty" 54, 59–60, 95, 124, 136, 243
175th F.A. Battalion 185
168th Infantry Medical Detachment Training Schedules 244
168th Infantry Regiment: 5, 7, 27, 68, 79–80, 127, 136–137, 142, 156, 161–162, 168, 170, 173, 178–179, 189, 200, 233
168th Infantry Medical Detachment Training Schedules 103, 120, 146, 245
133rd Infantry Regiment 5, 7, 27, *38*, 40, 63, 68, 73, 78, 137, 142

Pantano, Monte 5, 19–20, 81, 140–148, 200–201, 204, 232; *see also* Silver Star
paperwork (reports) 41, 124, 141, 206

Parker, Col. Dick 243
Paroxysmal Atrial Tachycardia (PAT) 180–181, 214, 219
parties 45, 109, 114, 123, 125, 153, 172–173, 185–186; *see also* dances
Patton, Gen. George 84–85, 97, 101, **105**
Pearl Harbor 1, 5, 12, 15, *34*–35, 37, *38*–*39*, *70*, 197, 235
Pierce, Lt. Spec T/4 243
pilots: flying/flying lessons 14–15, 29, 77–78; pilot's license 29, 78; WWI shell-shocked aviators 205–206; *see also* Hoyer, Jean Katherine; Ludwick, Jean Hoyer; World War I
ping pong 59, 153
polio 220
Power, Will 96, 243
Powers, Dr. Ivan 14
Powers, Larry 243
Presbyterian Church 49
Presbyterian Hospital, Waterloo, IA 14, *26*, 77, 187
prisoners of war: American 79, 96, 100, 111, 181, 233–234; German 25, 93, 100, 107, 134, 199–200, 202
Providence *see* God
psycho-drama 206
PTSD 84–85, 122, 164, 176, 189, 204–209, 211; collateral damage 2, 204, 209; psychiatric casualties 84–85, 204–205; treatment 84–86, 204–209; walking wounded 144, 146, 204–209, 211; *see also* wounded
Purple Heart 100, 114, 120
Pyle, Ernie 156, 170

quartermaster, U.S. Army 8, *38*, 167
Quinlivan, Chaplain 243
Quisling, Vidkun 36

"rackets" 62
radio 109, 119, 122, 125
Rathbone, Jack 243
Red Cross: emblem 100; girls/nurses 100, 120, 153, 173
Regimental Surgeon 3, 5, 10, 79–80, 86–88, 113, 155–156
replacement depots 191, 194–195
rest camp 146, 149, 152, 159
Rhythm Majors Swing Band 41, 62, 74, 109, 186; *see also* music

Index

Rion, Capt. Bob 243
river crossings 129–130, 140, 165
Robinson, Lt. "Robbie" 120, 243
Rogers, Sgt. 243
Rogers, 1st Lt. William 233
Rohlf, Maj. Ed 110, 243
Rommel, Gen. Johannes Erwin 6, 63, 78, 193; *see also* The Desert Fox
Roosevelt, Pres. Franklin D. (FDR) 6, 36–37, 66, 148
rotation home 118, 137, 139, 154, 159, 165, 169–170, 172–173, 180, 187, 190, 192–193; *see also* bureaucracy, U.S. Army
Rouse, Col. 243
Rudoy, Lt. Martin 83, 243
Russian army 65, 119, 124, 139, 169, 177
Ryder, Maj. Gen. Charles 97, 232

sanitation/hygiene 37, 41, 63, 65, 69, 87, 104, 157
Saturday Evening Post (magazine) 107
Schiffrin, Capt. 90, 243
Schuster, Capt. Emile 191, 244
self reflection 75, 164
752nd Tank Battalion 193–194, *237*
sexual desire 183–184
sexually transmitted diseases 146, 183
Sherman, Gen. William Tecumseh 56
sick call 25–26, 31, 37, 41, 46, 52, 63–64, 113, 123, 149, 176
Sigourney News Review (newspaper) 47
Silver Star Medal 5, 19, *20*, 145, 187, 231; *see also* Pantano, Monte
sleep 27, 33, 46, 52, 54, 59, 69, 91–93, 96, 106, 110–111, 131, 135, 138, 141, 149, 151, 156–157, 161, 164, 173, 178, 195, 209
Smith, Lt./Dr. R. Glenn 27, 52–53, 56, 195, 242, 244
smoking 119
Snyder, Kenneth 244
souvenirs 76, 112, 131, 153, 158, 194
Spanish Civil War 235
Spanish Flu epidemic 206
Spoo, Lt. Barney 148, 165, 184, 244

Stalin, Joseph 148
Stars and Stripes Weekly (military newspaper) 142, 184, 190
Straits of Gibralter 68, 194
RMS *Strathaird* 37
Sunday School 91
Surgeon of the European Theater 163
surgeries 42, 46, 61, 87, 216–217
surgical field instruments *144*
Swamp Island 44, 72, 109–112, 119–120, 153, 163, 168, 172, 186; *see also* Northern Ireland
swimming 33, 107, 109, 115, 120, 129

Taylor Light airplane 14, 78; *see also* Ludwick, Jean Hoyer; pilots
tents: pup 72, 76–77, 85, 129, 156, 164; pyramidal 164, 195
USS *Texas* (battleship) 37
Thanksgiving 140–141
34th Infantry Division Buddies 240–244
34th Infantry "Red Bull" Division 5, 23, 35–36, 70–71, 77, 80, 156, 160–161, 191, 209, 235; Gold Star Museum 210; *see also* 133rd Infantry Regiment; 168th Infantry Regiment
'39 Oldsmobile Coupe 24, 27, 157, 214
Thompson, Capt. Harry "Hank" 173, 244
Time magazine 146, 174, *236*
trench coat 120, *132*, 143
trench foot 145–146
Trussel, Maj. Henry "Pappy" L., Jr. 242, 244
Tunisia: Beja 199; Bizerte 98, 101, 104, 199, 200; Carthage 89, 108, 120; Eddekhila 100, 120, 199; El Haidra 108, 233; El Kef 70, 198–199; Faid Pass *71*, 78–81, 84, 86, 112, 198; Fondouk Pass 1, 70–*71*, 78–80, 86, 92–93, 97, 156, 198–199, 204; Gertie's place 111–112, 120; Hajeb el Aioun 78, 86; Hill 609 1, 70–*71*, 97–99, 147, 156, 199; Kairouan 112, 198; Kasserine Pass 1, 69, 78–81, 84, 86, 98, 112, 147, 198–199, 203, 233, 240–241; Maktar 198–199; Mateur 199; Rohia area 83; Roman ruins 89, 108; Sbeitla 87, 108, 19; Sbiba 78, 81, 87–88, *90*, 198–199, 243; Sidi bou Zid 81, 198; Sidi Nsir *105*, 199; Tunis 69, *71*, 82, 89, 98, 101, 108, 199–200; Tunisian Campaign *71*, 103, b, 199; weather 108; *see also* North Africa
typewriter/typing 8–9, 28, 32, 47, 51, 94–95, *102*, 108–109, 131, 152, 163, 190; *see also* letters/mail/packages

"Uncle Hoiman" 82, 95
U.S. Senators 133
University of Kansas (KU) 13, 222
University of Kansas Medical School 13, 218, 222–223, 226
University of Minnesota 14

V-mail 104, *117*, 121 see also letters/mail/packages
vaccinations 63, 97
Valley Forge 145
vaudeville shows 45, 75, 122, 171
Vesuvius, Mt. 153
Vickery, T/4 244
"Victory" ship 193–194
Victrolas 62
volleyball 59
von Ripper, Capt./Baron Rudolph Charles 146, 201, 235–*236*
Voorhees, Corp. 175, 244

Wagner, Nurse 74, 122, 125, 244
war: history 176–179; military leadership 176–179, 207; nature 150, 177
The War Department 8, 104, 233, 235
War of 1812 179
Washington (State): 64; Cascade Mountains 214–215; Columbia River 19, 214–215, 220–221; Highway 2; Lake Chelan 222; Mt. Rainier 222; Orondo 215; Spokane 215; WA ST Board of Community Colleges 220; Waterville 215, 224; Wenatchee 5, 19, 101, 214–*216*, 220–222, 224; Winthrop *228*; Yakima 215
Washington State Medical Association 5, 215
WASPs (Women's Air Force Service Pilots) 77

Waterloo, IA 14, 23–24, *26*, 74, 77, 185, 196
The Wenatchee World 215
West Point 81, 97, 158, 178–179, 201, 240
Williams, Capt. Marvin E. 244
World War I: bi-planes *205*; equipment *38*–39, 68; flight surgeons *205*–206; shell-shocked aviators 206–207
wounded: collateral damage 89, 204, 209; evacuation 134, 143, 145, 155–156, 159, 166, 204; treatment 31, 100, 103, 100, 114–115, 143–*144*, 155–156, 161, 165, *166*–167; walking 144, *146*, 204–205, 207; *see also* PTSD
Wright, Capt. Harold V. 237
Wry, T/4 244

www.ingramcontent.com/pod-product-compliance
Ingram Content Group UK Ltd.
Pitfield, Milton Keynes, MK11 3LW, UK
UKHW051850210426
5322IPUK00025B/644